The Sm..... Houdini, and Me

By Johnny Virgil

(This book is about)
The Snitch, Houdini, and Me

First edition

Table of Contents

Introduction

It was May 29th in the year 1963 when my front door burst open, a stainless steel claw reached in, grabbed my head, and pulled me toward the light. I was nine and half pounds of lean, mean, umbilical machine, and I didn't want to leave. With my sincere apologies to the Bobby Fuller Four, I guess you could say that I fought the claw and the claw won. I was brought into the world against my will, swearing vengeance upon both the steel claw and its operator. A vengeance that, to this day, remains un-exacted...so far.

It wasn't *all* bad, however.

For two years, I cried, I ate, I pooped, I slept – usually in that order. I was nothing if not efficient.

Two years and one day later (approximately), I formed my earliest memory. It's a little hazy now, but I'm pretty sure it was along the lines of "Hey, I could get used to this." In fact, I had it made. I had a mother and father who doted on me. I had grandparents who spoiled me. Every day, from the time I opened my eyes until the time I closed them, was all about *me*. I didn't even have to do anything fancy to keep their attention, but once in a while, I'd throw them a bone. For instance, upon seeing my first black guy in the supermarket, I loudly asked, "MOM! MOM! WHY IS THAT MAN MADE OF CHOCOLATE?" That one was a real crowd pleaser.

Unfortunately, just as I was settling into my role as an only child, my blissful existence and uncontested reign as King of the Universe was abruptly brought to an end. In May of 1965, The Snitch was born. It wasn't a complete surprise. I mean, I knew something had been percolating in my mother's stomach for a while, and I assumed that eventually, the odds were good that something would come out, but still – when you suddenly have to share your parents' affections with an ugly noob, it can be an adjustment.

According to available photographic evidence, I pinched him sometimes, just to show him who was boss. I maintain that these photos were doctored to cast me in an unfavorable light.

I didn't call him The Snitch right off the bat. He had many years ahead of him to earn that title, although to be fair he was telling on me long before he could talk – in fact, I was in trouble almost as soon as he learned to point at things. If there happened to be dirt on the floor and a broken flowerpot, all it took was a single sweeping index finger that went first to the dirt, then to me, and the next thing you know, I was being interrogated like a U.S. fighter pilot who had been shot down over China.

I immediately knew he was going to be a giant pain in the ass. All he did was cry, eat, poop and sleep. I hadn't realized until then just how incredibly annoying that sort of behavior could be. Eventually, he focused primarily on the crying and the eating, and by the time he turned two and I turned four, I knew that in a few years I'd be fighting him for my meals and holding my hand over his mouth to keep him from telling on me. I'd need to be careful, though. Even at two, he was a vicious biter.

Another two years went by, and like clockwork, I noticed my mother's tiny, five-foot-tall frame was once again harboring a watermelon shaped object that could only mean one thing: Another interloper. Life, it seemed, just wasn't fair. When would this end? Was she planning on doing this every two years for the rest of her life? Even though Snitch and I had unknowingly done everything possible to prevent this from happening, there it was. We had refused to sleep. We had escaped our beds and wandered into our parents' room unannounced at all hours of the night. We got scared and sometimes joined them in bed. When we got sick, we whined incessantly. We never gave them five minutes of peace.

To this day, I'm not sure when they had time to work on creating Houdini. But there he was, squeezed out like clockwork two days after my birthday. Shortly thereafter, he came home to live with us. Like The Snitch before him, Houdini earned his nickname at a fairly young age. He mimicked the famous magician by becoming a great escape artist in his own right. We'll get to that later.

You'd think that The Snitch and I would have immediately formed some sort of unholy alliance in order to vanquish the newcomer, but for some reason, that didn't happen. In fact, I kinda liked the little guy. I think a lot of my fondness for him was because by the time he turned two, he would do my evil bidding. Like his brother before him, he too was a vicious biter. If I needed someone bitten, he was my go-to guy. I could casually lean over and say "Go bite Snitch," and he would dutifully yet nonchalantly wander his way over to where Snitch was lying on the floor watching TV and then, without warning, he'd tear into him like a starving zombie. He wouldn't give up, either. That's what I liked about him; the kid had heart. He'd keep on it until The Snitch had teethmarks at least *somewhere* on his body.

When I became old enough, I got sent off to kindergarten, which, much to my mother's relief, tended to keep me from issuing directives to Houdini that might get him hurt or killed. That was also to come later.

Before I share the opening story in this book with you, I'd like to clear up a few things.

6

First off, this book isn't an autobiography. While the stories are primarily autobiographical in nature, in rough chronological order, and based upon actual events, they are by no means my complete history of growing up in the late sixties and early seventies. Instead, think of them as stories about the pivotal points in my life; points that determined the sort of person I was to become. These are stories that I hope will make you laugh, but mostly they are stories where I could have (a) died because of my stupidity, (b) caused the death of someone else because of my stupidity, or (c) *wished* I were dead because of embarrassment caused by, as you've probably guessed by now, my stupidity. In other words, hide this book from your kids unless you like visiting the emergency room.

After reading this, you might be shocked to know that I also have a younger sister. Sadly, she was a last ditch effort by my parents to pop out a female of the species, so she is quite a bit younger than I am. When she was very small, we did convince her to name her doll "Freddie" and allow us to cut it open and install internal organs made of tin foil, but unfortunately, I had moved out before she started having teenaged adventures of her own.

She's a great sister, and today she is a physical therapist, and mother to two children of her own, a girl and a newborn boy. Even though she's not featured much in these pages, this book should serve her well as a guide for what *not* to allow her children to do. At least I've given her that much.

Markie (our next-door neighbor and unofficial brother) is also featured heavily in the following pages. He was an unforgettable part of our early childhood, and I'm sorry to say we lost touch over the years. From what I hear, he's doing very well for himself as a general contractor. If he agrees not to sue me, I'm going to send him a free book.

Today, Snitch is a partner in a NYC law firm, Houdini has his PHD in microbiology and heads up a lab at a cutting–edge pharmaceutical company, and as for me, well...I'm an IT geek who writes a blog. Once upon a time in 2007, I wrote a post about a 1977 JC Penney catalog that I found in the rafters of my grandfather's house. Eventually, a million or so people visited my blog to read it.

I'm pretty sure I was either adopted or dropped on my head as a baby, because I'm sitting here ridiculing the fashions of 1977 instead of saving the world one court case and/or disease at a time.

Life's funny that way.

Education: The Formative Years

Lick'em if ya Got'em

They say that everything you need to know in life you learn in kinder-garten. While I'm not sure how true that is, I did learn a *few* things, and I'll quickly share them with you here.

(1) When you are forced to sit in a circle on the red dots on the floor and sing stupid songs while the teacher plays piano, it pays to check them all out until you find the warm one that has the hot water pipes running un-derneath it, and snag that one as often as possible. A warm ass is a happy ass.

(2) Always ask to go to the bathroom long before you are about to burst, oth-erwise you might not make it and then you'll be known as "that kid who peed in his pants" right up until you go off to college in another state.

(3) It's normal and fine to have a crush on your beautiful 24 year old teacher. In my class, all the boys did, even that one gay kid who didn't really know he was gay yet. To be fair, I think he just wanted to paint her toe-nails and do her makeup, but it still counts. What is *not* fine is trying to touch her boobs. That will get you into trouble.

(4) Lastly, I learned that if you wanted to play with a particular toy, and you were smaller than the other kid who *also* liked that toy, your best bet was to hide it behind the giant blocks so you could get to it first the next day. Otherwise, you'd be at the mercy of your teacher forcing the bigger kid to share, and that always ended badly for you when the teacher wasn't looking.

Another option was to catch the attention of the other kid, and give the toy a healthy lick to claim ownership. Cooties were a powerful deterrent. He might tell the teacher on you, but as long as you didn't leave a visible spit trail, it would be your word against his, and you would get the toy the next day.

Of course, that worked quite well for everyone else too, and once word got out, the place turned into a total lick-fest. It got so bad that nobody cared anymore, and you'd play with something you knew first-hand had been licked by 12 different kids and you wouldn't even blink. Finally, the teacher had to sit us down in a circle and tell us to stop licking toys. I'm not sure if she ever figured out why we were doing it.

And parents wonder why their kids are sick all the time.

Once I graduated from kindergarten, I had a rudimentary sense of right and wrong, a tenuous grasp on a few necessary social skills, and a technique for avoiding bullies that mostly resulted in me being pushed to the ground and forced to eat dirt.

In retrospect I guess it wasn't a very good technique.

I Think I Work for Mrs. Newhouse.

Last year, I got a Christmas card from my boss, and she signed it with her name, followed by a drawing of a smiley face that looked like this:

The second I saw it, I was transported back to the first grade, where my teacher Mrs. Newhouse graded our ham-fisted spelling papers in much the same way. In her case, there were three different versions, depending on the quality of your work:

Great Job! You give me hope for the future of mankind and make me think there's a slim chance I'm not wasting my life after all.

Not so great, but acceptable. You could probably do better if you actually tried, but we both know you're going to just skate by doing the bare minimum that anyone expects. You'll probably have a lot of fun along the way, though.

Wow, this paper is a train wreck. I'm no fortune teller, but I'm pretty sure your future involves wearing lots of high-tech communications equipment and becoming an expert in the latest computer touch-screen technology. To get a jump on your career, practice leaning out of a window and handing people paper bags.

A handful of those bad boys on the end and you were pretty much destined to become a burden to society, and she made sure you knew it. The pressure to achieve good grades was immense, even in the first grade. It's not that my parents beat me for bad grades or anything, but there was something about their expectations that made me demand better of myself. I didn't want to let them down. Studying was hard for me, even then, and I was the recipient of my fair share of frowny faces. Not wanting to end up picking fruit for a living, I did the only thing I could do. I buckled down and studied my spelling and – no, I'm obviously lying.

There was one other thing I could do and I did it – I chose to pay close attention to the type of felt-tipped pen that Mrs. Newhouse used to mark our papers. Then I found one exactly like it, theorizing that it would be relatively easy to turn a "burden to society" frowny face into the "he's a good kid, but will probably end up as the drummer in a rock band" semi-smiley, should the need ever arise. After I mastered my technique (which involved starting my line beyond the end of the frowny face and working my way back so as to avoid the tell-tale "ink blob" in the middle), this worked perfectly, and on the rare occasion that I actually pulled a frowny face, I was covered. That is, until the day this kid Pete saw me doctoring one of my papers, and asked me to do the same thing for him.

Being the kind of guy I am, I helped a brotha out.

Unfortunately, it turned out that Pete had kind of a big mouth, and since we seemed to have more than our share of dullards in our first grade classroom, I ended up doing quite a few "upgrades" for other students. After word had gotten around that I had the exact pen and an apparently foolproof technique, I became a pretty popular guy in the yard. I was like Andy Dufresne in *The Shawshank Redemption*.

Eventually, I decided that with great risk should come great reward, and I realized that other kids might actually *pay* me for these same services I had been providing for free.

It turned out I was right.

I started a small cash business on the playground, and was doing quite well for myself until some little assknob decided to cut in on my action with his *own* red pen. Unfortunately for everyone, it wasn't the same *kind* of pen, and he sucked at the art of forgery. After that, it was just a matter of time until the dreaded parent-teacher conferences brought some slight discrepancies to light. He got busted, and that brought down the whole house of cards. He ratted me out and – after a few brutal interrogations of some less-than-stellar students who corroborated his story – Mrs. Newhouse had what she needed. As you can imagine, my parents were less than pleased with me at their *own* parent-teacher conference, which went about as well as could be expected.

I was punished, required to admit what I did to Mrs. Newhouse, and then had to formally apologize to the entire class. After that, I was put on probation and not allowed to possess red pens of any type ever again for as long as I lived, which, as my father told me in no uncertain terms, wouldn't be for very long if I pulled any shit like that again. I still feel a little naughty when I pick one up.

That was the end of my short-lived forgery career. The next time I got in trouble in Mrs. Newhouse's class it was because I was drawing naked, vaguely humanoid female monsters with giant, saggy tits who, for some unknown reason, wore hoop earrings with the price tags left on. I think I may have had some sort of budding Minnie Pearl fetish.

Really, my parents should have just taken away all my writing implements and called it a day.

I learned a thing or two in the first grade, too. For instance, I learned that the threat of being forced to "stay after school" could make an entire class of students cry like their parents were being torn apart by wolves right in front of their eyes. I also learned that crime doesn't pay, especially if you get caught, and that making your parents proud is generally an easier thing to do if you don't cheat to get results. Lastly, I learned that a good teacher can make a difference in your life, no matter how young you are at the time.

Here's hoping every kid gets at least one "Mrs. Newhouse" in grade school.

The Artist Formerly Known As.

We did other things besides practice our writing and spelling. There was also "art period." Normally, art period was whenever the teacher got tired of riding herd over a bunch of sugared-up six-year-olds and wanted some down time. Out would come the construction paper, colored pencils, crayons and chalk, and both the kids and the teacher would have a little quiet time wherein the kids could sometimes draw whatever they wanted (which, in some cases, resulted in additional impromptu parent-teacher conferences) and sometimes not.

Most of the time, our teacher would assign us a drawing theme. Usually it was something very broad, like "family" or "upcoming holiday." This forced us to think a little bit, and gave the teacher an opportunity to catch up on the latest issue of *McCall's* or *True Confessions*.

I'm willing to bet that most of the "works of art" created during this time in a child's life are usually lost. They spend a few days stuck up on the fridge with a magnet, then they are surreptitiously tossed out with the used coffee grounds as newer and more immediate artwork takes its rightful place.

My mother, bless her heart, had the foresight to collect a scrapbook for each of us as we were growing up. They were full of our artwork and school-work from Kindergarten through sixth grade. As you will see shortly, I was apparently big on drawing pictures of my family, either by choice or direction.

Although I have no recollection of actually making any of these drawings, I believe I can say with almost 100% certainty that the teacher *forced* us to do this.

I say this for two reasons. One – as I mentioned in the last story – my normal subject matter was a bit more risque, and two, judging by the quality of my work, I think we're looking at nothing but blatant coercion here.

For instance, here's the first known portrait of The Snitch and Houdini:

As you can see from his grin, The Snitch was an extremely happy kid, even though he had clover hands and zero genitalia. Houdini was less happy because in addition to the same hand/crotch affliction, he also suffered the misfortune of having been born with no mouth or nose and a pair of floppy penis ears. It's tough to be a happy kid when you're walking around with penis ears. Especially when you're in a crowd of people and you hear your favorite song.

From my mother's detailed notes, this next picture is apparently a self-portrait:

This is a mystery to me. In my defense, I can only assume that at some point in my formative years, I wore a ten-pound beard of bees in lieu of actual clothes. Oddly enough, I also had propeller hands and the crotch of GI Joe. I'm glad I grew out of those because while I'm sure I would be able to swim like a mofo, performing ordinary tasks like typing and going to the bathroom would be difficult at best. Sadly, judging from all available photographic evidence, the Donald Trump hairstyle I am sporting in this portrait was not far from reality.

Here's another one I drew of The Snitch. This picture is clear evidence that The Snitch was replaced for a short time by Curious George.

I will have to go through some old photos to prove this theory, but I am about 90% sure that I actually remember that happening.

The Snitch again. You can see that my artistic talent has really started to flourish. I have no idea what kind of toxic paste fumes I was sniffing, but they were obviously doing fantastic things to my mind. The most confusing thing about this drawing?

I have no recollection of my brother ever wearing a tiny top-hat with two ants on it, who are *also* wearing top-hats. Never. Not even on weekends or holidays.

The other thing I can easily surmise from this picture is that my brother turned completely evil whenever he doffed his ant-infested top-hat. It's obvious from the wide, soul-devouring grin and the sinister, arched eyebrows. He looked a little like the crypt-keeper.

17

Here's an extremely realistic picture of my mother:

As you can tell, she was very well endowed. In both the chest *and* the hands department.

This picture of my father confuses me. It was drawn on the cover of a Father's Day card, so I *know* it's him. And it said "Dad" right on it.

The only problem here? My father didn't have a mustache *or* a beard. Ever, as long as I've been alive.

And his nose was, as far as memory serves, never an upside down peace sign.

The rest is pretty accurate, though. That's my dad. Always trying to hug everybody with his stick arms.

I think later on they tried to get us to draw activities we liked to participate in, like this next picture:

As you can see, one of the things I enjoyed was taunting sperm whales with a pork chop on a string. If you know anything at all about fishing, you know that's how it's done with sperm whales.

Other popular subject matter included getting us to draw "holiday themed" pictures. Here's one of Santa Claus:

At least I *think* that's who it is. It's hard to tell, because there are some discrepancies here. He has obvious crotch height problems, for example – probably because his giant, hairy scrotum is hanging from his chin instead of from where it should be. If I saw this individual coming out of my chimney hole, I think I would probably beat him to death with a fireplace poker and ask questions later. Don't even ask about the pope hat, the zucchini boots and the single white glove.

My professional opinion: Probably not the real Santa.

From what I can tell, this next one is supposed to be representative of Halloween:

Needless to say, I have questions. First and foremost: *What the hell kind of deformed, one-eyed, one-armed, ant-eater-lookin' witch is that?* Holy shit. I understand the magic wand bit, and I figured out that the X's indicate magic in use, but why is she straddling a small palm tree instead of a broom?

Also, I have no idea what the hell that giant black tentacle wearing a codpiece on its face could *possibly* be. If anyone has any clue, I'm all ears (as you can see from my self-portrait a few pages ago). I have to say, though, the shoes are pretty sweet.

Last, but not least, is the pride of my collection. It's one of the few "very good" scores I actually received:

I think maybe it's supposed to be a tree. Or a turkey. As for which holiday this picture is supposed to represent – I'm not exactly sure. I think it's either Thanksgiving or Penis-In-A-Tree Day.[*]

You probably want to find out for sure which one it is before you say yes to the stuffing.

---

[*] March 14th

Author Extraordinaire

It seems that I've always been making up stories. From looking at my out-put so far, it's clear that I was not much of an artist. I was, coincidentally, more of a writer.

The seeds of this creativity appeared around the age of seven, when the teacher made us write a story that covered exactly one page every day. My mother didn't keep all of them, but just a few from each month.

I am going to share some of my nascent genius.

> Today I went to the animal hospital and there was a lot of pets the man who guided us was Mr. Mitchell. I think my father and my dog went there. My dog had the worms.

I'm still not sure *what* ailment my father had, or why we would bring him to the vet. I do know we didn't get him neutered, because we have Snitch and Houdini as proof.

I did find out some things about myself that I'm not proud of. I would have made a good stoolie, for instance. I only know this because I found proof.

Also, I was very subtle:

> I don't like somebody in this room becuse when Miss Sabey was in our classroom he missbehaved. He has a green, yellow and white sweter on and He has a green sheit on and has a black boolt on just like mine. Can you gess who it is?

22

Here's one more. Given the chance, I clearly would have ruled with an iron fist:

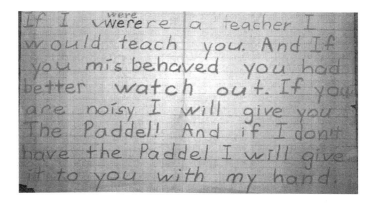

Ah, corporal punishment. The good old days. Just for the record, I still hate noisy people, especially the ones I am forced to deal with at work. I am thinking about bringing in the paddel, but no way am I giving anything to anyone with my hand. Not for free, anyway.

There were many more stories along these lines. Another thing I learned from one of these informative daily missives – apparently, "my gerbil is like a typewriter." That's a simile, I think. Or a metaphor. Or an early crack habit that I don't remember.

While my writing was improving, my art was not.

Here's a cat from my modernist period:

From looking at this, I am forced to assume that in order to create an authentic rendering of a cat, it is necessary to use *actual cat vomit* in the creative process.

Over time, I got slightly better. At the end of the school year, the teacher made us create an avatar, although that term probably didn't exist then. There was an end-of-year open house, and we had to make a full-sized drawing of ourselves and put it in someone else's seat. Our poor parents then had to try to select their own child from these hideously bad renderings.

No pressure, mom.

So here's me, in all my four feet of glory:

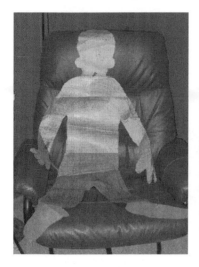

Because you can't tell, I'm wearing a green-checkered shirt and brown pants, and my feet are twice the size of my head. Speaking of my head, let's take a closer look:

Yes. I admit this to you. I only had four tiny, corn-kernel teeth, all on the left side of my lipless, banana shaped pie hole.

My ears were level with my mouth, and completely non-functional. Either that, or I actually *had* no ears, and simply listened through my gigantic goiters. Oddly, I have no memory of sporting a soul patch.

My nose? Well, I'm not complaining. You could cut yourself on the edges, but at least I had two nostrils. Sure, they're on the front instead of underneath, but I'll take what I can get.

To be fair, I've outgrown most of this, and my features are now slightly more conventional.

Lastly, let's take a closer look at my hand:

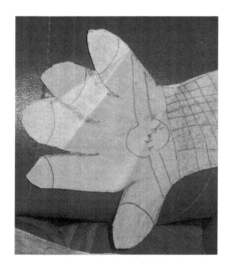

Holy penisfingers, Batman! It turns out that I actually *could* give it to you with my hand. I tell myself it's all about the girth.

It helps me sleep better at night.

Crime and Punishment

Just Wait...

I didn't get into too much trouble at school. For the most part, The Snitch, Houdini and I were well-behaved children, I think out of fear more than anything else.

It wasn't fear of our teachers, although there was some of that. Remember, when we went to school it was entirely acceptable for someone to pound the living shit out of your ass with a flat piece of wood; encouraged, even. And let me tell you something else – that shit *worked*. If you got the paddle, you never, ever wanted to get it again.

Our fear, however, had more to do with what would happen to us when our daily behavioral report was submitted, in triplicate, to our father.

My mother would tally each instance of bad behavior, and using an arcane mathematical formula handed down by my great-great-grandmother, she would then determine where on the relative scale of badness we deserved to be. If any of us exceeded a certain predetermined level, we'd have a serious problem, and that problem would be walking through the front door at the end of a hard day.

To us, there were no scarier words in the English language than "Just Wait Until Your Father Gets Home."

The Doghouse is Very Uncomfortable

When I was eight years old, and my brothers The Snitch and Houdini were six and four, respectively, we spent a lot of time in the dog house. Don't misunderstand. This was not by choice.

Whenever we misbehaved, that's what my mother would do to us. She would give us one or two chances, and if we didn't behave, that would be it. Into the doghouse we would go. Sometimes, it was just one of us, but most of the time it was at least two, because just as it takes two to tango, it also takes two to gang up on Houdini and tickle him until he pees in his pants.

This was considered the worst punishment my mother could dish out. First came the standing in the corner. I think they call this a "time-out" now, except we didn't get to sit. If that didn't work, she'd send us to *her* room (because our rooms were much too fun for the punishment to be effective) where we'd sit by the door dying of boredom and yelling "Can I come out yet? Can I? Can I come out yet? I'll be good, I promise..." until she threatened to spank us if we didn't shut up. If she let us out and we got into trouble again, it was the doghouse for sure.

This was the straw *after* the last straw. Yes, I know that doesn't make sense, but work with me here. Basically, this was the moment when she handed off our punishment to my father, and washed her hands of us. She would scream, "OK, That's it! I'm putting you in the doghouse!" and we instantly became the best children on the face of the planet. But by then it was too late. We had received our warnings. We had squandered our chance to avoid our fate.

When that happened, there was only one thing to do: *Beg*. Beg as if your life depended on it, because you thought it just might. Beg because our father would be home at six p.m., and if we were still in the doghouse when he came in the door, there would be hell to pay.

Now, before you go thinking that my mother was the most heartless person in the world for stuffing her children into the doghouse, let me tell you a little bit about it.

First, it wasn't an actual dog house. It wasn't even outside.

In fact, it looked like this:

FAMILY DOG HOUSE

WHO'S IN THE [VIRGIL] FAMILY DOG HOUSE
TO STAY OUT – OBEY THE RULES
TO GET IN ----TRY SOME SHENANIGANS

Dad   Mom   Johnny   Snitch   Houdini

It hung on the kitchen wall next to the phone. The hook inside the doorway of the doghouse was eventually replaced with a two-inch-long finishing nail, because the stock hook couldn't easily handle all three dogs, which it was frequently called upon to do.

Most of the time, unless my mother was *really* pissed, we could convince her to let us out of the doghouse a few minutes before my father walked in the door. He'd normally call before he left work, and we knew that we had about 15 minutes to work on her. It was like being on death row and waiting for a pardon from the Governor. There was an almost palpable sense of free-dom when it happened, and we were on our best behavior for the rest of the night, which was probably her plan from the beginning.

If you were in the doghouse and didn't make it out before he came home, most of the time you would end up in tears, but not because of anything physical. My father was a master of *psychological* punishment. He was scary in a serious, stern sort of way, and he certainly wasn't averse to a ritual spanking now and again, but he never really hurt anything but our pride. I can think of only once when he lost his temper and hit me upside the head, catching me a good one with his wedding ring by mistake. I can't remember what I had done to deserve that, but I'm sure it had to have been spectacular. He apologized to me afterward, told me it would never happen again, and it never did.

Normally, our punishment was of the non-physical type. His usual way of dealing with our transgressions was to use logic, something with which we were mostly unfamiliar. There would be a conversation like this:

"Your mother said you were bad today. What did you do?"

"I got Houdini's hair caught in the wheels of my race car."

28

"So that's why you're in the doghouse?"

"No."

"No? Why are you in the doghouse then?"

"Because I did it two more times after she told me to stop."

"Is that it?"

"No. He threw my car down the stairs."

"So what did you do then?"

"I punched him pretty hard. In the butt."

This line of questioning would continue for a while, but eventually we'd work our way down to the speech, which always centered on a common theme:

"Do you know how much your mother does for you and your brothers every day?"

"Yes."

"What does she do?"

"She cooks dinner and does our laundry and cleans the house and takes us places."

"You made her cry today, did you know that?"

"No."

"Do you think that's fair? That she does all that for you, and you make her cry?"

"No."

"I think you owe her an apology, don't you?"

"Yes. I'm sorry."

"Don't tell me, tell *her*. Come with me. You're going to apologize right now, and then your mother and I will decide what your punishment is going to be."

At that point I would usually start crying, and again tell him how sorry I was. After the apology, (and that was rough, let me tell you) he'd send me back to my room. A few minutes later, he'd appear at my bedroom door and just stand there, like a judge preparing to hand down a sentence. By that time, I was resigned to my fate, because (1) I knew the hardest part was over, and (2) I knew I totally deserved whatever it was.

So that's the story of the parental discipline in our house growing up. I've never been arrested or in rehab, so I guess it worked. There's still time, I guess. I can only imagine how much they laughed about it after we were asleep.

I can remember being in a crowded grocery store with my mother when she got pissed at Houdini and yelled, "If you don't start behaving right this instant, you're going straight into the doghouse when we get home!"

Today, screaming that sentence in public would definitely get you a stern talking to – most likely by social services.

Weapons of Recess

I wasn't much of a trouble-maker in elementary school. I never got caught with weapons, and other than running afoul of Big Dave when trying to break into the lucrative Bubble Yum and Charms Pop trade, I never had much of a problem with other kids.

I was in exactly two fights on school property. The first was broken up before it even started, and the second one consisted of me riding on a big kid's back and choking him, afraid to let go because I knew if I did, he'd pound me into dust. I never had one of those life-changing fights you always see in the movies where the newly-courageous nerd kicks the crap out of the school bully. I knew who the bullies were, and I steered clear. Of course, there was always "that kid with the switchblade" who would stab you just as soon as look at you, but the reality was a bit farther from the truth. Sure, that particular kid had failed third grade five times and had started growing a beard, but generally he was pretty harmless, as long as you stayed out of his way and handed over your lunch money when he or one of his henchmen asked for it.

When I was 12, yelling "You're dead!" or "I'm gonna kill you!" was perfectly normal and fine, because we didn't mean it *literally* like they do today. Most of the time, the worst thing that would happen is you'd get punched between the shoulder blades at recess and maybe have to lick some kid's sneaker. I think it's safe to say things have changed.

I got thinking about what sort of things we'd get in trouble for when we were 12, and other than the time my friend Danny brought in the severed deer leg and put it on Laurie's chair before she got there, we were a pretty tame bunch. We had our share of fads, and most of our trouble usually centered around those. One year the teachers would have drawers full of confiscated Duncan butterfly yo-yos, another year it would be clackers, Wizzers, or God knows what else.

Of course, there were other things we'd do to make giant pains in the asses of ourselves besides bringing in toys. Luckily for us, and not so luckily for our parents and teachers, some of these things were free.

Here's an annoying thing we used to make called a "Popper."

A classroom full of these things was a nightmare of noise. God help you if you were a substitute teacher and just there for the day, because every time you turned your back, the classroom would erupt with noise. It took me a while to figure out how to make one again, and the sound it makes is something you never forget. If you flip it down hard enough, the inside chute will open with a loud POP! The right kind of paper matters – thinner is better. I haven't folded a piece of notebook paper like that in a long time.

While most of the home-made stuff we got in trouble for was pretty tame, there were a few things we'd make when we wanted to inflict pain on a classmate. In our view, nothing was funnier than someone you knew getting hurt, as long as you knew it wasn't serious, and as long as you knew that it hurt a *lot*.

We called these "Chinese Snappers."

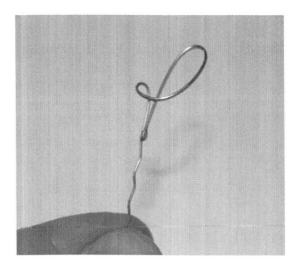

I have no idea what made them Chinese, instead of say, French or German. I know it looks pretty harmless, but that little bent piece of wire could raise a welt on your leg that you'd have for a week. And that's with a *small* bobby pin. If you used one of those mongo bastards my mom always had lying around, the finished product would end up at almost four inches from tip to tip. If you snapped someone on bare skin with that one, there was a good chance they'd end up bloody, especially if you took the little rubbery blob off the end of the bobby pin. When this fad was going on, you were in constant fear of getting hit in the ass or leg by the Giant Snapper. It hurt a lot more when you weren't expecting it. You'd just be walking down the hall minding your own business and a passing kid would reach out and the next thing you know, you'd be writhing on the floor and the back of your thigh would feel like someone just shot you with a nail gun.

Eventually, getting caught with one of these in your possession would get you detention. Using it on another kid and getting caught would get you suspended for three days. I never got caught, and that's because I didn't so much use them on other kids as I did manufacture and sell them to other kids. I had them in my possession only for as long as it took to deliver the merchandise to the buyer. I was nothing if not a careful businessman.

I never got hit by one of my own creations, and I never got caught with one in my pocket. I think that's because there's an old saying that goes something like "You don't bite the hand that supplies you with giant Chinese snappers for a quarter." This lasted until the crackdown, whereupon I closed up shop and was saved by plausible deniability. I was a solid "A" student selling to mostly solid "D" students, and so had the scales of justice artificially tipped in my favor. It may not have been fair, but it was and still is the way of the world.

Given my history of schoolyard money-making schemes, you'd think I'd be a rich millionaire by now, living off the proceeds of my famous inventions, or retired from my job as the owner of a high-end importing/exporting conglomerate. Unfortunately for me, you'd be wrong. I was always being shut down by the man, and my next invention was no exception to that rule.

I was always about taking a good idea and making it better. If you want to be kind, call it my innate ingenuity. If you want to be honest, call it my lack of originality.

Take spitballs, for instance.

Spitballs are timeless, and I'm pretty sure they're universal. Somewhere a billion light years away, little Grimgath Spracknog is sitting in a classroom on Xlagmat IV, with a giant wad of spotchkath in his mouth, working it around and getting it to just the right consistency so he can shoot it through one of his nasal tubes at the back of the teacher's second auxiliary head.

I constantly saw kids shooting spitballs through straws, and more than a few times I was the unwilling recipient of a sloppy smack in the back of the head that had been destined for the black board but had fallen short. The problem, I surmised, was one of range. An eleven-year-old didn't have enough lung power to create the pressure necessary to shoot a spitball very far with any sort of velocity. Once again, I jumped into this untapped market with both feet. I created this:

Compression Spitball Cannon

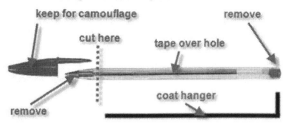

It looked like a pen, but worked like a tiny spud gun. Jam a spitball in, push it down to the end with the ramrod, then jam another one in and push that about halfway down. When you slammed the ramrod in hard, the first spitball would come out of the end at about 200 feet per second, and the next one was then in place and ready to go. It sounded very much like a pellet gun being fired. Aiming was an acquired skill, but after a while you'd get pretty good at it.

I never made much money on this one because unlike giant bobby pins, every kid had access to Bic pens and coat hangers, and once someone got a good look at it, it was easy to replicate. I only sold these to the kids who were too stupid or lazy or rich to make their own. Eventually, due to the counter-feiters and their knock-offs, I left the business.

I studied up on the blowguns of the Amazon, and tried modifications for longer range and more power, but they never got out of the prototype stage. I once modified one of these with a needle and flight stabilizer and then shot it into my brother Houdini's chest from 30 feet away as he walked out of the bathroom. While great for home use, I decided it was probably in my best in-terest to avoid introducing this particular modification to my school mates.

As the saying goes, "It's all fun and games until someone loses an eye. Then it's just one game: Find the Eye."

The Death and Life of Freddie

"I'm afraid it's serious. Freddie will die without this operation," I said.

"Oper...ation?" my sister asked.

"Yes. Freddie needs a new heart. The good news is, a donor heart just became available," I replied. "There's really no choice. Either she gets the operation, or she'll probably never wake up. She'll die and it will be all your fault."

"I don't want her to die," my sister said, tears starting to fall from her eyes. "I love her."

"I know you do. That's why I'm recommending that we go ahead with the surgery. It's really her only chance."

She was crying hard now. I waited silently for her answer. She attempted to regain her composure but failed miserably. "OK! Do the oper-... operbation!" she blubbered. Freddie was prepped and lying on the table, eyes closed. I wasted no time. I nodded to the attending who would be assisting in this procedure, picked up the scissors, and made a decisive yet careful incision from neck to abdomen. My sister saw this and ran from the room, wailing.

After a few moments of exploration, I glanced at my assistant. The situation was not good. In fact, things were a lot worse than I had anticipated. It wasn't just the heart. There were other problems as well. In fact, it looked like most of the organs were simply missing. I pressed on with the procedure.

"I'm ready now," I said. "Hand me the heart."

"Here, Doc," the attending Snitch said, carefully handing it over. I stuffed the heart in place. Quickly, I turned back toward the attending physician.

"What about the liver, lungs, stomach and kidneys?" I asked. I could hear wails of grief in the distance. We weren't going to make it. We didn't have enough time.

"I didn't make them yet. Hang on," Dr. Snitch said, glancing quickly at the door. "Oh crap. I think she's telling on us."

He worked faster. "Here, here, here and here," he said, handing me the rest of the organs.

We were out of time. I tossed the rest of the organs in quickly, and began sewing up the incision. I finished, and was just about to pronounce the surgery a success, when the worst possible thing happened. The hospital administrator showed up.

"WHAT are you three doing? Why is your sister crying?" my mother asked, standing in the doorway. My sister was peeking out from behind my mother's left leg, thumb in mouth.

Nurse Houdini reached out and quickly lowered Freddie's dress to cover up the crude scar.

"Freddie's all better now," he said.

"Yeah, we fixed her up good," I added.

"You three are unbelievable," my mother said. "What would possess you to cut open her favorite doll like that? Right in front of her, no less! She's only three years old for God's sake. How would you like it if I did something like that to one of your favorite toys? Your father is going to hear about this."

She paused a moment, then asked, "And why does she keep calling it Freddie?"

"We convinced her that was the doll's name." I said. "A girl doll named Freddie. We thought it would be funny."

My mother sighed and walked out of the room.

"She's ugly now," my sister said, grabbing Freddie from Houdini and fingering the roughly sewed scar down the middle of her doll's soft, fabric body.

"And bumpy," she added, scowling.

Houdini brightened. "We could operate again," he said. "This time I could do it."

"NO!" my sister said emphatically, clutching Freddie to her chest and fleeing the room.

Houdini and I looked at each other.

"It was a good operation." I said.

"Yeah." he replied.

"She'll get over it when she realizes we just saved Freddie's life," I said.

"Prob'ly," he said.

As far as I know, Freddie is still healthy and living a peaceful life somewhere in Massachusetts.

Holidays: Major and Minor

What Memories are Made Of.

My mother was Roman Catholic, and my father started out Protestant. I say "started out" because when they got married, my father converted to RC, which, as far as I can tell, just meant that he picked up another layer of man-agement, a new place to worry about called Purgatory, and a whole metric ass-load of saints that were now on his payroll and required by religious mandates to listen to his prayers. I guess when you're a Protestant, you have more of a direct line to the Man upstairs. With the RC franchise, it's bad form to ask forgiveness directly. Instead, you have the church and a bunch of Saints in there acting like your agents and putting in a good word for you. In the RC plan, God's more like Bono or Sinatra, I guess.

We went to church every Sunday, and on all the major holidays. I'm not sure how seriously we as a family took the whole thing, since a lot of the time we would either sit or stand way in the back so my mother could "beat the rush" and get out of the parking lot before everyone else. I think we went because my mother thought we were supposed to. At the time, I never really thought about it. It was just something we did, like cook pasta on Saturday and steaks on Sunday. I know I spent a lot of time looking around at girls and thinking lustful thoughts. I figured what better place to have lustful thoughts than a place with instant forgiveness? When I got tired of that, I'd stare at the overhead light until I had an afterimage burned into my retina, then I'd waste a few minutes watching the blue-green blob float around the room, trying to get it to stop over the heads of the cute girls whereupon the cycle would start all over again.

After I was old enough to drive, I'd take Houdini to church, which really just involved quickly running in to see which priest was giving the sermon that day in case my mother asked, and then sitting in the church parking lot for an hour listening to music and shooting the shit. I was a pretty bad Cath-olic.

In their defense, however, my mother and father were always reminding us about what they called the "true meaning" of the holidays. Christmas and Easter especially, because those generally involved presents and candy and it was easier for us to fall off the wagon. They taught us about the birth and re-surrection of Jesus, and we even went to Sunday school every week. In our secret heart of hearts, though, Christmas remained mostly all about the presents.

Thanksgiving was a little different, in that it was pretty self-explanatory. Thanks. Giving. You gave thanks for stuff. Pretty easy, right? You thanked God for your parents, your grandparents, your dog, your toys, Casey Kasem's top 40, the food you were about to eat – even the peas and the broccoli for some reason.

I hated peas and broccoli, so giving thanks for them didn't really make much sense to me. It was like giving thanks for wasps and poison ivy. According to my mother, however, there were starving kids in Africa who would love our broccoli and peas, so we should be thankful we had it instead of them. That sounded a little spiteful to me, and my kid logic immediately kicked in. I suggested that since we *didn't* like it and they *did*, we should just box it up and send it to them. Win-win, right? Unfortunately, my suggestion only got me sent to my room for being a smart ass.

Stupid logic. Always getting me into trouble.

The Balls Don't Fall Far from the Tree

We always had a real Christmas tree growing up. As a kid, I was fascinated by the entire tree-collecting process. It was a yearly ritual, and shortly after Thanksgiving we'd find ourselves packed into the station wagon on our way to a tree farm. The harvesting of the perfect Christmas tree varied slightly from year to year, but here's a rough breakdown of the steps involved:

1. *The cutting of the tree.*

We'd all stomp around in the snow looking for "the one." Not too fat, not too tall, not too crooked, not too small. Most of the time, we'd find the perfect tree, and start screaming to our parents to come and look. Five minutes later, when my mother and father concluded their quarter mile hike through muddy tractor ruts to get to where we were, the conversation that followed usually went like this:

"Dad! Dad! Let's get this one! Can we get this one? It's perfect! It's just the right size! Can we? Huh? Can we? Huh? Huh?"

"You see that red tag that says "Sold?" my father would ask.

"Yeah, we see it," one of us would reply.

"Do you know what SOLD means? That means somebody already bought it. It's SOLD."

"Ohhhhhhhhh."

This would evolve (or devolve, perhaps) into a ten-minute ethics discussion about why it would be wrong to just remove the sold tag and claim the tree as our own. Once we understood that we weren't to remove them under any circumstances, we'd run off to find the next perfect tree, which didn't have a Sold tag, but *did* have a piece of red ribbon, which after another quarter mile hike by my parents, we found out meant the same thing. We would do this for approximately 18 hours, or until my father just chopped down the one closest to the car. For some reason, it seemed like we always did this during the worst possible weather. Looking back on it now, I think that was my father's way of avoiding the crowds.

2. *The tying of the tree to the vehicle.*

If there was one thing my father always had an abundance of, it was rope. He would tie that tree on so tight it became one with the car. My mother had nightmares of losing a tree on the highway, so he did his best to try to reassure her, which generally meant the tree was tied down like Gulliver. Plus, my father really just *liked* rope, which was a shame, because most of the time – by the time we got the tree home – the knots would be frozen solid. Then he'd spend another 30 minutes trying to untie the knots so he didn't ruin the rope. In the end, he would almost always have to cut the tree from the car like he was a surgeon cutting out a failed kidney, and the car would end up with approximately 3,000 frozen little dreadlocks hanging off the sides of the luggage rack.

3. *The carving of the stump.*

Nine times out of ten, the tree ended up being too fat for the shitty little tree stand we had. That meant my father had to whittle it down slightly with the chain saw and chisels, which was pretty fun to watch (and listen to, if you liked to learn new and interesting curse words). By the time he was done cutting and chopping and whittling, the base of the tree usually looked like this:

It was ugly, but it fit in the stand and that's all that mattered.

4. *The dragging of the tree.*

For some reason, due to the design of the house I grew up in, it was neces-sary to drag the tree across every single carpeted surface in the entire place to get it to the living room. This resulted in pine needles being permanently em-bedded in the carpet for the next 12 months. My mother loved this. Between the needles and the sap, she was a wreck. It usually got so bad she'd just go outside and chain-smoke cigarettes until my father was done. And if you think that sounds bad, you should have seen it at the end of January when the tree was dry as dust and had to get dragged outside again.

By the time we moved out, a good archeologist could have accurately dated our house by the layers of pine needles in the shag rug. Our house had a vaulted ceiling so the trees were generally huge. Big ladders, eyebolts and picture hanging cable were almost always involved in keeping it upright. When we moved into a larger house with normal eight foot ceilings, it took us a while to adjust. The first couple of years we would bring home a tree that looked small outside, but ended up being way too big when it was finally dragged into the living room.

When my father attempted to stand it upright, it would invariably make a huge scrape mark across the ceiling. He'd grab the shears and be back at that tree like Edward Scissorhands – chopping an extra two feet off the top so it didn't hit the ceiling anymore. Picture a flat top haircut made of evergreen branches. Now picture an angel on top, jammed between the top of the tree and the ceiling so she looks like a mob informant in a car crusher, and you've nailed it.

5. *The stringing of the lights.*

This always started with "testing." Each string would be plugged in, and searched for burned out bulbs. Somehow, during the last 11 months in stor-age, approximately 25% of all the bulbs turned to shit. The thing is, the old strings were wired in series, which meant you had no way of knowing which bulb in the string was the culprit. If one bulb was bad, the whole string was out, and the trick was to find the bad bulb. You would do this with a "known good" bulb. By swapping it out with the bulbs that "looked bad," you would hopefully hit the right one and the string would jump to life. Of course, you were totally screwed if you had more than one bad bulb in the string, which was usually the case.

After that, you had no real choice but to use one of those window candles with a single socket and test every single bulb. Eventually, we would even hit the battered, taped-up shoebox, which is where we stored all the "old bulbs" – the ones that still lit up but had the color flaking off the outside.

(An aside about the bulbs: My mother was nothing if not a follower of Christmas bulb fads. Whatever bulb was popular the previous year, that's what we had. She would buy them the week after Christmas for half price. We had giant bulbs that looked like colored rock candy, we had spinners that used the heat from the bulb to spin a propeller, we had bubble lights, elf faces, blinkers, pastels, ones that were supposed to look like flickery candles but just looked like they were shorting out – you name it and at one time, we had it.)

My father hated all of them equally, but he hoped there was a special spot in hell for the antique lights. Because these were inherited from my grand-mother and consequently ancient, they got hot. Really, *really* hot. So hot, in fact, that they required the installation of a little scalloped metal pie plate thing around the back side of the bulb to limit its contact with things that might spontaneously ignite, such as pine needles or arm hair. The fun part about these lights was that my mother always wanted him to string them while they were lit.

Obviously, being a logical and practical guy, he always wanted to simply test the string, put them on the tree and THEN plug them in. Unfortunately though, it seemed like every time he took that approach only half the lights would come on due to one bulb getting jostled enough to fail. Then it would be "swap and replace" all the way down the line to find the bad bulb, which was much more of a pain when the lights were already on the tree.

Because of this complication happening more than once, eventually my mother got her way, which meant my father used to burn himself pretty regu-larly during this exercise. I can say with complete authority that most of the bad words I learned in my life I heard for the first time while watching my father put up a Christmas tree.

6. *The handling of the balls.*

Every year, my mother would decide whether or not to bring out the "new balls." These were the ones purchased on December 27th of the previous year. We kids, of course, all wanted the new balls.

Add the new ones to the huge pile of old nasty ones that had the color flak-ing off the outside, plus all the crappy construction paper and glitter-covered decorations we made in school – and you had quite an assortment of tree dec-orating crap. Of course, everything we had went on the tree. Usually after the first couple of boxes, we'd run out of those little hooks and start using un-bent paper clips. My mother and father would hit the high branches, and we kids would hit what was left of the low branches.

Since we all immediately grabbed the NEW balls, every branch below the four foot mark looked like this:

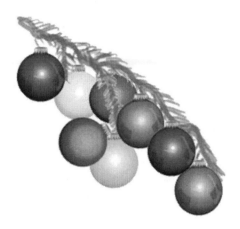

Now cover that already straining branch in tinsel and another pound of miscellaneous crap passing itself off as "ornaments" and you will come close to picturing an average Christmas tree at my house when we were growing up.

The ultimate psychedelic Christmas tree had to belong to my Grandmother. It's a shame I was never into hallucinogens, because this tree would have been a fantastic trip. It was an artificial tree, made completely out of shiny aluminum. It had blue-chrome balls on it, and it was in a base that slowly rotated the entire tree. On the floor next to it was a spotlight with a color wheel that would cycle between red, blue and green. I guess these vintage trees are quite collectible now.

I would stare at that thing for hours, all the while listening to the rrrrr-rrrrrr-rrrrr sound of the chicken rotisserie motor turning the thing around and around and around. It was truly mesmerizing.

About twice a day, we'd hear a metallic screaming sound coming from the porch, and one of us would have to run out there before the motor burned out. The slowly-spinning tree would periodically catch on the tree skirt and eventually get it so wound up on the trunk that it would stop the motor. It was like a festive Christmas snake eating its own tail.

The only bad thing about these aluminum trees (well, OK – not even close to the *only* bad thing, but one of the worst things) was that if your house happened to be carpeted, and you happened to add additional tinsel for effect, this tree would "reach out and touch you" if you walked too close to it. The first time Houdini caught a two-inch-long static electricity lightning bolt to the back of his head was also the *last* time.

We all learned to respect the tree.

Mission Unpossible

Christmas at our house wasn't just all about the perfect tree. There were other deeper and more important religious aspects to it. Presents, for instance. It seemed as if sometimes Christmas was a constant battle between good and evil. In case you need a hint – we were the evil.

OK, maybe not *completely* evil, just…very impatient. We knew that even though most of the Good Stuff would be coming from Santa, there would be some additional gifts from our parents and grandparents.

Our mission: To find them.

We stared up at the trapdoor in the ceiling.

"No way," The Snitch said. "Unpossible. No way I'm lettin' you boost me up."

"Come on," I replied, from atop the chair. "Don't be a butthead. I won't drop you. And it's *im*possible."

"Uh uh. Go get Houdini if you want to, but I'm not climbing up on your shoulders."

"He'll do it – you know why? Because he's not a chicken," I said. "But you're still helping us. You can hold the chair steady or something."

"What do you need me for?" he asked, his suspicion evident.

"If you help, then you can't tell on us," I said. He knew that was true, and reluctantly agreed.

I went to find Houdini. Time was running out.

I found him downstairs watching The Flintstones on TV. "Hey, Mom and Dad are out and I'm gonna stand on a chair and then you have to stand on my shoulders and look around in the attic," I said.

"K," he said, not looking away from the TV. "It's almost over, I'll be there in a second."

He didn't even ask why, he just agreed to it. That's what I liked about Houdini – he was always up for anything regardless of the consequences. I left and went back upstairs to the hallway, where The Snitch was standing with his flashlight in hand. "I got this," he said, holding it up. "In case the light bulb is out."

"Good thinkin'," I said, dragging the chair a little to the left so it was directly under the trap door. I climbed up on the chair again and yelled, "HOUDINI! COME ON!"

He pounded up the stairs and stopped when he saw me standing on the chair. "What's in the attic?" he asked.

"Our Christmas presents," I said. "We already checked mom and dad's closet, and there was nothing in there. This is the only other place they could be."

"Okay. Boost me," he said, taking the flashlight from The Snitch and shoving it in his pocket.

"Climb up on the chair," I said, turning and holding on to the chair back. "Then get on my shoulders, and we'll see if you can reach the door."

Two seconds later, he was sitting on my shoulders and I was standing up on the chair. I was trying to look up, but it was difficult with him on my back. "Can you reach it?" I asked.

"Yeah, just barely," he said.

"Push the trap door open then grab on to the edge," I said, knowing the "door" was really just a piece of plywood lying loose in a frame. "If you can get a good grip on the edge, pull yourself up and stand on my shoulders."

He did it easily, and before I knew it, he was standing on my shoulders with me holding his legs, his head and the top third of his body sticking into the attic. The Snitch was holding me steady on the chair.

"See anything?" I asked, wincing under the weight of Houdini's sneakers, which were starting to smash permanent Converse All-Star imprints on the tops of both my shoulders.

"I think I can reach the light," he said, fishing around for the string that was attached to the single, bare bulb. A click, and light streamed down from the hole. A pause. Then, "Nope. Nothin."

"That's impossible," I said. "Look in the back."

"I might be able to pull myself up," he said, and before I could tell him not to, he pulled his entire body up into the attic and disappeared.

"How's he gonna get down?" the Snitch asked, voicing exactly what I was thinking.

"He'll have to hang down and then I'll get under him again," I said confidently, having no idea.

"Anything?" I yelled up through the dark hole.

Houdini poked his head down and said, "Nope. Nothin' in the back either."

"Crap. OK, come down," I said. "Drop your legs down through and get back on my shoulders. Then drag the door over."

He dropped through the hole like a spider monkey out of a tree, and I barely got under him in time. He was facing the wrong way, hanging on the edge of the attic door frame, but at least he was standing on my shoulders. He moved the door most of the way over the hole, then without warning slammed down so he was sitting on my shoulders backward, giving me a face full of Houdini crotch.

"Jeez! Get the door closed, will ya?" I yelled, barely keeping my balance as I tried to avert my face. If it hadn't been for the Snitch steadying my legs I think we both would have been on the floor in a pile.

I got him to the ground in one piece and considered our next move. "Where else can we look?" I asked, not thinking I'd actually get an answer.

"What about the crawlspace in Dad's office?" Houdini asked.

I had forgotten all about that.

"Let's go!" I said. We put the chair back and ran downstairs.

Getting into the crawlspace was more complicated than it sounds, because it wasn't just a simple crawlspace. The crawlspace door had a home-made desk in front of it. The left side of the desk was supported by a chain, and operated like the flip up section of a bar that allows the waitresses and bartenders to get behind it. This fold-down section of desk blocked the crawlspace door. We couldn't just move all the crap on the desk and flip it up to open the door, because it would be obvious someone had been in there. We had to keep track of where everything was so my father didn't know we were snooping around.

I grabbed a pencil and pad, making a mental note of its original location. While The Snitch and Houdini waited, I sketched the desktop and the placement of everything on it. The stapler, the hole punch, the stacks of papers, the telephone – all documented. When that was done, we moved it all and swung the desk up, and opened the crawlspace door. I motioned for Houdini to make like a good soldier and take a peek while I held up the desk.

He crawled in with the flashlight and I heard him say, "WOW!"

"What?" I said, "Did you find something?"

"Yeah," he replied. "Tons of stuff. But it's all wrapped."

I was afraid of this. "OK," I said. "Don't touch anything. Just look. Do you see anything on the wrapping paper? Initials or anything?" My mother would always put our first initial in some inconspicuous spot so she knew who was supposed to get what on Christmas morning.

"Yeah. I see one that has a H on it. Can I pull it out?"

"No, we have to keep track of where everything is. If the pile gets messed up, Mom will know. Just take the easy ones off the top. If that one's on top, hand it out."

I turned to The Snitch. "Go into my room and pull out the bottom drawer of my dresser," I said. "Pull it all the way out, then lift up the bottom and bring me the little box underneath."

He took off to get it and I managed to get the desk section to stay up by itself by wedging it with a ruler. That way I could grab the presents Houdini was handing out the door. "OK, that's enough," I said when there was no more room to stack, and I had everything documented. "C'mon out."

He backed out of the hole and sat up. A moment later The Snitch came into the office with a skinny cigar box. In the box was The Kit.

The Kit consisted of a single-edged razor blade, about four or five different types of tape – gloss, matte finish, skinny, wide – even a small roll of masking tape, because sometimes my mother ran out of the clear stuff. The kit was used once a year to open, examine and then re-wrap Christmas presents.

We carefully examined the presents one by one, deciding which side to cut. It had to be the side where the paper was loosest, otherwise you ran the risk of tearing it when you tried to re-wrap. If you did it right, you could cut the tape, carefully open the flap, look to see what the gift was, then tape it closed again. I was the surgeon general of Christmas presents.

We opened almost all our presents, except for the ones we deemed too hard to re-wrap, taking care to re-tape using the same type and width my mother had initially used. Unless you looked with a magnifying glass, you wouldn't know they had been tampered with. As Houdini was backing out of the hole after putting the gifts back in their places, he jostled something and the desk section came smashing down on his back and head.

"Ow." he said. That was it. A four foot long, 30-inch-wide hunk of 3/4 inch plywood had just bounced off his melon, and all he said was "Ow." The kid was indestructible.

We got the desk fastened back in place like it was supposed to be, and referenced our drawing to make sure everything was back where it belonged. Lastly, the pencil and pad went back to their original locations.

There was only one more thing to take care of.

"Let me see your surprised look," I said to The Snitch. "Christmas morning when you open that radio you wanted, what are you going to do?"

He said, "WOW! A radio! Just what I wanted!" and his face lit up. Not bad. A little cheesy. Not Oscar worthy, but not bad. I turned to Houdini.

"That G.I. JOE in there," I said. "Pretend you just opened it up. Act surprised."

He gave a performance that would have made Jimmy Stewart proud. In fact, I think an angel may have lost its wings that day.

I'd like to tell you my parents never caught on to our little yearly mission, but to this day, I'm not really sure. Either The Snitch let something slip, or we weren't as careful as we thought we were, but the following year my mother told us that all our presents were being stored at a neighbor's house until Christmas morning. It's entirely possible it was just motherly intuition.

We never got in trouble for it, so my guess is they were never 100% sure we had been snooping. Maybe they just let us slide, but I prefer to think of it as a Christmas Miracle.

Clear and Presents Danger

The house we grew up in was a raised ranch. When you walked in the front door, you found yourself standing on a small landing with a set of stairs going up and another set going down. In our house, the bedrooms, kitchen, dining room and living room were upstairs, and the "family room" was downstairs. In order to keep some heat on the bottom floor, we had a magnetic vinyl accordion door at the bottom of the stairs. In the winter, this was almost always closed. It also made quite a racket when you opened and closed it, due to the metal track and the magnetic latch. That door was the only thing separating The Snitch, Houdini and me from our Christmas tree and the glorious treasure Santa brought us on Christmas morning.

For quite a few years, we were forbidden to go down there until our parents were awake. That wasn't really such a good plan on their part, seeing as how all three of us were usually up and out of bed at 4:30 a.m., and there was no way in hell they were going to sleep through *that*. Finally, in an effort to get more than two hours of sleep, my parents decided to simply pick what seemed to us to be an arbitrary time. It varied from year to year, and thinking about it now, I believe it was dependent upon several variables, including our behavior and how late Santa had stayed awake on Christmas Eve deciphering Korean assembly instructions.

Most of the time we were allowed downstairs by seven or eight a.m.. If we made giant pains in the asses of ourselves, that could be pushed to nine, with dire threats of "stop bugging me or you'll have to wait until after church," and nobody (except maybe my parents) wanted that. There was some quiet whining, but for the most part we were never better-behaved than we were between the hours of five a.m. and nine a.m. on Christmas morning. I'm still not sure which was worse – going to church first and trying to sit still for an hour in utter anticipation, or seeing it all first, and then being forced to leave it behind and sit in church for an hour just thinking about the stuff you barely had a chance to play with.

I think there were two main reasons we weren't allowed downstairs – one, our parents wanted to take pictures and witness us being surprised and two, Santa, being sort of a slacker, never wrapped anything. We'd always search to find the presents my parents had hidden under the stairs or in the attic, but the ones we found were never from Santa. All Santa's presents appeared magically out of thin air while we slept.

We could never quite figure it out. Apparently, we weren't too bright, and we never questioned why my father always showed up at my grandmother's house a few hours after us on Christmas Eve, because he had to "work late."

I am pretty sure the two phrases my father most dreaded to see on that night were "some assembly required" and "batteries not included." He would get home from work and frantically build stuff until he had to meet us, then, after we got home and went to sleep, he'd finish everything up and put it under the tree. No wonder the poor guy wanted to sleep in a little.

As far as the whole Santa thing went – I had some suspicions, but, on the other hand, I also believed in magic and that everything in the Johnson Smith catalog worked as advertised. I was a firm believer in Santa long after all the kids in school were telling me he was fake. I distinctly remember slipping out of bed late one Christmas eve and eavesdropping on a conversation between my mother and father. They were sneaky and evil. Instead of yelling at me to get back to bed, they pretended they didn't know I was there, and had this conversation:

"I'm starting to get a little worried."

"You think he's not coming?"

"I'm not sure. Normally, he'd have been here by now. Maybe he had problems with the reindeer and he's running late."

"That could be. Or maybe someone upstairs isn't really asleep yet. I'd better go check."

To this day, I can remember from experience that there really *is* a way to force yourself to go to sleep by sheer willpower, but I seem to have forgotten how it's done. It's a shame, because it could really come in handy on some Sunday nights when I can't sleep and have to get my ass up for work the next day.

The only chimney on our house was four inches in diameter, and went directly into a natural gas furnace in the downstairs hall closet. I knew Santa wasn't getting in that way, because I had seen that thing with the door off, and unless Santa happened to be fireproof, those solid walls of blue flame looked pretty impenetrable.

I raised that particular concern one year, thinking we should maybe leave the back door unlocked for him, and it turned out that our particular version of Santa just needed a fireplace – and not necessarily a chimney – to magically appear.

It's a good thing he wasn't picky about it either, because this was our fire-place:

Every year, my father inserted cardboard tabs into cardboard slots, locked them in place with brass-headed fasteners, and paved the way for our magical back-door Santa. Behind the "logs" there was a small orange light bulb and holder for a little pinwheel. The heat from the bulb would cause the pinwheel to rotate, casting weird shadows behind the logs. Voilà! Ultra-realistic "flames." It had to be wired to the wall so it didn't fall over when you hung full stockings on it, so it was completely plausible that a 300-pound fat guy in a red suit with a giant sack of presents would have no problem at all simply appearing inside of it without so much as popping tab A from slot B.

One Christmas morning, we decided we'd had enough of the aforemen-tioned iron-clad rule to stay upstairs. *Do not go downstairs, do not go near the accordion door. In fact, do not even go down on the landing.* Otherwise, our parents swore to us, they would take everything Santa gave us and donate it to the less fortunate. And while we had nothing against the less fortunate, we knew the big man usually did pretty good by us, and there was no reason to get carried away.

Plausible deniability was always our game. We tended to follow the *letter* but not necessarily the *spirit* of the law. They said we couldn't do *that*, but they never said we couldn't do *this*. So, while we couldn't go down on the landing, there were other ways to skin a fat guy in a red suit.

There was one thing our parents didn't count on, and that was Houdini and his really small head. Well, two things actually, since Houdini's small head was of no use to us without my Ready Ranger mobile field pack.

READY RANGER
mobile field pack

AURORA

Self contained: Communications/Power Pack, Periscope, View Signal Unit, 7/A Horn, Star Finder, Console and Holder, Courier Pouch, Compass (Ranger Direction Finder), Inventer Skate

I was nothing if not a Ready Ranger. I know, that sounds really geeky in retrospect.

"I have an idea," I whispered. "You guys want to see what we got from Santa?"

"We'll get in trouble," Snitch said. "We can't sneak down. Dad will hear the door."

"Yeah, but we don't have to," I said. "Houdini, go in my room and get my Field Pack." A few moments later, he came back with the kit, and I opened it up.

If you're not familiar with this piece of all-plastic, ultra-high-tech spy/survival gear, all you need to do is look at that picture and figure out what the tall black thing in the center is. I popped it free.

I held the periscope through the railing and tried to angle it to point through one of the little triangular openings in the top of the accordion door, but it wouldn't work. I couldn't get the angle right. If I adjusted it so I could actually look through it, all I could see was the door. In order to tip it so I could to look through the tiny openings in the top of the door, I had to hold it out beyond the railing, and then I couldn't get my eye close enough to look through it.

"Houdini," I whispered. "Does your head fit through the railing?"

He immediately tried it, and it popped through like we had buttered the sides. I already knew mine wouldn't fit, mostly due to my fat head and obscenely large ears. Also, I still had recurring nightmares about the one time I had actually managed to get my head jammed between the wrought iron balusters on the stairs. I screamed bloody murder for what seemed like an eternity while my mother ran around frantically trying to figure out a way to free me. Eventually, she really *did* have to butter my head, and I wasn't going there again.

After he pulled his head back out, I said, "OK, now lay down and stick your head back through, and when you're set, I'm gonna give you the periscope."

He lay down on the floor, stuck his head through the middle two balusters, and put his arms through the openings on either side. I handed him the periscope.

"Don't drop it," I said.

"I'm not gonna," he whispered defensively.

Of course he wouldn't drop it. Why should he drop it? He was only lying on the floor with his head sticking through the railing, barely able to move his arms.

"OK, now hang it down a little bit, and see if you can get it pointed through one of the little openings in the top of the door. Then tell us what you see."

It took him a second to get situated, but then he struck the mother load. "Whoa," he said, breathlessly.

"Jeez, c'mon, tell us! Whattaya see?" The Snitch said, desperately hoping for a two wheeler.

"I see a lot of stuff. A bozo bopper. Battling Tops. A big wheel, I think. Snitch, you got a *bike*!!"

The Snitch did a little dance of joy. "What else?" I asked impatiently.

"Rock'em Sock'em Robots!" he said.

Score! That was all I needed to hear.

"OK, give that to me and come on back through," I said, as I sat on his back and pried the periscope from his hands. He didn't want to give it up, but he was in no position to resist. Luckily, he didn't have an "outer ear" problem like I did, and when I got off his back so he could move, his head popped out effortlessly.

"Good job," I said, already deciding in my head that Red Rocker was going to remain undefeated forever. We packed up the field pack, and immediately went back to being the best behaved kids in the world for another three hours, secure in the knowledge that our magical back door Santa had come through for us once again.

I'll Take Three.

I am not sure how many times in my father's life he's said those words, but that was his solution to a particular dilemma – how to shop for me and my brothers. To avoid in-fighting, present stealing and general envy, he would just simplify his life and buy three of whatever it was. If we didn't like it, well, tough.

Initially, this strategy worked pretty well. That is, until my brothers' toys started turning up mysteriously broken while mine were still perfectly fine. That was odd, since I was clearly much rougher on my possessions than they were. While Houdini's powers of destruction were closer to my own, this was definitely not true of The Snitch. His stuff was always immaculate. His toys didn't even look like he used them. I swear to God he would wash the dirt off his dump truck at the end of a hard day's play. If someone had given him access to car wax, I'm fairly sure it would have made his day.

Oddly, it was his stuff that showed up broken most of the time. He couldn't prove it, but he believed that I was somehow responsible. After a while, he figured out that I was sneaking into his room at night and swapping out my broken whatever for his good one. After that, he started writing his initials on his stuff with a black Sharpie.

At a very young age, I discovered that rubbing alcohol will remove Sharpie ink without harming plastic in the slightest. I also became quite adept at forging my brother's handwriting.

The Snitch was beside himself when his clearly marked talking GI Joe suddenly went all Jack Bauer and refused to say a word no matter what you did to him, while mine was still talking up a storm.

In retrospect, I was a terrible brother. I think the culmination of my under-handedness was when my portable cassette player stopped working. This obviously wasn't fair, since I used mine all the time and The Snitch hardly ever used his, and consequently, his was in perfect condition. By this time, The Snitch had gotten wise to my methods and started scratching his initials in everything he owned.

I got around this little obstacle by opening his player up and swapping the guts. I'm not sure if he ever did figure that one out. Snitch, if you're reading this, I owe you a Walkman.

Anyway, to back up a bit, after my father realized that buying us the identical thing wasn't working to keep the peace, he decided to buy us the *same* gift, but in different configurations.

So for instance I got this:

and my brother got this:

As you can see, there was very little guts-swapping potential there. In this case it didn't matter because I didn't want his. Mine was obviously way cooler. At least mine didn't look like a giant girl's bracelet. Toot-a-Loop? Really?

I loved my radio. It was AM only, and sounded like shit, but I hung it from my bike handlebars and listened to it constantly when I rode around. I put it on the pillow next to my head late at night and listened to the skip signals from far away cities. I listened to it religiously every time the top-40 countdown was on. I burned through nine-volt batteries so fast my mother started rationing me.

As I've said, I was rough on things. I dropped it while riding around and cracked the plastic dial window, so I pulled the broken pieces out. I painted it orange, but didn't bother masking the dial, so the numbers were gone. I put stickers all over it, then peeled them off, leaving it gooey with adhesive, which obviously collected dirt. During its final days, the outside was the approximate color and texture of an inner-city basketball. I tried wiping the adhesive off with acetone and a towel, but that just smeared the paint and exposed the blue plastic, which the acetone then began to melt, causing the towel fibers to stick to it. After that it was just sticky all the time. God forbid that it touched the rug. With the cat and dog hair, the thing would routinely come up from the floor looking like a blue and orange elephant testicle on a chain. (If you are an elephant nut expert and know for a fact that they don't have hairy balls, then feel free to edit that last sentence and substitute your favorite large-testicled mammal of choice.) I don't know from elephant junk. I just know this radio looked horrible and I barely wanted to touch it.

Eventually, it just sort of gave up on belonging to me, similar to every pet I had back then. I have no idea what happened to it, although I think I may have just chucked it when I discovered FM.

Fast forward 30 years. I'm on e-bay, and I see the exact radio I had when I was a kid. I flip out and buy it for about five times what it probably cost new, but it's a perfect specimen, in perfect shape. When it finally shows up via UPS, it stinks like an old ashtray, like so much stuff you find on e-bay. I air it out for a few days and it's fantastic.

As a result of this successful purchase/bid, and maybe because I still feel a little guilty about my parts-swapping past, I decided to find a Toot-A-Loop for The Snitch. I figure it'll make a fantastic Christmas present. I find one, bid on it, and win it. It shows up discolored and smelling of cigarettes, so I ship it back for a refund, which I don't get. I find another, make sure it's as advertised and I win that one too. It shows up in a well-packaged box, and unbelievably, I don't have to knock cigarette ashes out of the box before I re-move the radio.

It's not in great shape, but it's pretty good. It has one big gouge, and the dial is scratched, but hey, it's 35 years old. I spend about a half-hour cleaning and polishing it. Then I throw a battery in it, and discover that it has some tuning problems. Even so, it's still exactly like the one he had when he was a kid.

I'm pretty excited – I figure if he has even one nostalgic bone in his body, he'll love it. I take it over to my father's house, and tell him all about my idea, which he thinks is great except for the one thing I didn't count on, but in retrospect, probably should have.

He says, "follow me," and starts up the stairs. I follow him to my brother's old room, and he opens the closet door and pulls my brother's *ori-ginal radio* from the top shelf. Not only that – the damned thing looks *brand-new*, like it just came out of the box.

At that point, I didn't care. I was tired of bidding on shit and sending it back and wasting a fortune in shipping. So I just gave him both, and told him the story. I'm not sure if he liked it, or if he thought it was corny. In any case, about five minutes after he unwrapped them, his three-year-old threw his original one and it hit the kitchen floor and broke in half.

Not his father's son.

I offered to swap the guts out into the spare for him, but he never took me up on it.

Happy "Valintines" Day.

Remember the excitement you felt when Valentine's day rolled around? Remember how you would stay up late on February 13th, writing out your cards and making sure to put a little "extra effort" into that one for the girl or boy you had a crush on? You don't? Well screw you, then. I didn't want a card from you anyway.

In my stash of childhood artwork, I found an envelope full of cards from my second and third grade class. I did a little digging through the pile, and even found one I had made for my mom.

Let's take a stroll down memory lane. A trip back to a simpler life; to a time when your teacher forced you to give a card to everyone in the class – even the fat kid who smelled like sour milk and threw up all over his desk that one time. Yes. Even him.

You could always tell the kids who had thrifty parents – their valentines would always be reused from last year. They'd take an old card, glue it to a piece of paper like it was art, and then fold it in half and write something in it. Here's an example of a card like that I received from Susan:

Because of a clearly inferior glue job, I could see that the back of the original card said "To Susan." That hurt me deeply, since I knew I was getting a recycled card. But that wasn't the worst part. Oh no. Not only was the card itself recycled, the *text inside the paper it was glued to* was *also* recycled:

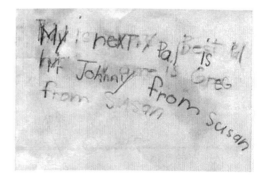

In case you can't make out what's going on there, that bitch Susan had originally written "This is for my best pal. His name is Greg," but apparently Greg pissed in her Frosted Flakes or something, because she decided to give

62

it to *me* instead. However, rather than expend the minimal effort to actually get a new sheet of paper, she just did a half-assed erasing job and sent it to "Her next pal" who was apparently yours truly. So it was Susan, then Greg, then me. Can't you feel the love? I know I can. I guess it's only fair that I don't remember her.

Then there were the kids who clearly had no help at all from their parents. A folded piece of paper was the best you were going to get from them. Here's one to me from a kid named Danny:

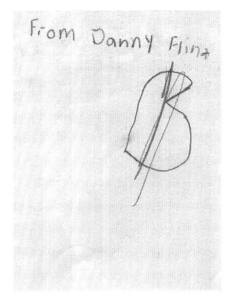

That was it. Nothing inside. In fact, there *was* no inside. It was just a single sheet, with a deformed sideways heart on it. The heart was scribbled out in an apparent act of defiance against teacher-forced boy-love.

I don't blame Danny for fighting the establishment, although he always was a troublemaker. He may be in jail now.

That would be sort of ironic.

Remember how I was telling you about going the extra mile for someone you really liked? Check out this painstakingly rendered work of art created just for me:

You're hard to beet, Valentine. Do you carrot all 4 me?

That's true love right there.

At first, this one made me all warm and fuzzy inside, because there seemed to be quite a lot of work, thought and feeling put into it. Then I opened it and immediately thought, "No, STEVE, I most certainly DO NOT carrot all 4 you, you little homo."

I kid. After all, it was a simpler time. I realize that Steve had no idea that his Valentine might have been a little inappropriate. He was just being a nice guy. It reminded me of that one Simpsons episode when someone asked Ralph Wiggum if he were gay or straight and he replied, "I'm not anything yet!" That was us.

Last, but not least, here's one I made for my mother when I was in third grade:

Dear Mom, Happy Valintines Day. Thank you for all the grand things you did for us.

Grand Things? Who the fuck was I? Little Lord Fauntleroy?

"Thank you ever so much for all the grand things you've done for us, mummy. Now, if you don't mind, The Snitch and Houdini and I are off to play a quick game of cricket in the courtyard. Perhaps before we retire for the evening you'd be so kind as to read to us from the Illustrated Chaucer? Very good, then. Ta ta!"

I don't know what I was thinking. I have no recollection of making any of that.

I'm still not sure about that Steve kid, though.

All Hail The Easter Bunny! Bringer of Candy, Hider of Eggs.

Houdini still believed in the Easter Bunny. I knew the truth, and The Snitch was on the fence about it. He had already figured out the tooth fairy, since he caught my mother putting money under his pillow once, and didn't buy her "doing a favor for the tooth fairy" excuses. Some of the kids in his class had told him that Santa Claus wasn't real, and that wasn't sitting well. He still believed, but only because he had asked my mother flat out about all the mythical beings that brought him stuff, and received her assurances that they did indeed exist, and the kids in his class were just making up stories.

He even asked me about Santa once, and under dire threats from my mother, I did what I had to do and lied my ass off. After that, he was pretty sure on the Santa thing. He was finding it a little harder to believe in a six-foot-tall rabbit that delivered candy replicas of itself and hid your colored eggs, though. That shit didn't sit right, whereas apparently a fat guy in a red suit who flew around in a sleigh pulled by reindeer and slid down non-existent chimneys into cardboard fireplaces was still perfectly logical.

Even so, he wasn't *quite* ready to let the Easter Bunny go. Maybe it's because of the lengths my father went to in order to preserve the myth.

On the night before Easter, we'd always leave a carrot and a bowl of water out for the Easter bunny. I don't know why we left a bowl, since I'm sure a human-sized, vest wearing bunny who walked upright could have handled a drinking glass without much trouble, but that's what we did. We made him drink his water out of the bowl like some kind of domesticated animal. When we had gone to sleep, my father would nibble chunks out of the carrot and leave some stray pieces of bunny fur stuck to it. (I *still* don't know where those rabbit hairs came from, and I'm not sure I want to.)

Houdini, however, believed in the Easter Bunny with his heart and soul, and all he could talk about for the preceding week was how many eggs he was going to find in the Easter egg hunt. Every year, we'd color a few dozen eggs, and the Easter bunny would hide them all around the house. The next morning, whoever found the most eggs would be declared the winner.

There wasn't any actual *prize* if you were the winner, so looking back on it, I'm not sure exactly why it meant so much to us to be the one who found the most eggs. Maybe because it meant you were the best at finding. I think that was a recurring theme of our childhood. If you had the most X, you generally won, unless X was equal to something like chickenpox or mosquito bites. There were even occasional fist fights over the eggs, which isn't really in the spirit of the Christian Easter celebration – although since we're talking about Easter eggs here, maybe the pagans were more lenient when it came to fertility and fisticuffs.

The fights in our house were usually of the "I saw it first" variety. House rules were drawn up, and it was decided that whoever touched the egg first owned it, regardless of who "called it" upon visual discovery. I do know that nothing bad ever happened to the second and third place winners. At least in our fights, the beta male didn't run the risk of being killed or exiled from the village.

We were coloring eggs at the kitchen table, a row of white coffee cups filled with warm vinegar water and food dye lined up before each of us. A giant bowl of hard boiled eggs sat in the center of the table, each one with a perfect, pin-pricked hole in the large end. My grandmother had a little device that poked this hole, and she swore by it. It was supposed to let the air out and keep the shells from cracking when you boiled the eggs. For the most part it worked well, and we rarely lost one.

We loaded up our cups, one egg in each. As the eggs steeped, we constantly checked the color with the wire egg holder. The goal was to achieve a deep, primary color with no uneven areas. It was a true art form. In our view, the deeper the color the better. Two-tones were the holy grail and required exquisite mastery over the wire holder, because the one thing you didn't want was an overlap mark in your colors. That was just shoddy workmanship.

As each was deemed finished, we'd transfer it to the drying rack, and then to its final resting place, the Easter Bunny's basket. When the final egg had been dyed, and the basket was full, we'd set it in the center of the kitchen table.

The next challenge was to keep my grandfather from eating them. He *loved* hard boiled eggs, and my mother always tried to make a few extras for him, but he'd inevitably end up sneaking into the ones we colored. If he got caught, you'd hear shouts of "MOMMMMM! GRANDPA'S EATING ONE OF MY EGGS!" as another masterpiece was cracked on the edge of the kitchen table and consumed. The upshot of this is that we never knew how exactly how many eggs were left in the basket at any given time.

The year after I found out the truth about Mr. E. Bunny, my parents enlisted me to hide the eggs. Up until that point, I always thought the Easter Bunny was a little soft in his bunny head, because his hiding places truly sucked. Half the time, you'd see the supposedly-hidden eggs just by looking around in the room. After finding out that it had been my parents hiding the eggs, it all made sense. They wanted them to be easy to find so that the hunt would be over in time for lunch.

As a newly drafted egg-hider, I took my responsibility seriously. I decided that the hiding places should be more challenging. I didn't share this belief with my mother, however. It was a clear case of UNODIR (unless otherwise directed), and I was flying solo on this one.

I took the eggs and hid them all over the house, making sure there were none in plain sight. I hid them in shoes, behind pictures frames, under the TV stand, even in the pockets of coats hanging in the closet. And I considered those the *easy* ones to find. I must have hidden close to three dozen eggs.

When I had finished, I told my mother that my mission was accomplished and I was going to bed. She then told me that in the morning my job would be to "find" a few, but then let The Snitch and Houdini find the rest. Maybe even give Houdini a few hints because he was still pretty small. I felt like this would be the best hunt ever.

When I got up the next morning and came down to the kitchen, my mother said, "So, how many eggs did you hide last night?"

"Uh, all of them?" I replied.

She looked at me in disbelief, wondering how she raised such a dummy.

"You mean you didn't *count* them?" she asked.

"No," I said. "You didn't tell me to count them. I just took the basket of eggs and hid them until there were none left."

"Tell me this, Einstein," she said. "How are we going to know when they've all been found?"

Unfortunately, that was a question to which I did not have a good answer. She tried to find out how many eggs my grandfather had scarfed, but he couldn't remember – or more likely wouldn't cop to it. We estimated that there were somewhere between 20 and 30 eggs hidden around the house.

Houdini and The Snitch came running down the stairs. Houdini ran right to the plate we had left out.

"Look!" Houdini yelled. "The Easter Bunny ate the carrot!" We all gathered around to look at the gnaw marks my father had left behind. Then we went straight to our Easter baskets to check out what sort of candy we had received. Sometimes the Easter Bunny would leave us a toy as well. (One year, I remember the Easter Bunny had left us wrist-rocket slingshots. That was a good Easter, although getting hit in the back of the head with a marshmallow peep flying at 200 feet per second hurts more than you'd think. Sadly, the slingshots were confiscated until summer vacation. In retrospect, perhaps they hadn't been the Easter Bunny's best idea.)

After breakfast, it was time for the egg hunt. The Snitch and Houdini mentioned how the Easter Bunny did a better job of hiding this year, and I was secretly pleased. After they had found all they could, we were still quite a few eggs short. I started giving out suggestions in the guise of brilliant deductions. "I wonder if the Easter Bunny would hide any eggs in the closets?" I'd ask, heading toward one of the closets. "I'll check this one, you guys check the one in the hall." A few seconds later, you'd hear Houdini or The Snitch yell "Found another one!" and the hunt would go on.

Finally, we had them all. Or at least I thought we did. I hadn't been keeping great track of all my hiding places the night before, and with Houdini and The Snitch running around the house at full speed, I wasn't sure which ones they had actually found. My mother looked at me, and quietly said "Well?" I gave her a little shrug of my shoulders. "I dunno," I said. "I think so."

In August, my mother complained to my father that the downstairs bathroom smelled a little like sewer, especially over near the sink. My dad is one of those do-it-yourself kind of guys, so before he called the plumber he went and had a look. He emptied out everything underneath the cabinet so he could get at the drain pipe to see if he could find the problem.

He found the problem. In case you're wondering, it was bright blue.

Summer Vacation vs. My Parents

What your Parents Don't Know Might Kill You.

There's one thing about my childhood that still amazes me to this day: The fact that I'm still alive. I never killed anyone else either, although that was a close thing.

We grew up in a suburban area, a growing series of developments that were basically surrounded by forest that had sprouted up in what used to be farmland. As a result, we spent a lot of time out of the house, running around on the trails that were cut through the woods. This was especially true in the summer, when we were let loose at eight in the morning and didn't come home until dinner time or dark, whichever came first.

Things were dangerous in the woods – more dangerous than we or our parents probably really knew. They trusted us to stay out of trouble and to look out for each other, and we mostly did the first, and sometimes did the second, if you don't count all the times one subset of us tried to ditch the odd man out. Sometimes it was me, sometimes it was Markie, but most times it was The Snitch. We dodged death and/or serious disfigurement more than a few times due to nothing more than sheer luck. That's why you probably shouldn't let your kids read this. They will swear up and down that they would *never* do anything in this book, but keep in mind that I said the same thing when I was their age.

Granted, most kids today are probably more interested in playing *Gears of War* or *Modern Warfare II* than actually getting outside and running around, but just in case, tell them not to do these things. I disavow all responsibility for the safety of your children. You're on your own.

The First Time

When I was probably ten or so, I got on a booby-trap kick. Markie, The Snitch and I loved the woods, and as little kids, we hated and feared the big kids who also hung out there. It was contested territory, sort of like the Gaza strip, only with a more stable government. Their single purpose in life seemed to be torturing us with their motor bikes, and if they caught us in the open, it was like watching someone hunt buffalo from a helicopter.

They liked to do donuts around us and kick up dust until we were choking, or come cruising down the trail at an amazing rate of speed and try to get as close to us as they could before swerving. Apparently, their goal was to make us crap ourselves, and then laugh about it later.

Eventually, we had enough of this. We started out simple – pulling logs across the trail. Shortly thereafter, we discovered that if we did this on a blind curve, we could actually get these dirt bike assholes to slow down. We were hoping one of them would hit the log and mess up his motorcycle, but I don't think they ever did. For the most part, they just took a quick spin around the trails at a slow speed and removed all the obstacles before riding.

That all changed when we saw our first jungle warfare movie. The almost poetic simplicity and overall effectiveness of camouflaged pits with punji stakes at the bottom was not lost on us.

At the very first opportunity, we went out to the trails to dig a hole. We quickly realized that there was no way three kids under the age of ten armed with a single shovel were going to dig a hole big enough to swallow a motor-cycle, so a new battle plan was quickly drafted. We would opt for something smaller.

Our ten-year-old logic told us that a motorcycle with a flat tire can't be rid-den until it's fixed. So we dug a 12" deep, 24" wide, 36" long trench across the center of the trail. We didn't really think through our goals here, but ba-sically we were just after some light destruction, a flat tire at most. With that modest goal in mind, we took a few strips of plywood, pounded some nails through them, and placed them in the bottom of our shallow trench, points up – mini-punji stakes, specially designed for motorcycle knobbies.

We then bridged the trench with small branches and placed a sheet of newspaper over this. The last step was to cover the entire thing in sand. We stepped back and looked at our handiwork. It was perfect. You could stand right on top of it and never see it. Now all we had to do was hide in the woods and wait.

So that's exactly what we did.

We sat there slapping at bugs, all three of us jacked up on adrenaline and unable to stay still. It was pure torture. Just when we couldn't stand it any longer, we heard the whine of a dirt bike approaching. We recognized the sound of that particular bike. It was Victor Bradford, and he was coming right towards the booby-trap. We waited, holding our breath in anticipation, our hearts pounding in our scrawny chests.

It was right about then that The Snitch, who was actually two years younger than me and just one year younger than our friend Markie, put the entire picture together. He was the first of us to figure out that maybe, just *maybe*, someone could possibly get hurt or killed with this plan, and that it was a very bad idea. I don't think that was what he was really worried about, however. I think it had more to do with the fact that if someone got hurt, we would be "In Trouble."

The one thing my brother did NOT like to be was "In Trouble." He feared it completely. It was like a miniature death sentence for him – it totally freaked him out, and I still have no idea why. His visceral response to being in trouble for doing something bad was generally way out of proportion to the actual trouble we were in. I'm sure that whatever the reason, it has a lot to do with why he's an attorney now.

In retrospect, he was the smart one, but at the time, we all just thought he was a big wimp who had nothing better to do than hang out with us until things went south, and then run home and tell our parents about how it was all our idea and he didn't have anything to do with it. It didn't take much of this behavior for him to solidify his reputation as a "Teller," and make us not think twice about ditching him.

At any rate, he panicked (or wised up, depending upon your perspective), stood up, and tried to wave Victor off. By that time, however, it was too late. He was too far away, and Markie and I were still crouched in the woods. The motorcycle was coming fast, in reality probably doing no more than 25 mph or so, but it was so loud that it seemed to be almost flying.

The collision happened in slow motion, exactly like it did in one of the war movies we had been watching. The bike's front tire hit the pit and Victor went flying, followed closely by his motorcycle. He landed hard on his back, the bike crashing down next to him.

Time had stopped. We were frozen in place, our mouths hanging open, our eyes as big as ping pong balls. On the one hand, we couldn't believe it had actually worked. On the other hand, we were scared shitless. Victor's bike had shut itself off, and he was lying there, not moving, not even breathing. We didn't know what to do. We were absolutely sure he was dead. The only sound was the ticking of the cooling motorcycle engine, and the Nelsons' dog barking in the distance.

My brother was the first to break the silence. Of course, he did so by whispering the oft-repeated mantra of the snitch. In a shaky voice he said, "We're gonna get in trouble for this, you guys." Markie immediately hissed back, "You better not tell!"

Markie and I stood up, and started slowly walking toward Victor. We were about half way to his dead body when he sat up abruptly and looked directly at us. We completely freaked. He jumped up, and screamed, "You little fuckers are dead! DEAD!" and started running after us. Markie screamed, "RUN!!" which was totally unnecessary, since we had started doing that the exact microsecond Victor had been miraculously resurrected.

Like good little soldiers, we had our contingency plan, and we managed to stick to it either by luck or circumstance. If we were being chased by a single enemy, SOP was to split up. He couldn't catch us all. If he caught one of us, the others would either circle around and attempt rescue, or run home and Get An Adult, which was always the back-up plan if things went to shit on a mission. If we managed to escape clean, we were to meet at the tree fort.

In this case, it worked. We all got away, and (as agreed) we met up at the tree fort, climbed up and pulled the rope ladder in after us. This tree fort was parent-approved, in that it was really high, so my dad insisted on checking it to make sure it was structurally sound. We compensated for this indignity by making it virtually inaccessible without a rope ladder and an iron constitution. Once inside, we collapsed in relief, both in knowing that we had gotten away, and that we didn't kill Victor after all.

A few minutes later there was a huge BAM! on the side of the fort. Victor was smarter than we figured. He had managed to follow one of us.

Markie and I both looked at The Snitch.

"What?" he said. "It wasn't me, you guys. I got away clean."

We didn't buy it, but right then we had more important things to worry about than pummeling him. That would come later. Regardless of whom Victor had followed, we were now treed like raccoons.

He couldn't climb up without a ladder, but he was patient. The first noise we heard was him throwing rocks at us. We poked our heads out of the fort window, and he immediately tried to take them off with another rock. He had a pile of them by his feet. Clearly, he had thought this through, unlike us, the treed idiots. Each granite fastball was punctuated with obscenities that all seemed to revolve around our respective moms and our supposed sexual escapades with them. And apparently none of us had fathers, either.

Eventually, Victor tired out, or ran out of rocks, or both. To this day, I'm not really sure why he left, but he did. He shouted a few more F-bombs in our general direction, then walked away to get his bike. We waited there until it was almost dark, just to make sure Victor wasn't coming back. When we were sure he was really gone, we dropped our rope ladder and ran like hell to our respective houses.

To my brother's credit, he didn't tell on us. I'm not sure whether he was too scared to actually implicate himself in this one, or if he took our threats of a savage beating to heart, but either way he kept his mouth shut.

Even so, our parents got a call from Victor's parents the next day. We were summarily grounded, and not allowed in the woods for a week or until my mother couldn't stand having us underfoot any longer, whichever came first.

Worse than the grounding was the fact that we had to listen to the "What the HELL were you kids thinking" speech from our father. (The answer, of course, as everyone who has ever received this speech already knows, is: "I don't know." This is immediately followed up by "You WEREN'T thinking, and that's the PROBLEM.")

Kids are stupid.

So Victor lived. We lived. We had to pay for a new tire and tube out of our allowances. There was an uneasy truce. Victor didn't screw with us much after that, although we always suspected that he was the one who had flung the fresh dog shit at the side of our fort. We couldn't prove it though, so we just scraped it off with a stick and waited for the stink to fade.

You'll notice that the title of this story was "The First Time." Unfortunately, we weren't very fast learners, and the second time we almost killed a guy it was Markie's stepfather.

The Second Time

This simple bit of ingenuity got me into a LOT of trouble:

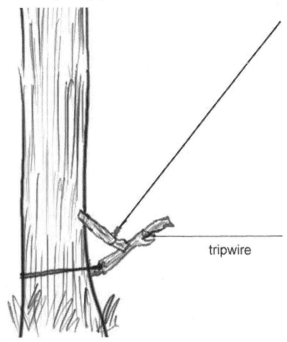

tripwire

I discovered this little piece of magical backwoods engineering in a hunting and trapping book when I was about 12 or so, and couldn't wait to actually apply it to something. I immediately shared the idea with Markie and The Snitch.

Of course, the first thing we thought of to apply it to was the same thing we always thought to apply things like this to – our sworn enemies, the big kids in the woods. That's what we called them, like they actually lived there or something.

After the incident with Victor, you might think we'd have learned our lesson. You would be wrong. The need was too strong. We were industrious, and full of brilliant ideas just waiting to be implemented. Ideas that would, we were sure, put a world of hurt on our tormenters.

The way we saw it, the problem we had last time was that we were too close when we stuck around to see the results. Well, that and the fact that my brother blew our cover by standing up at the last second, trying to warn Victor away. That would not happen this time. Obviously, we would still want to see the results, but we would remain well-hidden and – new to this plan – far away, no matter what happened.

Our parents had told us *to never do that again* which, by our logic, meant that punji stakes and covered trenches were out. In our infinite wisdom, we reasoned that they didn't exactly tell us to not make *any* booby traps, just to never do THAT again. We reasoned that as long as we stayed away from punji stakes, the possibilities were still endless.

That, right there, is an example of pre-teen male logic, and why you should always make sure your male children understand the broader implications of what you are saying, and are not simply registering the literal meaning of your words.

If you are too narrow in your definition of what they are not to do, they will weasel around it. Then, when you express your disapproval, they will come back at you with the following retort:

"Well, YOU SAID we couldn't do THAT, and we DIDN'T."

To which you will always be forced to reply "You know DAMN well what I meant!"

At that point it is over. You have lost. You may not *think* you have lost, but you have. You have failed to get your child to think, and you have become reactive. Your only recourse is the punishment of the ruling dictator, and your kid will, until the day he has kids of his own, think he was right and you were wrong. It's like trying to get three wishes from an evil demon. You have to be very careful how you phrase your commands, or they will come back to bite you in the ass.

Since the punji stakes were out of bounds now, we decided we'd go in the other direction – up. More specifically, into the trees. We figured that the dirt bikes went by so fast there was virtually no chance anyone would actually get caught in the trap, since they'd be long gone before anything happened. On the plus side, we'd still have the fun of getting to see the booby-trap tripped, and maybe give the dirt bike assholes a good scare and something to think about.

We needed an object to drop from the trees, but we were unsure as to what.

We considered a rock. Too round. Too hard to tie a rope around.

A bucket of water. Not bad, but not really as destructive as we wanted, and we knew that any bucket stolen from the garage would be instantly noticed by my father.

There was no way you could even touch something in the garage without my father immediately knowing about it. It was like some sort of disturbance in the G-Force. If you took something, he'd jump from his chair and run to the garage, quickly scoping things out with his "something-is-missing" radar. Regardless of how messy it appeared, he knew where everything was. There was a certain chaotic orderliness about it that I cannot, to this day, explain.

Eventually, we ended up raiding the fort of the big kids. Dangerous work, but at that point, necessary. We scored a cinderblock they had been using as one leg of a bench. One of those big, I-beam shaped ones with the double holes. Perfect for getting a rope around.

We scoped the woods until we found what we needed. Two trees, one close to the trail, with some overhanging branches, and one a bit farther back into the woods. We rigged the trigger on the tree farthest in, and the trip wire ex-tended across the trail to a tree on the other side. We used a nice black nylon 60 lb-test fishing line that Markie took from his stepfather's tackle box. Markie's stepfather lacked my father's sixth sense, so we were OK in that re-gard. My father may have actually felt a twinge and checked his own tackle box, but he probably thought it was just a false alarm since everything seemed to be in its place. When we were done, we had something that looked similar to this:

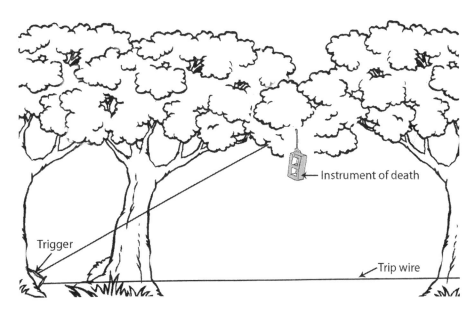

We were set. This time, there would be no getting caught. We had smartened up, and had brought a pair of binoculars to watch from a distance.

The Snitch got them for his birthday, and he was paranoid about getting them dirty or damaging them in some way, but Markie and I had finally convinced him to bring them with us for the good of the mission.

We set up on the crest of the hill going into the woods on the other side of a large field. This gave us a birds-eye view of the trail, and everything around for about 180 degrees. The sun was behind us, we were up on a ridge, and we were in the shade, not easily visible. A perfect vantage point.

We waited for the dirt bikes. We took turns looking through the binocs. I glanced around for almost 30 minutes, but didn't see anything in particular. Except for a few crows, the continual buzzing of the bumblebees and the occasional grasshopper, it was dead. I was bored, so I gave the binocs to Markie. He was looking through them for a while, but didn't see anything either. This surveillance crap was borrrrring.

It was almost six p.m., so we figured we were done for the day. The sun was going behind the trees, and it was getting a little harder to see. Just when I was ready to suggest that we leave, Markie spoke.

"Oh shit," he said. That was never a good sign.

"What? I asked him. "What? Let me see."

He didn't answer right away, but then he whispered, "Oh..*fuck*."

This was a much *worse* sign, since Markie's step-dad told him if he ever heard him use that word, he would whip his ass, ground him for a week, and wash his mouth out with Ivory soap. As a result, it was not a word he used lightly, or often.

I grabbed the glasses away from him, and focused them across the field. I saw this:

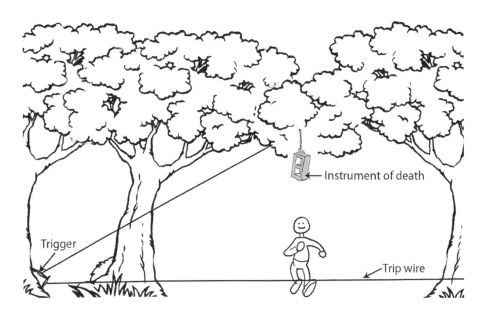

Markie's step-dad, Doug, coming up the trail toward us, only about 12 feet from the booby trap.

He'll see it. He has to. Nothing will happen, I thought. Just to be safe, we started yelling, and running across the field toward him.

He saw us, but didn't understand what we were saying, since we were still about 600 yards away.

We were going to be too late. Our only hope was that he either saw the trip wire, or just happened to step over it, and not trigger the booby trap.

No such luck.

We ran as fast as we could, yelling at him to stop, but he didn't. We reached the edge of the field and had started down the trail just as he reached the trap.

His left foot kicked out and got hung up in the trip wire. The trigger worked as designed, and we watched in horror as the rope holding the cinder-block whipped up into the air and the block dropped. This obviously wasn't going as well as we had hoped.

We thought for a second that his forward momentum might carry him past the point of impact, and we were hoping the block would land behind him, no harm, no foul. Just a simple yelling fit, a grounding, and no serious injuries to contend with.

This also did not happen.

The only small stroke of luck was that it missed his head. Not by much I'll grant you, but at least he's not dead or a vegetable today. It did, however, catch him a glancing blow to the left shoulder.

He yelled something that should have, by all rights, resulted in his mouth being washed out with Ivory soap. He grabbed his shoulder and almost fell to the ground. I distinctly remember him yelling at us, "WHAT DID YOU DO? WHAT THE HELL DID YOU KIDS DO? YOU COULD HAVE KILLED ME!!"

We knew it was useless to discuss the finer points of intent at this time, so we kept our mouths shut.

We stood there until Doug finished yelling at us, his hand held gingerly to his shoulder. There was no blood, and nothing was broken. At worst, he would have a bruise for a few days.

It was then that Markie spoke.

"We didn't do it," he said.

I looked at him with a mixture of awe and disbelief, and not a small amount of raw admiration and new-found respect.

A bald-faced, transparent lie.

If I had learned anything by that point in my short life, it was that the phrase "I didn't do it" was never, ever, under any circumstances, something that was actually believed by any sane parent, even if it happened to be true. In this case, it was patently *un*true, and he read it on our faces.

"DON'T YOU LIE TO ME!" Doug screamed. Using his good arm, he grabbed Markie by the back of the neck. He looked at me & Snitch and said, "YOU TWO! GO HOME!"

I didn't need any more incentive than that. I took off like someone was beating my ass with a riding crop. When I got home, I went directly to my room and waited for my mother to call us for dinner.

An hour after dinner, I heard the doorbell ring. Another thing on the list of things that are never a good sign. It was Doug and Markie, and they stood at the front door and talked to my father for almost five minutes. I knew what was going on. Markie had ratted me out. He told Doug that it was all my idea, and now the chickens had come home to roost.

After they left, I waited. The waiting was the worst. I waited to hear my father yell, "JOHNNY! GET DOWN HERE!" In fact, that's what I was *hoping* for. That meant he wasn't too pissed. If he actually made the trek *upstairs* to my room, then I knew I was in what we liked to refer to as "Really Deep Shit."

Unfortunately, the yell never came. Instead, I heard him coming up the stairs. The most dreaded sound in my young life. The slow, methodical footsteps that meant I was completely screwed.

I then had to explain to my father that it *wasn't* my idea – Markie was lying, and we had *all* come up with it. I stressed that I was simply the mechanical engineer that made it work.

Unfortunately, the nuances of that argument were lost on him. I was grounded. I lost my TV privileges and he took my bike and skateboard away. I got the requisite "What The Hell Were You Thinking" speech – the one I had, sadly, pretty much memorized by that point in my young life.

We also had to apologize to Doug, and promise that we would never do that, or anything remotely like that, ever again. We mostly kept that promise.

So that's my story, and I'm sticking to it. It wasn't *all* my fault, but I share responsibility. In retrospect, not one of our finer moments of brilliant thinking.

That being said, to this day I can't help remembering it without feeling a touch of pride.

After all, that bitch actually *worked.*

The Third Time

My brother was a tough kid. During his terrible twos, he had so many accidents that – had he been born in the 90's instead of the 70's – my father surely would have been arrested on suspicion of child abuse.

In the space of one year, he was rushed to the emergency room no less than five times, and the doctors had started giving my father funny looks. The partial inventory is as follows: A gash in his head from running full speed under a kitchen counter overhang and not quite making it, a burnt and cauterized lip injury from sticking an unfolded paperclip in his mouth and then subsequently into a live electrical socket, third-degree burns on his hands from grabbing a hot lawnmower muffler, another head injury from getting beaned by a fly ball at a little league baseball game...the list goes on.

By the time he was six or so, I don't think he could actually feel pain. He was invincible, and he would tell you so. You couldn't hurt him unless you punched him in what he called his "mortal weak spot," which was generally any part of his body hit hard enough to actually make him cry. This was a hard thing to do, and quite frankly if there wasn't at least *some* blood, he usually didn't shed a tear.

As his older brothers, The Snitch and I felt it was our duty to keep him in his place. We would do the normal things when he was being a pain in the ass, like hold him down and tickle him until he couldn't breathe, give him wedgies, noogies, indian burns, pink bellies and on rare occasions – mostly after we had eaten hot dogs for dinner – we would sit on him and make him smell our farts.

I'm not proud.

By chance, that all changed one summer day. The Snitch and I were watching television and Houdini was, as usual, bugging us. There happened to be a blanket on the floor, and I had an idea. I conferred with the Snitch, and we asked Houdini if he wanted to play "mummy." When we had finally convinced him that it would be a blast, we rolled him up in the blanket and once he couldn't move, we tickled him until he couldn't breathe. This way was much easier, since his kicking ability was seriously impaired. He could still do a mean worm-kick, but it was much easier to avoid.

This was also the start of a series of what I like to refer to as Very Dangerous Situations.

It just so happened that this blanket discovery was right around the time that Houdini learned about escape artists, and earned his nickname. To this day I am not sure what his fascination with escape was about, but he would brag to us that there was nothing we could put him in, tie him up with, or bury him under from which he could not escape.

We, of course, were happy to test this theory of his on a regular basis. We would only favor his requests if he agreed that no matter what we did to him, he wouldn't tell, and if he didn't get free within a predetermined amount of time, he would have to do our chores for a week. As a result, we used to torture him regularly, because one, it was really fun, and two, we really hated our chores.

We started him off easy, although we didn't know this at the time. We rolled him up in the blanket again, and then tied rope around it, and left him in his bedroom. Somehow, 20 minutes later, he burst triumphantly into the TV room, sweating like a pig, with rope burns over 80% of his body. He had escaped.

This would not do.

The next time, since we weren't all that original with this game yet, we wrapped him in the blanket again, only this time we made a few changes. First, we gagged him, and then when we wrapped him up, we made sure his head was tucked in the blanket as well. That way he couldn't see what we tied him up with, or even where he was. We then dragged him into the laundry room, stuck him in the little space between the washer and dryer, and went back to watching TV. Every once in a while, over the laugh track of *Bewitched,* we would hear a series of loud grunts and straining noises very similar to those made by someone trying to give birth quietly. Soon, these grunting noises were followed by a rhythmic, metallic thumping that sounded exactly like a washing machine spinning an uneven load.

We were extremely surprised when about half way through *The Munsters,* out popped Houdini. He was no longer wearing a shirt, and I am pretty sure there was a small patch of hair missing from the side of his head.

This was truly amazing to us. He had done it *again.* We didn't want to admit it, but we were beginning to be impressed, and I have to say that we were starting to believe his hype.

This is where things escalated out of control. We needed to win this contest of wills.

So did he.

When we finally goaded him into trying his next escape, The Snitch and I decided to forgo the blanket altogether, and we simply hog-tied him. We tied his hands behind his back, then tied his ankles together, and then connected them both.

We gagged him, and finished it off with a backwards ski mask. Then we hauled him outside, and dumped him on the floor in the backseat of the station wagon.

You know, that one over there sitting in the driveway in the sun.

In late July.

We left him there. To this day, I cannot believe that he did not die. That possibility never even *occurred* to us. If you ever wonder how kids get locked in the trunks of abandoned cars and suffocate, well, it happens just like this.

About an hour later, my mother called down to us from the kitchen and said, "Is Houdini down there with you? I can't find him anywhere."

"No," I said, panicking, and trying like hell not to show it. "But I think he's back in the playroom. We'll go get him."

We ran out the back door, around the house to the car, and opened it up. Houdini was still where we had left him, but he didn't have much fight left. We yanked off the ski mask and took off the gag. He was pretty out of it, and consequently a little more pliable than was optimal. We had a hard time getting him to stand up once we had hauled him out of the car and untied him.

I'll give him credit though. Once he found out that our mother was looking for him, he shook it off and put on his game face, even though he was barely conscious. After he told her that he had been down by the pond running around (and we were all off the hook), he admitted to us that he thought we had probably won that round. He did say, however, that he totally would have gotten free if he had been able to breathe a little better.

After that little scare, we backed off on the gagging thing. We figured it would be a good idea to allow him to yell for help if he needed to.

His next great escape was from the pole in the basement, where we had tightly fastened him by winding a few 60-minute cassette tapes around his body, head to toe. I think his hands and feet went numb on that one, but he did get free eventually, by chewing through the tape on his shoulder. He was truly a force to be reckoned with.

A year or so later, things changed again. Not the basic relationship – that was still kill or be killed. This was more in the nature of the contest. I had discovered electricity, and Houdini had discovered money. He would do anything for a couple of quarters. I could get him to clean my room, do my paper route and all my chores for a week if I paid him 50 cents.

I had also developed a deep fascination with electronics. I was taking apart radios and electronic equipment of all kinds at this point, and even though stuff generally never got fixed or put back together again, I learned a lot.

One of the things I took apart was an electronic camera flash. If you don't know what's inside one of those bad boys, it's basically a huge capacitor. That whine you hear when you turn one on is the capacitor charging up.

You know where this is going, right? Depending on the size of the flash, the capacitor can discharge tens of thousands of volts. In other words, this is essentially the same circuit that powers a stun gun or Taser, except it normally puts the electricity to a xenon flash tube instead of a pair of electrodes. I took the flash tube off, and soldered in a couple of long wires instead. I would routinely weld pennies together with this thing. Charge it up, touch the two wires to the edges of a couple of stacked pennies and WHACK! I'd be temporarily blind for ten seconds, and was probably doing bad things to my retina, but it was worth it because the edges of the pennies would be melted together.

This device, coupled with my brother's newfound greediness, was an instant recipe for disaster.

As usual, this part of our story starts with a spectacularly bad idea.

Using the electronic flash guts, a couple of quarters, some solder and a shoebox, I built the stage. I soldered some wires to the bottom of the quarters, and ran them through holes in the top of the shoebox so it looked like the quarters were sitting on top.

Inside the box, I connected the wires to the capacitor, and then charged it up. After it was charged, I carefully placed the top back on the box, and made sure the quarters were lying flat. The box provided enough sound proofing so that the high-pitched whine of the capacitor was no longer audible.

I called Houdini into the room. His eyes were instantly drawn to the two quarters sitting on top of the shoebox.

"What's that?" he asked, eyeing me suspiciously, and eyeing the money greedily.

"Magic quarters," I replied.

"What makes 'em magic?" he asked.

"Well, you can't touch them both at the same time. They won't allow it. In fact, even though they're close enough to touch with two fingers on one hand, nobody can do it," I said.

"What if I do?" he asked.

"Well, if you do, they'll be yours. They will have accepted you as their new master."

This was the part I was waiting for. He reached out two fingers of his left hand, and hovered over the quarters. He brought his index finger down slowly. It touched the first quarter. He did the same with his middle finger, lowering it slowly toward the second coin. It was millimeters away and then...

He touched it.

His arm was thrown violently into the wall, and he instantly started bawling. I felt bad because I had really hurt him, but I was also scared shitless. He *never* cried. He was the toughest kid I knew. It must have hurt like hell.

I calmed him down a bit, and we assessed the damage. He couldn't feel his hand. The fingers were numb. I was shitting my pants thinking that I had just paralyzed my little brother, and goddammit I was going to be in Big Trouble.

I begged him not to tell. I told him it was only temporary, and that the feeling would come back in no time. Lucky for me, this turned out to be true, and a few minutes later he could move his fingers again. He had two small burn marks, one on each fingertip, and I was pretty sure his fingernails would never grow the same way again, but he was going to be ok.

After about another half hour, I had finally negotiated him down to ten bucks and a radio. I considered myself very lucky. It was an old radio.

You might think this would have taught me a lesson, but you would be wrong. I was loathe to give up on the electricity entirely. The humming, buzzing, siren song was too much for me to resist.

A little while later, I found a transformer in someone's garbage. This transformer stepped down the 120volts AC house current to about 40 volts. Not enough to really hurt you, but enough to give you a decent shock.

I wanted – no, I *needed* – to apply this voltage to Houdini. I don't know why. It was just something that had to be done.

I shared my transformer discovery with The Snitch and we came up with a plan. We would tie Houdini up and throw him in the closet to attempt an escape, which he would think of as unworthy of his talents. He'd done it before, and he'd do it again, in no time flat. Not even a challenge. This time, however, there would be a twist.

I took the transformer, some rubber cement, some bare copper wire and some insulated copper wire, and went to work on the closet doorknob:

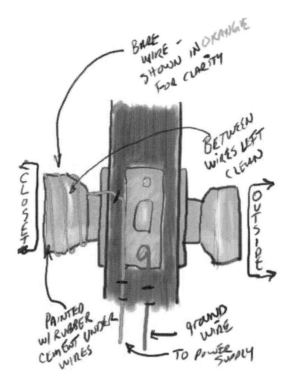

The Snitch and I figured it would be dark in the closet, and when Houdini finally threw off his shackles, he would triumphantly grab the doorknob and hilarity would ensue – for us, at least. We hung a shirt over the doorknob to disguise it, and went to work on convincing Houdini to give the closet escape a shot. He agreed to escape for the paltry sum of two dollars, and the game was on. We tied him up – loosely, to assure his quick success – and tossed him in the closet, yanking the shirt off the knob as we did so. I think the loose rope may have tipped him off, since we usually made sure it was brutally tight. We waited outside the door, the stereo on to mask the sounds of struggle. The closet however, remained silent. He was waiting. Assessing. Trying to figure out what was next. It had been too easy, and he knew it.

Finally, we heard the knob rattle. "OW!" A pause. "OW!!!"

A shuffling sound, another rattle, and then the door opened. We were impressed. At first we thought he just toughed it out and turned the knob through the pain, but he was smarter than that. He had grabbed a shirt off one of the hangers and used it to open the door.

He stepped out of the closet and glared at us.

"Gimme my money," he said.

Goddammit he was the best brother in the universe.

After we got a bit older, we actually became friends in addition to being brothers. Turns out we were a lot alike, my fascination with electricity not withstanding. When I was in high school, we would hang out and listen to my records, something that we do to this day. We live in different states now, but when we get together it somehow always gets down to music, and what's new, and what we've both been listening to lately.

The stuff I was listening to in the 80's was before my time – mostly 70's British invasion rock and progressive rock. As a result, he cut his teeth on bands like Genesis, Zeppelin, The Stones and the Kinks. Not too shabby for a 13 year old kid.

Later on when I had a band, he used to hang out and listen to us practice. I'm actually surprised he's not deaf. The reason I say this is not because we played particularly loud (although we did OK and I have the hearing loss to prove it) but because of his chosen method of listening:

I shit you not. He used to lie there for hours. I mean, seriously, that *had* to do some damage.

I got him drunk once on New Year's Eve when I was 19. I had just broken up with my girlfriend, and we sat around commiserating on life, the universe and why relationships are such a pain in the ass.

Trust me, it's no fun sitting at the breakfast table the next morning trying to explain to your mother how your 15 year-old brother got a hangover straight from hell.

Dead brain cells from the NYE drinking binge notwithstanding, he turned into one of the coolest and smartest guys I know. He obviously had more brain cells to spare than I did, because now he conducts genome research, which I'm pretty sure has something to do with Travelocity.

I miss having him around, even though he's only three hours and a phone call away. He's a great friend and brother, even if he is half deaf and has an irrational fear of electricity.

What a wuss.

Air Assault

It amazes me that we used to get away with so much when we were kids. I'm talking about the things we used to do as kids that, if kids today did them, would probably land them in juvenile detention until they were old enough to vote.

Let me give you an example. We showed up at our fort one day, and it was trashed. Pulled-down-out-of-the-tree-and-strewn-upon-the-ground trashed. Of course, it never occurred to us that the actual landowner might have done it because he didn't want kids nailing shit up in his trees. We had no concept of private ownership that extended past our Hot Wheels Sizzlers cars. As a result, blame was immediately and irrevocably pinned on the big kids – specifically, Victor Bradford and his crew.

They had a ritual during the summer that involved partying on the hill overlooking the field. This usually occurred on a Saturday night. They would build a bonfire and bring in a couple cases of beer and some weed, and hang out up there until they either ran out of beer or the cops came and busted it up. We used to go up there the day after the party just to see what we could find. Mostly, the cops never bothered, so it was just empty beer cans, broken beer bottles and torn up chip bags. If they actually did get raided by the cops, or thought they were getting raided, they would split in a hurry, as soon as the cop cars started driving across the field. They may have been close to the legal drinking age, but the weed was a definite no-no.

On those mornings, we would sometimes make a major score, and go back to the fort with a haul of well-thumbed Penthouse mags, some unopened beers, or – once – a pot pipe. I actually didn't know what this was until later, and the only reason I found out then was because my mother was doing laundry and found it in my pants pocket. That was a fun conversation, let me tell you.

One mid-June evening, Markie showed us his stash of fireworks. The Snitch and I had little experience with such things, since our parents were of the "fireworks are dangerous and illegal" mentality when it came to things that exploded or burst into flames. If we were lucky, they'd let us light off a few of those smelly, smoky, do-nothing, lame-ass snakes. (I can still remember that sulfuric stench.) Basically, things that shot up into the air or could blow your mailbox off its moorings were *definitely* out.

Not so for Markie though. He had the good stuff. The best of the lot were the whistling bottle rockets, and a bunch of what we called M-80s. I don't know what the real name for these things was, but they were about two inches long and made out of hard cardboard tubing with glued ends. They had a green, woven fuse sticking out of one end or sometimes the middle. They would blow a six-inch wide hole in the ground about three inches deep. They sounded like TNT, and they could completely destroy a mailbox or blow the lid of a milk box 20 feet into the air. They were, in a word, awesome.

As was usually the case, Markie got into some of the stuff early. He came over in the morning, and when he flashed the stash, The Snitch and I nonchalantly headed out the door to "go play in the woods." He had a bundle of bottle rockets and a couple of M-80s.

The first thing we did when we got out to the woods was head over to the hill, to see what was what. The place had been cleaned up nicely.

We didn't find anything, but Markie had a brilliant idea. He wanted to bury one of the M-80's in the fire pit, and cover the wick with a few of the old pieces of charcoal that were left from a previous fire. We figured this would be ample payback for trashing our fort. When they had the party later that night, they would build a fire right on top of this thing, and eventually the fuse would light and that mother would explode all over the place.

Obviously, we had no concept of forest fires, permanent disfigurement or blindness, or even what it might feel like to get hit in the face with a burning log the size of a baseball bat. We carefully buried the M-80, then went down in the field to launch some bottle rockets.

We found an old beer bottle and used that for a launching pad. We angled the bottle slightly, dropped the rocket in, and lit the fuse. The rocket launched into the air with an ear-piercing whistle and exploded with a flash and BANG! high overhead. It was daytime, so the effect was a bit subdued. The smoke trail was pretty cool though. We did a few more, and then fate intervened. As Markie lit one of the fuses, he caught the bottle with his hand, and it tipped to a 45 degree angle. The rocket launched and screamed its way toward the other side of the field. It bounced off the dirt just shy of the woods, then exploded.

Holy shit. We looked at each other. A perfectly conceived plan immediately jumped, fully formed, into our 10-year-old minds.

We had just discovered anti-big kid artillery.

This was way better than wasting an M-80 that may or may not go off. We sent The Snitch back to the fire pit to dig up the M-80. When that was done, we got to work.

The next step in our plan was to determine range and repeatability. Luckily, Markie had brought two packets of rockets, and there were a dozen rockets in each pack. We walked to the side of the field opposite party hill. We tipped the bottle to what we thought looked like the right angle, and tried two rockets. Those Chinese were pretty damn meticulous, because those things landed within 10 feet of each other. They were a bit short, but that could be fixed. A few more tries, and we had the bottle adjusted so we could pretty much shoot a rocket within 20 feet of the fire pit 70% of the time.

I had another idea. We hunted for more bottles. We found two in the woods, and then raided Markie's garage for another ten. We half-buried them in a single row, all duplicating the exact angle of the initial test bottle. We even curved them slightly to make sure they were all pointed in the same exact direction. We ran a few tests from the outside bottles and when we were happy with the results we locked them in, packing dirt on all sides.

We were ready. Now we just needed a way to light 12 fuses more or less simultaneously. We tried tying the wicks together with other pieces of wick, but that generally didn't work too well. Either the trajectory was thrown off or the firing of one rocket blew out the wick of the one next to it.

Eventually, after much discussion, the solution to this vexing problem came to us. Ironically, it was all thanks to my father. I remembered that he would routinely light our sparklers with a propane torch or a road flare, since it was easy to set them down and not have to worry about flicking a lighter or using matches every time one of us was handed a new sparkler. It was the perfect solution. There was no way we would be able to sneak my father's propane torch out of the garage without him sensing a disturbance in the G-Force, so we took Markie's step-dad's. He would never miss it.

In preparation, we asked our parents for permission to spend the night camping with Markie in his back yard. We set up the tent, and around six p.m. we brought our sleeping bags over to his house. We figured it would be way easier to sneak over to the field from his yard, since it backed up to the woods.

After dark, we periodically sent out a scout to see if the party had started. Since The Snitch was the youngest, it was always him. He finally came back from his recon with reports of enemy movement.

"You guys! I seen the fire! And I can hear'em talkin' and laughin'," he said, out of breath. "Sounds like there's a bunch of'em. Some girls, too," he added.

Markie pulled the bottle rockets and the propane torch from under his sleeping bag. He even had one of those sparking flint torch lighters, so we didn't need matches to light the torch.

We put the pinhole covers on our army flashlights (we all had the olive green, right-angle flashlights from the Army-Navy store), and headed toward our launch site. Luckily the trails were wide so it was a pretty easy walk, even using nothing more than the feeble beams of our covered flashlights.

Markie carefully placed one bottle rocket into each bottle, making sure the fuses were all facing up. We could hear the big kids whooping it up across the field. They were about to get their payback for tearing down our fort, and in a big way. I sparked the torch, and adjusted it down to a mean, almost invisible blue flame. "Ready?" I asked. Markie and The Snitch nodded. "Here goes. Markie, get ready with the next batch." We weren't sure exactly what was going to happen, but we wanted to be prepared in case we could get off another salvo. He broke out another twelve and stood ready.

I ran the torch across the row left to right. There was a SHOOOSH! sound as the first rocket went up, but the rest of them were drowned out by the screaming whistle of the previous rocket in line. It happened in the space of a few seconds, but it was perfection. Not a single rocket left behind. We saw the arcing rocket trails heading toward the hill, and a split second later, there was a series of loud explosions all up and around the trees surrounding the fire pit. There were immediate screams of terror from the girls, and simultaneous profanity from the guys.

It was utter pandemonium, and *we had caused it.* It was, in our minds, the best thing we had ever done.

Markie was on the ball. He already had the second batch ready to go. I whipped the torch flame across the wicks and a second later another batch headed on its way. We were running before they even hit. We were hard pressed to be completely quiet, but figured with all the exploding, we didn't have to worry too much about it. We managed to make it back to the tent without killing ourselves.

We made a quick stop to grab our sleeping bags, then headed straight for the back door to the garage. We put the torch back, then went in the house and sat down in the family room to catch our breath. There was no way we were sleeping outside. Not with only a flimsy piece of nylon between us and certain death.

When Markie's mom came down to see what all the noise was, we were just hanging out, watching television. She asked us why we weren't outside, and we said we heard lots of bangs and yelling and stuff we thought that maybe the big kids were having a party over at the hill. She agreed that perhaps it was best that we have our sleep-over inside instead.

Two days later, we managed to get over there to see if there was anything good left behind. Other than finding a few red sticks from the bottle rockets, there wasn't much.

That was good enough for us, though.

Nobody ever found us out. Even The Snitch never said a word. For some reason, I think he took the trashing of our fort even more personally than Markie and I did.

It was the perfect mission. We never found out the real story of what happened up there. I'd love to talk to one of the kids who were on the hill that night to find out what was going through their heads when the air started exploding around them.

On second thought, maybe I don't want to know. Now that I've told you all this, I really hope nobody died that night and I just never heard about it, because getting arrested would really suck. If that turns out to be the case, I'm counting on you all to make my bail.

The Legend of Granny Grunt

We stood astride our bikes at the edge of the trail, hiding behind a hedge. We were waiting to make our move. Me, Markie and The Snitch. We were 11, 10 and nine, respectively, and it was just the beginning of summer vacation. School was out, and the summer stretched before us like a highway into the desert.

"I seen it, no kiddin'," Markie said. "I was sneaking through yesterday and I seen it."

"You did not," I replied. "It was prolly just her cane, you dork."

"No, it wasn't no cane. I'm tellin' ya it was a shotgun. And she pointed it at me. *Right at me*, you guys. I thought I was done for, but I pedaled really fast and made the woods before she could draw a bead on me. I wasn't gettin' shot, no way. You buttheads don't know what rock salt feels like when you get hit with it."

"Yeah, like you do," the Snitch scoffed.

"Well, no...but Marty Jackson told me," Markie replied. "It hurts like, well, ...it hurts a lot. And if it's close enough, *it can kill you.*"

We were starting to buy his story. After all, everyone knew that Granny Grunt had shot that kid with rock salt a few years back. Everyone knew it, and everyone knew someone who had a cousin or brother that had been friends with the sister of the kid who got shot. Granny Grunt had also killed her husband and dog, and buried them in the back yard and then planted flowers on them. You could still see the spot. Just because our parents didn't believe she was a double murderer and a witch to boot didn't mean it wasn't true.

"Well, she's not outside now. I think it's safe," I said. "You guys ready?"

Markie eased his bike out a little farther on the path, and gave the house the once over with his critical eye. He shared his professional opinion. "I think we can make it," he said. "I don't think she's home. Either that or her car's in the garage."

"OK. Ready?" I asked, my voice tight. "One...two...three...GO!"

We pedaled as if our lives depended on it – because in our hearts, we knew they did. We were only out in the open for maybe twenty seconds, following the faint trail that ran along her fence, but it seemed an eternity. We were completely vulnerable, and we knew it. On the one hand, we wanted to zigzag to throw off her aim, but on the other hand, making a beeline for the woods seemed most prudent from a pure speed standpoint.

"The front door's opening! I think she sees us! FASTER!" Markie screamed.

"I SEE IT! I SEE THE GUN!" The Snitch yelled back, looking over his shoulder and almost steering his bike into mine. He had apparently opted for zig-zag, consciously or not.

"Jeez! Watch where you're going!" I yelled, barely avoiding him and re-doubling my pedaling efforts. "You're gonna get us all killed!"

We were flying in a pyramid formation, Markie in the lead with his brand new Schwinn Orange Krate bicycle. This thing was tricked out – shock absorbers, five-speed stick shift, banana seat, monkey-hanger handlebars, and flared chrome fenders over the fat back tire and small chopper-like front wheel. The Snitch and I followed, me on my junkyard special and he on his no-name gold single-speed 'unisex' bike with the optional bolt-on bar that turned it into a boy's bike.

Then it was over, and we were back in the trees, heading down the trail at top speed. We kept going until we were out of Grunt's woods, and safe in our own. Our hearts still in our throats, the adrenaline pumping through our veins, we coasted to a stop. We dropped our bikes and sat down on the side of the trail, our legs shaking from equal measures of exertion and exhilaration. We had made it. Alive. We felt like heroes.

We were on our way to "The Jump."

Granny Grunt's house sat between Mayhall Street and the woods where the jump was. "The Jump" was a permanent dirt ramp at the bottom of a huge, ski jump-like hill. It was created by the older kids who owned minibikes and dirt bikes, but they stopped using it because Granny kept calling the cops on them. Since we were younger, and our regular old pedal bikes didn't make any objectionable noise, Granny Grunt opted to periodically take care of us herself rather than get the cops involved.

That particular day, we were heading over to the jump for a competition. We would be going for distance, and I was going to win. There was no actual prize, other than bragging rights and the well-earned respect of your peers, but that was enough. I didn't know it then, but it was going to be my last competition.

We weren't wealthy growing up, but we weren't poor. Comfortably middle class, I guess you'd say. My father worked hard to put a roof over our heads, and we didn't have a lot of fancy things, but we had all of the basics. New clothes and shoes for school and enough money so we didn't have to do without much in the way of necessities.

My father was a big believer in saving for a rainy day, and in this case, that rainy day was our collective college educations. As a result of his aggressive saving behavior, he was also extremely frugal. (OK, let's be honest. He was cheap, and he taught me well.) He knew the value of a dollar and he always knew when we could "make do" with something, and so we often did. Case in point: I had a bike, but I also knew that there was no Schwinn Orange Krate in my future – not unless I was going to buy it myself.

My first bicycle came home in an old cardboard box, as a collection of bike parts. I'm not even entirely sure they were all parts of the *same* bike. I remember my father coming home from work, and telling me "Hey! I got you a bike today."

I ran outside to see it, and my heart sunk as I watched him take a bunch of dirty bike parts out of the back of the station wagon. I didn't have high hopes for this bike, but I'd seen him work miracles before, so I withheld my immediate judgment. My father lived by a few simple rules: Nothing couldn't be fixed, and epoxy and Rustoleum paint should be integral ingredients of any repair. If something had been broken, you could glue it, and if it were rusty, you could paint it. If those two things failed, you could, as a last resort, replace it. I had seen this pattern time and time again over the course of my young life. A certain green garden cart comes to mind – toward the end, I don't think there was any metal left in it. It was just an exoskeleton of epoxy and paint.

The first thing he did was sand and repaint the bike frame a dark metallic blue. Then he replaced the tubes in the tires, put some black electrical tape over the torn seat, oiled up the chain, and it was done. It had no chain guard, so I had to ride with a rubber band around my right pant leg. I learned this lesson after getting yanked off my bike by my own pants and catching hell for ripping up a perfectly good pair of Tough-skins. My father told me to tuck my pant leg into my sock, but I thought that looked ridiculous, so I opted for the rubber band, which, to my mind, was much more stylish.

So let me tell you a little more about Big Blue.

In addition to having no chain guard, my bike also had no fenders, so one not-so-enjoyable side-effect of this was that if the ground were the least bit wet, I would end up with a brown stripe of mud that started at my butt and went all the way up my back. I used to wear a backwards baseball cap just so the mud and water didn't get on the back of my neck and in my hair. The rubber part of the pedals had long ago fallen off, and all that remained were the center steel sleeves rotating on stationary pegs. As a result, your sneaker could easily slip off the pedal if you weren't paying attention. This problem reared its ugly head quite frequently, since the bike had rear coaster brakes.

I don't even know if they make bikes with this sort of braking mechanism anymore, but the way they worked was that if you wanted to stop, you would jam the pedals backwards, and that would engage some sort of brake in the rear hub. A favorite pastime of ours was to find a dusty, gravelly patch on the side of the road, get going as fast as we could, then slam the brakes on just as we hit the gravel patch and see how long of a skid we could produce. Yes, our tires were bald. The problem in my case however, always came back to the damn pedals. I would slip off them about one time out of twenty, and end up in a heap on the side of the road, with my bicycle either lying 20 feet in front of me, tires spinning, or directly on top of me, with my pant leg jammed so far into the chain that it would take the jaws of life to extract it. Normally, on any other bike, this also would have resulted in a brutally pain-ful bashing of the family jewels on the center bar.

Not in this case.

In this case, it didn't happen because…

…*it was a girl's bike.*

Yes. I admit this bit of humiliation to you. I rode a girl's bike for much of my childhood. I didn't know this at first, but as everyone who has ever been a kid can attest, kids can be cruel, and it didn't take long for them to start giv-ing me crap about it.

I didn't care much, at least at first. It rolled. It got me where I was going, and I could leave it anywhere and not have to lock it. This lesson has stayed with me to this day, and if you saw my current canoe you would understand. Sometimes, it's good to own a functional piece of crap that nobody wants to steal, because you can leave it anywhere and drag it across anything, and you don't even think twice about it. My bike was like that. I'm not saying it didn't get to me sometimes, and I did do a fair amount of whining to my fath-er, especially after The Snitch got a new and better bike – one with a bolt-on bar. Bolt on or not, at least it was there.

After a while, just to avoid the ridicule, I started telling the other kids that I had borrowed Markie's sister's old bike because mine had a flat tire. Nobody but Markie and The Snitch knew I was lying.

There was only one benefit to owning this rolling turd, and it made up for all the abuse I was forced to take.

King of the Jump

Since my bike consisted of nothing but a thin, girl's bike frame, two tires, a seat and handlebars, it weighed next to nothing. I was a scrawny kid, so I *also* weighed next to nothing. These two things combined to give me the hang time of a giant Frisbee.

When I was growing up, Evel Knievel was huge. He had just tried to jump Snake River Canyon on *a rocket bike* for god's sake, and he was the hero of every kid between the ages of 10 and 14. We had all breathlessly watched him jump cars, buses, tractor trailers, bodies of water and buildings, both flaming and not, and we were among his most ardent fans, especially when he failed with a spectacular wipe-out. We would talk about it for weeks, arm-chair quarterbacks to the last, like we knew exactly what went wrong. "He almost made it," we'd say. "If only he pulled up just a half-second earlier when he hit the lip of the ramp, he woulda made it."

Every kid wanted to *be* him. And every kid that wanted to be him wanted to jump over things with their bikes.

We all had the playing cards in our spokes held on by clothes pins – sometimes five or ten of them at a time. When we pedaled down the street, it sounded like a machine-gun fight. The only time we tilted them out of the way was when we were making a break for it through Granny Grunt's place and we wanted to be quiet, or when we needed to minimize the drag on a particularly daring jump. A few of the kids tried the under-inflated balloon procedure to get more of a "lub dub" sound, but the balloons never lasted long, and it was always back to the playing cards. Coincidentally, Bicycle brand cards were the best. They had some kind of plastic coating on them that made them last.

When you wanted to jump at Granny Grunt's hill, here's the way it worked: You'd walk your bike to the top of the hill, picking any debris off the trail on the way up, while all the other kids waited at the bottom. You got one practice jump, and then you jumped three more times. The best jump was the one that counted, assuming you didn't wreck.

There were quite a few things to remember in order to complete a successful jump. You had to have a feel for knowing when you had enough speed and when you didn't, especially if you were trying to clear an obstacle versus going strictly for distance. If you weren't going quite fast enough, you could inadvertently land on whatever it was you were attempting to jump over. Not such a big deal if you were jumping over a pile of bikes or some empty garbage cans, but quite a bit more serious if you were attempting to jump over a line of other kids lying on the ground. In the latter case you really needed to know when to bail and try again. The other important thing to remember was that when you hit the ramp, you needed to pull up hard, just as your front tire left the ground, and raise up off your seat a bit to turn your legs into shock absorbers in order to stick the landing.

You needed to be *absolutely, positively sure* you landed on your rear tire, or you were completely screwed. We had all seen it happen. Some poor bastard would land on his front tire, collapse the spokes and end up bloody, if not broken, and wouldn't even be able to walk his bike home because the front wheel was so bent that it wouldn't turn. Too many kids ended up this way, which is why we were strictly forbidden by our parents to even *think* about jumping our bikes over anything higher than the curb. Needless to say, I had to keep my involvement a secret. If my father even suspected we were doing this, he would have taken away our bikes until we were 35.

The final jump of my life happened like this. I was trying to beat Paul Davis for distance. He had just made a spectacularly perfect three-and-a-half-board jump, and had stuck the landing like a pro. (I say "three-and-a-half-board" because that was how we measured distance. We had found a six-foot section of 1x4 in the woods, and we used it as a giant ruler.) He thought his second jump was unbeatable, and he was feeling pretty cocky. He had a junk-yard bike too, spray-painted flat black.

I was up next, and I walked my bike to the top of the hill, inspecting the trail for any and all debris. It looked good. I ran through my pre-jump status check. Pant leg rubber banded: *check.* Seat tight: *check.* Tire bolts tight: *check.* Shoe laces tied: *check.* Big Blue and I were ready.

I took a deep breath, tipped over the lip and started pedaling hard, tucking down low at the same time. About a quarter of the way down, I was already going too fast for my pedaling to keep up, so I balanced my feet and kept my eyes on the ramp. I was a blue bullet. All I could hear were my tires on gravel and the wind, which was pulling tears from the corner of both my eyes. I hit the ramp perfectly, and as I launched off the end, I heard a clunk. I simultaneously came out of my tuck and pulled the front of the bike upwards. A picture perfect launch. Evel Knievel would have been proud. As I was sailing through the air, congratulating myself on a great jump, I looked down and realized something.

I could no longer see my front tire.

No, scratch that – it wasn't just the tire that was gone – it was the *entire front end of the bike.*

I was still holding the handle bars, but they were no longer connected to anything but my hands. I could feel the bike drifting sideways out from under me, both of us in free fall. The front fork – tire and all – had separated from the frame when I had pulled up, and it was somewhere under and slightly be-hind me. I was flying through the air connected to absolutely nothing.

I hit hard, somehow almost managing to land feet first. I still had the bike partially under me, however, and the frame and I crashed down together, the handlebars bouncing off my shoulder right before my face hit the hard packed dirt. I am pretty sure I passed out for a minute or two, because I don't remember much about that part. I remember feeling like I couldn't breathe, and it was hard to see, and my shoulder felt like it was on fire. I had never had the wind knocked out of me before, and I felt sure I was dying. All I could think about, when I was finally able to think at all, was that if I didn't die, my father was going to kill me.

At that point, I think I would have walked home on a compound fracture of the tibia in order to avoid having my parents find out what had happened. In retrospect, I am *very* glad my bike had no bar.

I actually beat Paul Davis. Distance counts, even if you don't stick the landing, and most of my bike and body went farther than he did. My front fork came in a little short, but that didn't matter. We had a judge's ruling on it, and Paul graciously allowed me the victory, since I was bleeding from both palms and one elbow and he thought my crash was the most awesome one he'd ever seen. (He was a good guy, even though we drifted apart when we got to high school. In junior high, he started running with a rough crowd and smoking pot, but we still hung out sometimes. He once stole a copy of *Jonathan Livingston Seagull* from the bookstore and gave it to me as a birth-day gift. To this day, I am not sure why.)

When I had recovered enough to stand up, if not walk, I inspected the carnage that had been Big Blue. It didn't look repairable. I was able to stick the fork back into the frame and walk it home, but it was like trying to push a shopping cart with a bad wheel. It didn't want to stay pointing in the right direction. I got it home and back into the garage without anyone seeing me. Even though the handlebars and the fork were no longer linked, it looked fine as long as you didn't pick it up.

You can't keep a busted bike a secret for very long when you're a kid. When my father asked me about it, I lied. I didn't say anything about jump-ing it. I just said I hit the curb and it broke. For a microsecond, I felt bad about not telling him what really happened, but I had hopes of getting a new bike, and so that feeling of guilt didn't last long. I had visions of a Schwinn Orange Krate of my very own. Hey, a guy can dream, can't he?

What I got instead was a generic gold unisex one-speed with coaster brakes and a bolt on bar, just like the one The Snitch had. Oh well. A new bike was a new bike.

My jumping days were over, however. I had learned my lesson, and besides, I knew from The Snitch's attempts that the new bike was heavy as hell and it didn't jump worth a damn.

A few years later, when I was about 13, which is *miles* from ten or 11, I got an olive-green 3-speed with 26" wheels that I bought for myself with money I had saved from my paper route. Because (for some unknown reason) it was cooler to ride your bike all hunched over, I replaced the new handlebars with some used 10-speed racing handlebars I bought from a kid down the street for three bucks. I wrapped them with black electrical tape, and called it good. One day when I went to the driveway to get my paper bundle, a funny thing happened.

Whenever you got a new customer that was in your covered territory, the home office would stick a little printed index card on top of your delivery pile with the name and address of that customer typed on it. You were supposed to go introduce yourself and find out if they had any special delivery requirements. I looked down at the address on index card and I knew the street, but not the house. It wasn't far, so I got on my new bike to check it out. After I figured out what side of the street it was on, and started riding slowly down the road, trying to find it. When I stopped my bike in front of the new customer's house, I couldn't believe it.

My subscription request was from Granny Grunt.

I hadn't been down to the old jump in a long time. I pulled into her driveway, got off my bike and walked up to the house. I rang the doorbell, and a few moments later, Granny Grunt opened the door. I explained that I was her new paper carrier, and we had a nice chat. She told me where she wanted the paper, and I told her when I would most likely be coming around to be paid. She asked me where I went to school, and how I liked it.

It was funny, standing there in the presence of someone who had evoked so much fear in me just a few years earlier, conversing with her as if she were nothing more than a friend of my mom's. It also occurred to me that I had never actually *seen* her before. She was smaller than my old memories conjured her up to be, and she certainly wasn't holding a shotgun. Turns out she wasn't the horrible witch I thought she was. She could be curt, and sometimes she'd complain to me about "those damned kids" but that's just the way she was. At least she always paid on time.

A couple of years later, when I was close to passing down my paper route to The Snitch and getting a real job, I got a cancellation notice for her on top of my pile. I showed it to my mother, and she told me that she thought she heard that Granny had died.

A little while later, her house went up for sale. An older couple bought it, and I got the subscription notice on my pile of papers shortly thereafter. The new people were rarely home, so sometimes it would be weeks before I could collect. For the most part they weren't very friendly, and they never tipped.

I think because they were never home, the legend of Granny lived on. Sometimes, when delivering papers, I'd see the younger kids cutting through the side yard on their bikes, mortal fear telegraphed in their every movement, pedaling for all they were worth. They were always glancing over their shoulders at the house, and didn't stop pedaling hard until it was out of sight.

Wherever Granny is now, I hope she's still scaring the hell out of the kids cutting through her yard, and still laughing her ass off every single time.

Caterpillar Roulette

"Push it, I dare ya," Markie said.

"No way. *You* push it," The Snitch replied. "Besides, what if it starts?"

"It's not gonna start."

"I dunno," The Snitch replied doubtfully. "The button says START right on it. 'Sides, we might get in trouble."

"For doin' what?" Markie asked. "Who's gonna know? If it starts, we just take off."

"He's not gonna push it," I said. "He's chicken."

"I'm *not* a chicken," The Snitch said, shooting me a dirty look. "And I don't see *you* pushin' any buttons," he added.

He had a point. I looked at Markie.

"I'll push it if you do," he said, then smirked. "But I ain't goin' first."

I took a single, nervous step toward the bulldozer.

I looked around. There was nobody in the field but us. It was a Sunday, and all the workers were gone. The week before, they had started construction in our woods. They were building a road – the road that would eventually be lined with new houses. The road that meant the end of our woods, our fields, the big hill, the end of...well...of everything.

"OK. Here goes." I said, resting my finger on the big red button on the side of the massive diesel engine.

"Do it," Markie whispered, the excitement in his voice barely contained.

I pressed it slowly, until it clicked home.

The dozer made a sickeningly loud RRRRR-RRRRRR! noise, and lurched. I instantly yanked my hand away from the button, as if I had been burned.

"Holy crap, it moved!" I said, looking at Markie. "Maybe you'd better not. I think it's in gear."

"So what?" he said. "A deal's a deal. I'll still push it, but Snitch is goin' after me." He grinned evilly as another thought occurred to him. "Then we go around again," he added.

Over Snitch's loud protestations, he reached out and quickly pushed the button. It made the same Rrrr-Rrrr sound – only shorter this time – and lurched forward another foot.

"It's your turn," Markie said to The Snitch. "You gonna do it?"

"No way," The Snitch said. "You can't make me."

We could, and we did. Somewhere between poking him in the chest and calling him a yellow-bellied chicken-liver, a wimp and any other name we could come up with to indicate the length and width of the yellow stripe going down his spineless back, he caved. In those days, peer pressure was an unstoppable force.

"OK! I'll do it, just cut it out!" The Snitch yelled at us, his eyes beginning to water. He wouldn't cry though. He knew if he did, we would never let him live it down.

He wiped his eyes, then stepped toward the dozer. He snapped his arm out and slapped the start button like he was slapping at a mosquito or a fly. The engine made a clicking sound, and the dozer didn't move at all.

Markie snorted. "Do over. That didn't count."

"Do over? No way! I pushed it! You guys saw me!"

"You didn't barely touch it!" Markie said. "It didn't count. Do it again." He looked at me for confirmation.

"Yeah, you hardly touched it," I agreed reluctantly. "Give it a real push this time. Don't just smack at it."

The Snitch reached out and pushed it harder. The engine made the Rrrr-Rrrr-Rrrr sound, lurched forward a good two feet, then backfired. We all jumped, and The Snitch let out a little yelp as a single, dirty puff of black smoke belched out of the stack.

"HOLY JEEZ!" Markie said, wide-eyed. "I think it almost started!" He looked at me expectantly. "Your turn," he said.

"I dunno," I said doubtfully. "It almost started."

"I *know*," he replied, a wild look in his eyes. "Wouldn't that be *sooo cool?*"

I had seen that look before. It was the same look he always got right before things went up in flames, exploded, collapsed, disintegrated, or otherwise went south in a major way.

I stood there for a second, doing nothing, deciding my next move. I had two choices – push it or don't push it. The first choice had two possible outcomes. If it didn't start, it was Markie's turn again, and I was off the hook. If it did start, well…it was best not to dwell on that possibility too deeply. The other, much less palatable choice was to do nothing at all. If I refused my turn, I would look like a coward. I was torn.

"What're you... chicken?" Markie asked.

That was all I needed to hear.

Before I could change my mind, I reached out and slammed the button, holding it in. The bulldozer lurched forward and I took a step or two to keep up with it. The engine clattered, backfired, then roared to life. We stood there, motionless and slack-jawed, as the driver-less bulldozer started moving, very slowly, toward the woods.

We had absolutely no idea what to do – none of us had actually expected it to start moving. There was no way we could jump on it, and even if we did manage to get on it somehow, we had no idea how to shut it down.

Markie yelled, "RUN!!" and instantly bolted for the road. We followed a split second later. I ran faster than I had ever run in my life, before or since. We ran until the bulldozer's noisy diesel was eclipsed by the sound of our Chuck Taylors slapping the ground, our ragged breathing and our pounding hearts. Through the Marketts' backyard, across the street to the Nelsons' house and along the fence to the pond trail, we ran. When we were physically incapable of running any farther, we collapsed on the grassy bank on the far side of the pond, all gulping air and shaking legs. We sat there for few moments to catch our breath and digest what had just happened.

The Snitch spoke first, looking at Markie. "We gotta tell *somebody*." he said. You could actually see the normal, almost expected, after-job Snitch-paranoia surfacing. I could never figure out why the hell we even brought him with us, other than the fact that he was my brother, and you had to make certain allowances.

He was clearly beginning to flip out. "Oh jeez. Oh jeez, you guys! What're we gonna do?"

Markie went ballistic. "*Do?* Are you freakin' nuts? *Nothin'* is what we do. If we even say a word to a grownup, we'll be in so much trouble you wouldn't believe. We don't say nothin, we don't do nothin." He paused, then leaned closer to The Snitch. "An' if you tell, you're dead meat." He put the period on the end of his sentence by giving The Snitch a knuckle punch in the arm. The Snitch said, "OW! That hurt, you...you...asshole!" He had just learned that one. He looked over at me for back up. Younger brother or not, he wasn't getting any support along those lines from my corner. The punch was just added insurance.

"Yeah, an' besides, you pushed it too," I said. *"Twice."* I didn't bring up the fact that I was the one who actually started it. I needed to make it abundantly clear that he was in this as deep as I was. He was a teller, but he usually responded well to logic. All we had to do was get him to see it our way, and after a long session of reason, alternating with threats of physical harm, he finally did. He reluctantly agreed that, in this instance anyway, silence and not honesty was probably the best policy.

Sitting there on the grassy bank, looking out over the stagnant, tea-stained water, we made a pact. Markie and I threatened The Snitch with bodily injury one last time – just to make sure – then we all did a pinky swear.

We vowed to Never Speak of This Incident Again.

And as far as I know, none of us ever did.

Well....until now, anyway.

Sorry, you guys.

Bending 101

We were seriously, extremely, completely bored. As usual, Markie, The Snitch and I were taking turns riding our bikes full-speed down the street, then slamming on our brakes and trying to see who could make the longest skid. [The key to winning, if you want to know, is to make sure you hit the dusty gravel on the side of the road and then keep your bike perfectly straight.]

"This isn't fair you know," The Snitch said to Markie. "You have a five speed and we don't. You can get going faster."

"So use my bike," Markie said. "Don't be a crybaby."

The Snitch thought about this for a second, then said, "I'm not a crybaby, so stuff it. It's too hot anyways. You guys wanna go over to the woods?"

It was the first day of August. We had an entire month before school started. Thirty-one, long, sweltering days that stretched out endlessly before us, September just a distant smudge on the horizon. We had reached the point of summer vacation where we weren't even sure what day of the week it was, and we didn't care.

We didn't have air conditioning, so it was too hot to stay in the house and watch TV. Most of the time you could find us riding our bikes around the neighborhood, jumping curbs, pulling wheelies and kicking up dust clouds with our skids. The clackclackclackclackclack noise of the playing cards in our spokes was just another part of summer, like tree-forts and catching bullfrogs.

Once in a while, we'd swing past our house or Markie's house and grab some squeeze pops or Fudgesicles. We'd stretch out on the grassy hill on the shady side of the Mondells' house and eat them, watching the clouds drift by and feeling the prickly, freshly-mown grass poking us through our t-shirts and tickling the backs of our necks.

Other days, we'd ride our bikes through the woods and down the steep path to the edge of the pond and sit around in the shade under the trees, swatting mosquitoes and talking about Important Things. Things like which cereal was better: Quisp or Quake. (Quisp) Or whether Evel Knievel was going to make it over the canyon, or even which part of the Dickie Goodman song interview was the funniest. (Mr. President, what really caused the energy crisis? "Smokin' in the boys room.") When things got really bad, we'd make up fictitious battles, like who would win in a fight between Steve Austin and say, 50 Sleestaks. (Steve Austin, no contest. Sleestaks are slow.)

The mosquitoes were brutal down there by the water, but sometimes we'd let them bite us until they were fat and red with our blood and then we'd slap them hard and pop them all over our arms, just to gross each other out. Donny from up the street told Markie that if you squeeze the skin around where they are biting you, they can't pull out and they'll just keep getting bigger and bigger until they explode. We never were able to replicate this, so I'm not sure if there is any truth to the legend. I know I always felt a little cheated when one managed to pull out, fully loaded, and fly away before I got the chance to slap it.

On most of the really hot days, we'd leave the pavement behind and ride our bikes around in the woods because it was much cooler under the thick canopy of leaves. We could always find something out there to keep us occupied, and no matter what we did we figured it was better than sticking around the house and taking the risk that my mother might think up "Something Constructive For Us To Do."

Normally, only my father gave us one-off chores and house projects, and that was generally only on the weekends. My mother was more or less content to let us run off into the woods and play from the time we woke up until the time we came home for dinner. As long as we stayed out of her hair, and she had a vague idea of where we were, we were ok. If we were hanging around the house, however, and started fighting with each other, or whining that there was nothing to do, she would always threaten us with "Something Constructive."

This, in direct opposition to our normal behavior, which lay decisively on the "Something *De*structive" side of the fence. Something Constructive generally involved "special jobs," thought up on the spur of the moment. We got an allowance, but that was for set, weekly chores. Feed the dog. Clear the table. Take out the garbage. Clean your room. The SC was more of a punishment tool – if we were bad, we would end up cleaning the garage, weeding the garden, raking the lawn or even shoveling up ossified dog poop. And if after all that we still didn't behave, off to the doghouse we'd go.

In order to avoid Something Constructive, we tended to stay as far away from the house as we could.

Being boys, obviously one of the things we liked to do when we were bored was climb trees. Big trees, mostly, but when we were really bored, we'd climb *small* trees – trees that became so spindly at the top that we were basically shinnying up them until we had nowhere else to go. We would have contests to see who could climb the highest before chickening out. Let me tell you, when you're waving in the breeze 30 feet up in a tree and you've got your full weight resting on two branches that aren't much thicker around than your thumb, you chicken out a lot sooner than you might believe you would.

I think it was Markie who first discovered that if you went a little *farther* than the point where you thought you were going to shit yourself, something interesting happened. Your weight exceeded the tree's ability to support you, and it would start to bend slowly toward the ground. When the downward force of your body weight was equal to the springiness of the tree, it would stop. At that point you'd be hanging there like a hairless lemur, usually about 20 feet off the ground.

From here, there were many, many options available. If you added about a Snitch-worth of weight to the trunk, you could actually bend the tree to the ground whereupon someone else could grab the top branches. The tree acted as a spring, and if you got under it, held onto a branch and then jumped straight up, you'd be able to leap three times higher than you normally could. It was like being Steve Austin. You'd jump up six feet in the air, then sort of float down.

The other thing you could do was to swing yourself around so you were sitting on the highest arc of the bent-over tree, legs hanging down on either side of the trunk. Obviously, this became a game called "Bucking Bronco." One of us would sit on top and hang on for dear life while the other two did their best to dislodge the rider.

We called this overall activity "bending" and I'm sure the actual owners of the land loved us as we went from tree to tree and bent them into arcs.

One morning our doorbell rang, and I heard Markie yell through the screen door. "Can Johnny and Snitch come out to play?"

We went outside and Markie said, "You guys wanna go bend?" We didn't have any other great ideas, so we agreed. We grabbed our bikes from the garage and the three of us pedaled towards the woods.

Markie had done a recon run the previous day, and had picked out the tree he wanted to bend. I looked at it, and expressed my doubts. "It's too big. There's no low branches. Even if we could get up there, it would take all three of us to even think about bending it. Plus, we'd have to be really, really high."

I wasn't being negative, I was just laying my professional bending expertise out there. The trunk had to be a good eight inches thick at the bottom.

"I can boost you, then the Snitch can boost me, then we can pull him up," Markie said, still not yet willing to give up on his new potential conquest.

The Snitch and I gave it some thought, then reluctantly agreed. Markie interlocked his fingers and lowered them. He braced himself, and as I stepped in, he heaved me up to the first branch. I grabbed it and swung up easily. The bark was smooth and slippery; very wax-like. We immediately named this species of tree for all of kid-kind.

Henceforth, they were known far and wide by the name of "wax trees."

Original, I know.

The Snitch boosted Markie, and within a few seconds he was sitting on the branch opposite me. We looked down at The Snitch. "I don't think we're gonna be able to pull him up," I said.

Snitch looked up at the first branch and said, "I bet I can shinny up, you guys. Just climb a little so I have room."

We did, and true to his word, The Snitch clambered up and joined us in the branches. He gave himself a giant wedgie doing it, but at least he was up.

With that, we started our ascent.

When we were as high as we could go, and all three of us were standing on the same few branches and holding the trunk, we started leaning this way and that, trying to feel if there were a certain direction in which the tree wanted to go. I'm not sure which particular tenet of the Bendological Sciences we were applying – it was either a branch of good old civil engineering or something more akin to Feng Shui.

When we found what we felt to be the right direction, we started swinging back and forth like a three-monkey pendulum, concentrating all our efforts in a single direction.

The tree started to bend.

"We got it!" I yelled. "It's going!"

"It's bending!" Markie yelled, "I knew we could – "

CRACK!

If you've never heard a tree snap cleanly in half, it sounds very similar to a gunshot. The ground came up to meet me, and the next thing I remember is waking up amid a sea of green leaves. I must have only been out for a second or two, because I looked up through the leaves and saw Markie draped across the trunk of the fallen tree. He was making a noise like a leaky air mattress. The Snitch was sitting on the ground holding his arm and trying not to cry.

I sat up, and as I did, Markie took in a huge, sucking gasp of air.

"Holy crap, you guys...we *broke* it." I said, a certain amount of awe in my voice. The tree trunk had broken in half about ten feet from the ground.

"No shit, Sherlock," Markie said, "I couldn't breathe. I thought I was gonna die."

"My arm hurts," The Snitch said. "I think it's broke," he added hopefully.

"It's not broke," I said. "If it was busted, you'd be bawlin' your eyes out."

He touched it gingerly, then moved it in and out experimentally. "Yeah, you're prob'ly right. I bet it's sprained though."

We allowed that it could be sprained and then took a more thorough inventory of ourselves, which revealed that – other than a few bumps and scrapes – we appeared to be just fine. We had been lucky.

Even at this young age, we were smart enough to learn from our mistakes, and we all knew that there was something for us to learn here.

What did we learn? Well, we learned that bending trees is dangerous and destructive and – no, I'm kidding.

Our actual lesson that day was voiced by Markie, about ten minutes after we had brushed ourselves off and were walking our bikes down the path toward his house.

"We ain't bendin' no more of them wax trees," he said.

Street Luge with Houdini

We found the wheels in the woods, connected to a rotted out red flyer wag-on. We pulled them off along with the axles and took them home. They were the last part we needed. We had a serious case of go-kart envy, and these wheels were the final piece of the puzzle. Come hell or high water, we were going to build ourselves a go-kart. The only thing is, we had no idea what we were doing. The one thing we *did* know was that it needed wheels, and now we had some.

It all started when we saw Burnsie drive his go-kart out of the garage for the first time. His dad had been working on it with him for months. It had a bright red, shaped-plywood body, a front-mounted lawn mower engine, air-filled tires, and an actual steering wheel. It looked something like this:

He'd ride it up and down the street, but would never let us try it.

It was maddening. We vowed to build our own, even though we knew it wouldn't compare. We didn't have a motor, or even rudimentary carpentry skills, but we were determined. We were only ten years old and Mike was 14, and our parents wouldn't let us have anything to do with any vehicle that wasn't pedal powered.

Burnsie wasn't a *complete* dick. Every once in a while, he would let us hang with him if he had nothing better going on. I remember the first time he let me come in and check out his new stereo. We were in his basement bed-room listening to the radio and Golden Earring were singing *Radar Love*. I told him the words didn't make any sense, and he said, " You're too young to understand."

115

I remember thinking at the time that he didn't know what the hell the song was about either, but I kept my mouth shut. I was just happy to be there hanging out with a big kid who had a go-kart. (I looked up the lyrics the other day and apparently I'm still too young to understand, because that song makes no fucking sense whatsoever.)

We took the wheels and axles and fastened them to the bottom of a thin rectangle of 3/4 inch-thick plywood. How did we accomplish this precision task, you ask? By hammering nails into the plywood on either side of the axle, and then bending them over, trapping the axle between the nails. Simple, yet barely effective. Obviously, we had absolutely no idea what we were doing.

We didn't have a seat, or a steering wheel. Or *steering*, for that matter. We nailed a chunk of 4x4 to the top to stop you from sliding backward, and we stuck a 2x4 to the front edge to brace your feet against. The 4x4 was kind of sharp, so we nailed some old carpet down on it. A few holes and some rope-loop handles and we were done. It looked something like this:

Since we would be pulling it behind a bike, we figured we wouldn't need to steer.

We figured wrong.

Normally, whenever we needed a guinea pig for an untried piece of potentially dangerous equipment, we immediately went looking for Houdini. This time was no exception. We needed someone fearless, light enough to be pulled behind a bike, and unable to feel pain like a normal human. He was the perfect candidate.

We got some rope, tied it to a hole we drilled in the leading edge of our rolling slab of plywood, and tied the other end to the back of my bike. We found Houdini, and had no trouble convincing him to lock in. We told him we'd go slow, and he actually believed us.

I inched my bike forward until the rope was taut, and Markie and The Snitch started pushing Houdini to get up some momentum and allow me to start pedaling. Pretty soon, I was riding hard with Houdini following about 30 feet behind my bike. Markie and The Snitch jumped on their own bikes and brought up the rear, keeping an eye out for cars.

Everything went pretty well at first. The kart was pulling a little to the left, but for the most part it was tracking better than expected. I would swing over to the right every once in a while to correct his path, and we started picking up speed. Unbeknownst to Houdini, we were heading toward Broderick Street, and the hill on its back side. About 3/4 of the way there, Houdini guessed where we were bringing him and he started yelling for us to turn around.

Our duty as his older siblings required us to ignore him, so we did.

We got to Broderick Street, hung a wide left and started down the hill. Since the go-cart had no steering, every turn was wide, fast and uncontrolled.

At that point, Houdini gave up on his yelling, and decided to simply concentrate on not falling off. We were going about as fast as I could pedal, and Houdini was humming along at a pretty good clip.

Suddenly, I heard Markie yell "CAAAAARRR!"

Every kid who has ever played kickball or baseball in the street knows the drill. Someone yells "CAAAARRR!!" and everyone runs to the side of the street until the car passes, then the game continues. Unfortunately, it was a little more difficult to stop this particular activity in the middle.

I cut over to the right and started to slow down. Houdini, on the other hand, did not. In addition to having no steering, we had also neglected to provide him with brakes. My cutting to the right had the unfortunate effect of tugging Houdini back on track, which meant he was then running straight down the middle of the street. To complicate matters, he was catching up to me quickly, since I had slowed down.

Markie screamed, "Jump!" but there was no way I was ditching my bike. I didn't want it dragged to the bottom of Broderick Street behind a plywood go-kart carrying my younger brother. I didn't realize until later that he had actually been yelling to Houdini.

The driver of the car caught on pretty quickly and slowed down before he flattened any of us. I *also* caught on pretty quickly, and I stood up on my pedals and tried to take off again to avoid the train wreck I saw coming. Unfortunately, I wasn't quick enough. Before I pedaled twice, Houdini's kart passed me. Along the way, the kart had run over its rope, and the rope tangled up in the front wheel. The wheel started winding it up like a spool, which yanked the kart hard toward the left curb.

I thought for sure I was going to get dragged down the street along with my bike. The only reason this didn't happen was because two *other* things happened simultaneously: The left front wheel of the kart came completely off the axle, and Houdini decided that he had enough of this shit. He figured that dying in an attempt to reach the grass was better than dying from road rash, or under the wheels of a car, so he jumped. He made the grass, aided by the fact that the left side of the kart dropped to the pavement and pretty much launched him in the right direction.

When he jumped, the mass of the kart was reduced considerably, which was a good thing for me. He had just taken a meaningful chunk out of $p = (m \times v)$, and for that I was grateful. The rope reached its limit and twanged like a guitar string, yanking my bike forward. I was braced for it, but not well enough. The back of the bike jumped off the ground just hard enough to knock me off my pedals. I fell crotch-first on the bar, and went down hard on the grass, tangled in my bike. I didn't see what happened to the kart, but The Snitch said it jumped straight into the air, spun around and then slammed into the pavement upside down.

The driver of the car had slowed to a crawl. It's possible that he was looking to make sure nobody was seriously hurt, but I think it was more likely that he just wanted to hang around long enough to watch this little single-act play of ours come to its spectacular conclusion.

When I had recovered enough to stop rolling around on the ground holding my crotch, I stood up and looked around for Houdini. Markie and The Snitch were just helping him up. He had some grass stains on his back, but other than that and a few scrapes, he looked fine. I limped over.

"Hey," I said. "You OK?"

"Yeah," he answered, still out of breath. "That was wicked cool. But I ain't goin' again without some steering." He thought for a second, then added, "And some brakes, maybe."

We found the missing wagon wheel in someone's bushes, and took everything back to the garage. We reattached the wheel, and then refastened the axle to a piece of 2x4 using the same bent nail method. We then fastened the entire assembly to the bottom of the platform with a large bolt.

This allowed the 2x4 to rotate, at least until the wagon wheels hit the sides of the platform. We then tied a rope on each end of the axle, which gave us the equivalent of horse's reigns and provided us with some rudimentary steering. To address the lack of brakes, we nailed a few hunks of 2x4 to the tops of the platform on either side of the seat, level with the sides. We then nailed a length of 2x2 to the side of this block. When Houdini pushed them forward, they would rub on the back wheels and slow him down.

This worked pretty good, and after the inaugural run (sans bike), he did two more with no issues. He said that the only hard part was letting go of the steering ropes to use the brakes. If you tried to only use one, you had a tendency to quickly pull to that side, and had to compensate by steering in the opposite direction. Not ideal, but with the steering improvements, (namely, that we had some) it was possible to just skip the brakes completely and coast to a stop at the bottom of the hill. Once we had the technique down, we all took turns, one guy riding and the other three watching for cars.

It wasn't motorized and it wasn't bright red, and it sure as hell wasn't safe, but it was ours, and we had built it ourselves. Burnsie may have had tons of fun driving up and down the street in front of his house showing off, but he didn't have Houdini, our fearless test-pilot. Even though it didn't always seem like it then, in the long run it turned out to be a pretty good trade.

Mostly.

Summer Jays

Through a haze of sleep, I heard the door bell ring, then ring again almost immediately. I heard it ring a third time, and even in my sleepy state I could tell there was an urgency about it.

My mother yelled "Come in, it's open!" because that's what you did in suburbia in the 70's. You just left your front door unlocked, and when someone stood on your doorstep and rang your doorbell or knocked on your door, you just yelled for them to come in. It didn't matter if it happened to be the kid next door, the mailman or some dude wearing a hockey mask and holding a chainsaw. You yelled for them to come in, and if they were uncomfortable with that, (and some people were) it was too bad for them.

In this particular case, it wasn't a guy with a mask and a chainsaw – it was just Markie. I could hear his voice drifting up to my room from the front door. "Hi, Missus Virgil," he said. "Can Johnny and Snitch come over?"

She told him we were still sleeping, but that she'd send us over once we got out of bed and ate breakfast. I looked at my clock, and it was only 8:30 in the morning. It wasn't like Markie to make it across the street from his house until after 10 a.m. at the earliest, especially during summer vacation, so I figured something must be up. I threw on some clothes and walked down the hallway toward the kitchen, stopping at The Snitch's bedroom on the way.

I opened his door and he woke up instantly. We didn't have locks on our doors, and he was ever-vigilant against me trying to sneak in there and put his hand in a cup of warm water to make him piss the bed. "Get up, turd." I said. "Markie was just here and he wants us to come over." He grunted and sat up. "*You're* the turd," he said. He was clever like that.

After breakfast, we asked my mother if we could go across the street, but before she could answer, the doorbell rang again, and there was Markie.

He had his face pressed up to the storm door screen, and was shading his eyes in order to see in. He saw us looking back at him, so he yelled in. "Hey you guys! Come on out! I wanna show you something."

My mother sighed, gave us the nod, and we were out the door. "Be home for dinner!" she yelled after us. "And don't spoil your appetite by eating junk!"

(She was always worried about our appetites, and how they might be spoiled, even though the reason we pushed our dinners around on our plates was not because we were full of Ring Dings. We pushed it around because it was fried liver, or because it was dried-up pork chops and Spanish rice that even the dog wouldn't eat. On those days, we were lucky to have had the

Ring Dings. My mother was not a great cook. I distinctly remember sitting on the kitchen counter at Markie's house and chain-eating 11 Reeses peanut butter cups pretty much as fast as I could unwrap them. Hey, don't judge me. (Seriously, if the chocolate is crisp and the peanut butter is fresh, how could you *not* eat them?*)*

Markie jumped on his Schwinn Orange Krate, and we ran to the garage to get our inferior specimens.

"Where we goin'?" I yelled to Markie, who was already riding across the lawn, a habit which my father absolutely hated. "Follow me!" he yelled back, heading down the street toward The Path.

"The Path" was a narrow, hard-packed dirt track that ran between two houses and into the woods and field beyond. It was used by every kid in the neighborhood; sometimes on foot, sometimes on pedal bikes and sometimes on motorcycles, or as we called them, dirt-bikes. It was a pretty busy path, and during the summer we'd scope it out before using it to avoid running into any of the big kids. If things looked like rush hour, we'd forgo the bikes and just walk through the woods directly behind Markie's house and then cut over. Even doing that, there were certain risks involved, but at least you wouldn't get your bike taken away from you. He was in a hurry, and we weren't sure why.

We hit the path, pedaling hard behind Markie. His bike wasn't made for trail riding, shock absorbers notwithstanding, so we managed to keep up. Ours weren't really made for that either, but at least our front and back tires were the same size. His front tire was the size of a dog dish, and it didn't do well in the sand.

He cut to the right in order to stay on the hard pack and avoid the soft, sandy part of the trail that ran out into the middle of the field. Before the pricker bushes and sand wasps took it over, the sandy part used to be a home-made baseball diamond, but now it was mostly a circular dirt-bike track. Nobody was using it just then, so we continued on without incident, moving toward the right to an adjoining path that led around the outside perimeter of the field. We passed the short trail to The Pit, and about half-way to the Big Hill, Markie stopped his bike in a cloud of dust. We stopped behind him and dropped our bikes beside the path.

He walked into the woods a little ways and then pointed up. "Check it out!" he said, pointing to a thick pine bough about 10 or 12 feet off the ground. We followed his pointing finger with our eyes, and saw a large nest sitting out on the end of the thick branch.

"It's just a bird nest," I said. "Big deal."

"Yeah," Markie said, *"but there's eggs in it."*

That changed things. That made it cool; irresistible, even.

"How do you know?" I asked. "You seen the birds?"

"No," Markie replied. "I climbed up and looked."

The tree wasn't what we'd consider a great climber. There was only a single branch reachable from the ground, and it was a dead one. We learned early on it wasn't a good idea to rely on a dead branch unless it was at least as fat around as your arm and wasn't rotten. Luckily, this one looked fairly sturdy, and I used it to get into the tree, climbed a bit farther, then swung a leg up so that I ended up sitting on the branch with the nest out on its end. The nest was a long way out, and there was nothing to hang onto but the branch itself.

"Shinny out," Markie said helpfully. "That's what I did."

I was pretty sure I could get out, but not too sure I could get back. I didn't want to look like a chicken though, so I wrapped my thighs around the branch, hunched forward, and started inching my way out. Other than getting the crotch of my pants caught on a small broken-off branch, I made it out to within viewing distance of the nest unscathed. It was tucked behind a spray of pine needles, and I reached out to move them aside. It was a pretty big nest.

"Eggs still there?" Snitch asked.

"Yeah," I replied. "There's six. Kinda tan with spots."

"Told ya," Markie gloated.

"I wanna see," Snitch said. "Come down."

I began working my way back from the nest, and when moving backward it seemed like the branch had somehow become three times longer. My pants snagged on the broken twig again, only this time it wasn't as easy to get myself unstuck. The branch was angled forward, which made it relatively easy to get past on the way out, but on the way back it was like the barb on a fishhook. Finally, I was able to lift myself up a little to get over it, but for a while there I thought I was going to have to chance dropping from the branch, which was just high enough so that I had second thoughts about doing it. After what seemed like an hour moving an inch at a time, all the while listening to commentary from Markie and Snitch about how best to accomplish the task, I made it back to the main trunk, let myself hang from the broken branch below and dropped to the ground.

The Snitch repeated my actions, right down to getting his crotch snagged on the same broken twig. He checked out the eggs and then made his way back, and then he too dropped to the ground.

"I'll bet we can hatch'em," Markie said excitedly. "See what kind of bird comes out. My sister told me if you put them in shoebox with a lightbulb, they'll hatch."

"No they won't," I said. "They'll just die and then start to stink. Remember the duck eggs?" My father had found some abandoned duck eggs on our lawn once, and decided to try to hatch them. He bought some little incubator thing that looked like a yellow flying saucer with a clear dome on it, and we dutifully turned the eggs twice a day for however long we were supposed to, but nothing happened. When they hadn't hatched, he told me to get rid of them. Instead of throwing them out, I wrapped them in a plastic baggie and buried them in a wooden cigar box. I had visions of egging a house with the rottenest of rotten eggs when Halloween rolled around in four months. Unfortunately, when I dug them up, I discovered that they had exploded in the bag and most of the rotten egg had leaked out. Even so, they were still juicy enough so that the stench was indescribable.

They both remembered that fiasco. "So whatta we do with'em then?" Markie asked.

"Nothin'," I replied. "They won't hatch if we mess with them. But I'll bet we can come back every coupla days and look. Maybe we can see when the babies come out."

So that's what we did, except instead of every couple of days, it was more like every single day, and sometimes twice a day. After a period of a week or so, we discovered that it was a blue jay nest. Every time we'd pull up on our bikes, the blue jay would fly to a nearby tree and yell at us. We also had made a pact that none of us would go to the nest without the other two, and we'd take turns being the first to look. I'm not really sure why we made this pact, or which one of us came up with the idea. It just seemed like a good idea at the time. After a short while, we became experts at the particular moves needed to get out to the nest, take a quick look, then get back down.

Finally the thing we were waiting for happened. It was Snitch's turn to look first, and when he got up to the nest, he flipped out. "THEY'RE HATCHIN!" he screamed. "I can see four out, and one more with his head stickin' out of a hole in the shell! The last one is still just an egg."

"Come down, it's my turn!" Markie said, and Snitch edged backward toward the tree. The mother blue jay was in the tree next to us, screaming loudly.

After we all had taken a turn, we rode our bikes back to the Markie's house. We were beside ourselves with excitement. None of us had ever seen birds hatch before, unless you counted a field trip to a farm, but those eggs weren't sitting in a nest. They were in a big chicken wire box under glass, and when we saw them there wasn't much going on but a bunch of unhatched eggs and a bunch of fuzzy chicks running around.

The next day, it was my turn to go first, and when I climbed out on the branch, I saw that there were only four chicks left. One chick and the un-hatched egg were nowhere to be seen.

"The last egg is gone," I said to Markie and Snitch, who were standing be-low me. "And one of the birds. But the other four are still here."

We checked on them every day for probably a week and a half, and watched them change before our eyes. They went from unrecognizable lumps of mush to prehistoric looking monsters. Eventually we could hear them cheeping from the ground when we rode up. When we climbed the tree to look, they'd all have their mouths open, expecting to be fed. This nest had become the highlight of our summer so far. When we weren't riding our bikes over there to look, we were talking about riding our bikes over there to look.

One Friday afternoon, Markie came over and gave us some bad news.

"I gotta go to my grandmother's camp for a week," he informed us. "You guys have to promise you won't go to the nest until I get back."

We thought this wasn't in the spirit of our agreement, but eventually we caved and reluctantly agreed – mostly because Markie seemed desperate. I think part of him didn't want to miss out on anything, but another part of him was more concerned that we might see something he didn't and hold it over his head, like when we found the dead pileated woodpecker. I think he was tired of listening to us say, "You shoulda been there, it was sooooo cool!" every time we got talking about it. I think another one of those situations would probably have killed him, so we agreed to stay away until he got back.

As it turned out, his parents ended up inviting us to go as well, so it didn't really matter. We had a great week of water-skiing, swimming and fishing, and the nest temporarily slipped to the back of our minds. As an added bo-nus, I got to see my first real boob through a knothole in the wall. It belonged to Markie's mother, but hey a boob is a boob, even if it's a really *long* boob.

When we got home, of course, the first thing we did was plan to meet up the next day and visit the nest to see what was up.

The next morning was hot and humid, and there was no breeze at all. We decided it was too hot to ride bikes, so we walked out to the nest. At 10 a.m., it was already shaping up to be one of those energy-sapping days where the last thing you wanted to do was, well, *anything*. Just moving around made you hot and sticky, and the bugs were everywhere. In the field, our footfalls on the powdery sand raised little dust clouds that just hung in the air, then dissipated slowly as we passed. The cicadas buzzed relentlessly in the trees. We could hear the distant sounds of traffic on Central Avenue, and the hum of faraway lawnmowers.

We didn't talk much. There was a hush in the woods, almost as if every living thing had decided that today was a day to kick back, endure the heat, and wait for it to cool off before doing anything that involved expending energy. Even the baby birds, normally raucous upon our arrival, seemed subdued. If it hadn't been for the mother blue jay scolding us from her normal perch a few trees away, we might have thought the nest empty.

It was Markie's turn to go up first, and even though it was hot and buggy, he couldn't wait to start climbing. He jumped up and grabbed the dead branch, pulling himself up into the tree, eventually lowering himself into a sitting position on what we had begun to refer to as the "nest branch."

As he worked his way out toward the end of the branch, we noticed that the commotion was becoming louder. A second blue jay had decided to join in the scolding, and we figured it was the father bird. By this time Markie was almost to the nest. When he got into final position, he reached out and moved the spray of pine needles from his view. Four baby birds looked directly at him.

Then they all jumped out.

He freaked and almost fell out of the tree. The Snitch and I stood there with our mouths hanging open while baby birds ran around us in circles. The Snitch moved first. "We have to put them back! We have to put them back!" Snitch screamed, and desperately began trying to catch the baby birds. From out of nowhere, the mother and father had been joined by a pack of about a half-dozen other blue jays, and now they were *all* screaming at us. We were catching baby birds and tucking them into the front of our T-shirts, then climbing up and handing them to Markie, who was lying out flat on the branch. Every time he'd put one back, another one would jump out. The nest had turned into a clown car, and the blue jays were getting increasingly agitated. The babies were jumping out faster than we could pick them up, and we were beginning to panic. Cries of "Get that one!" and "Another one just jumped out!" and "There's one by your foot!" echoed through the woods.

After five minutes of watching us try to bail this sinking boat, the ever-increasing crowd of blue jays decided they had seen enough.

One of them dove at Markie, pecking him on the top of the head. He lost his mind and either jumped or fell out of the tree, landing hard, but was apparently unhurt. I base this solely on the speed at which he regained his feet. He probably could have suffered a broken ankle and I doubt if he'd have noticed, since he was more than a little busy. The rest of the blue jays had joined the attack, and it was like watching an Alfred Hitchcock movie come to life. I'm not sure why, but they had Markie in their sights, maybe because he was the one who had been out on the nest branch. He was running in circles and screaming, "GET'EM OFF! GET'EM OFF!" while slapping wildly at his head, which was surrounded by a flapping, pecking, whirling dervish of pissed off blue jays.

The Snitch and I were still trying to pick up baby birds, but now we had nobody to hand them to. Markie finally wised up and started running in a straight line down the trail, a half-dozen screaming, diving birds over his head. He was still ducking and waving his hands around, but at least he was leading the majority of them away from us. I just stood there and watched him run until one of the remaining birds dove at my head, and then I started running too. I'm not sure when the Snitch decided he wanted to stop picking up baby birds and run for his own life, but he eventually did the same. We ran as fast as we could, and after a minute or two, the birds gave up the fight.

When we got back to Markie's house, we took inventory. Other than a few scratches from running through branches, and some small holes in Markie's head, we were relatively unscathed. When we noticed Markie's head was bleeding a little, we had to tell his mom.

As she dabbed his lacerations with peroxide, she asked us what happened, and we told her our version of the truth – We were just walking by the nest and the birds attacked us.

"Were you bothering them?" she asked, knowing full well that we were. "I hope you didn't touch them. Birds carry diseases, you know." She paused. "And if you handle the chicks the parents will smell you on them and won't feed them anymore," she added, to solidify our guilt.

We didn't tell her that currently their odor was probably indistinguishable from that of three sweaty kids, and as for the diseases part, no, that was news to us.

As we sat there digesting the fact that we were all probably going to die of some heretofore unknown bird disease, we agreed it would be best not to go back to the nest for a few days. We had handled the crap out of the baby birds, and we were hoping against hope that even so, they would live.

When we finally went back, the nest was empty, and there was no sign of the blue jays at all.

"Think they got eaten by something?" Snitch asked, voicing the fear that we all had but didn't want to talk about. "You heard Markie's mom. Since we touched them, the mother bird won't feed them. Something prob'ly ate them."

"I don't know," I answered. "They looked pretty big. Like they were almost ready to fly. And I asked dad and he said it wasn't true about the mother bird smelling you on them and not feeding them."

"Yeah, I think they lived, too." Markie said with confidence, ignoring the fact that I basically just told Snitch that our father had inadvertently called his mother a liar. "I bet anything they just flew away."

I thought about it for a few seconds, then said, "Yeah, you're probably right." The Snitch looked relieved.

It's amazing how easily kids can convince themselves of something. In that moment, we knew, for real and for true, that those baby blue jays had just up and flown away.

I dreamed about being attacked by blue jays for years. Even today, when I hear a bunch of them lambasting a squirrel or hawk for getting too close to a nest, I can't help but look up at them and think back to that hot, dusty, endless summer day when three little kids got their butts handed to them by a flock of those same fearless birds.

It always makes me smile.

Dog Days of Summer

"Here. Eat one," Markie said.

"No way," I replied. "That's gross."

"Don't be a wimp. Try one," he mumbled, his mouth full. "They're pretty good." This coming from the kid who used to eat daddy long legs when he could catch them. He handed me a bone-shaped object the color of a brick.

"Jeez, it's dog food," I said. "Why would you wanna eat'em?"

"I told you. Cuz they're good," he said as he bit off another piece and started chewing.

I looked at the biscuit. It had "MILK-BONE" stamped on it and it looked harder than my teeth. I smelled it. It had an odor that wasn't entirely unpleasant, and reminded me a little bit of Cheerios or corn flakes. I wasn't sure about this.

I licked it tentatively, not knowing what to expect. It had an odd flavor, but didn't taste bad, really. Not good, not bad. Sort of bland, actually. I took a bite. It was hard to chew, but actually tasted better once I started in on it. It sucked the spit out of my mouth, but I finished it and he handed me another one.

"Good, right?" he said, grabbing another one out of the box and chomping on it. "I like the green ones best."

"They're different flavors?" I asked.

"No," he said, shrugging his shoulders. "I just like the green ones best."

I bit off another hunk and chewed it up. They were a little salty, like potato chips. You couldn't eat just one. I was getting the hang of it, and once I was over the fear of it breaking my teeth, I got into it. I felt like I was getting away with something -- doing something I knew I wasn't supposed to do. Eating them rocked your brains. When you crunched them, that was all you could hear in your ears, and it made your eyes vibrate in your head.

After he had polished off four or five green ones, and I had eaten my third red one he said, "Check this out." and stuck out his tongue. It was the color of a fresh lime. Green, like a holly leaf. "Stick yours out," he said.

I stuck out my tongue. "What's it look like?" I asked.

"It's all red. Looks like you ate a hot ball," he said.

"Are you sure these things are ok to eat?" I asked. "We're not gonna get sick or nothin'?"

"Nah, I eat'em alla time. Nothin' bad happened," Markie said.

"OK, gimme another red one," I said, and he did. I burped a long, biscuity burp and bit the corner off, chewing contentedly. Dog biscuits weren't bad. Who knew?

We ate probably half a box, and then went inside to watch TV. A little while later, the phone rang, and it was my mother. I had to go home for dinner.

I wasn't hungry for obvious reasons, so I didn't eat much. "You ruined your appetite at Markie's house, didn't you?" my mother asked. "Did you fill up on junk? What was it this time? Friehofer's chocolate chips? Ring Dings?"

I couldn't tell her what we really ate, so I lied. "No," I said. "Just a couple of Doritos."

Two days later, I thought I was dying.

I was sitting there watching TV when it hit. The mother of all stomach cramps. I ran for the bathroom and made it just in time. To put it in scientific terms, I was experiencing a serious fluid dynamics problem.

According to Wikipedia, the solution to a fluid dynamics problem "typically involves calculating various properties of the fluid, such as velocity, pressure, density, and temperature, as functions of space and time." I'm not sure what the actual equation would be, but suffice it to say there was lots of pressure, way too much velocity, not enough density, and nowhere *near* enough space or time.

I cleaned myself up, and stood up. When I saw the blood, I completely panicked. The bowl was full of it, and I screamed for my mother. She practically knocked the door down trying to get to me. I was standing there with my pants around my ankles, pointing at the bowl, hyperventilating.

When she saw the bowl, she freaked out, and went into total mom mode. She started machine gunning questions at me. "Does your stomach hurt? Do you feel light-headed? When did this start? Did you eat anything you shouldn't have?"

When she got to that last question, something clicked. *Did you eat anything you shouldn't have?* In fact, I *had* eaten something I shouldn't have, and now I was going to die. It served me right for listening to Markie.

I confessed, tears streaming down my face. I told her everything; how Markie had convinced me to eat dog food, how he liked the green ones best and how I ate all the red ones. When I got to that part of the story, she visibly relaxed.

"You're going to be fine," she said, trying not to laugh. "It's the food coloring in the dog biscuits. You ate all the red ones, and that's what made you poop red. It's nothing bad."

I wasn't fully convinced, but I stopped crying.

"Remember when Doc ate all the blue dog biscuits and the yard was full of blue poop?" she asked me, trying to soothe my adrenaline-jacked nerves. "It's the same thing. I'm still going to call the doctor to make sure, but I don't think we have anything to worry about."

My mother also called Markie's mother and explained the situation. Markie's mom corroborated my story, and told her that yes, she agreed we were both idiots, and yes, coincidentally enough, Markie was dropping number twos the color of sweet pickles. No fluid dynamics problems though.

My embarrassment at calling my mother to look at my poop was offset by the good news that I wasn't going to die. I also stopped taking culinary suggestions from Markie.

I should have known better. The kid ate spiders, for Christ's sake.

Muscle Bound

"I found another one!" The Snitch yelled, holding up a perfect, white clam shell with a pinkish inside. We were at Seaside Heights, New Jersey, and scouring the beach looking to add to our extensive seashell collection, which we had begun about an hour before. It was low tide, and the beach was littered with shells and little jellyfish that looked like clear pancakes. I picked one up and chucked it at The Snitch. "Hey cut it out!" he said, contorting wildly to avoid the flying jelly.

I didn't figure they would actually sting you since you could seemingly pick them up without any adverse effects, but the official kid lore was that if you got one slapped on your back it would burn like acid. We never tested this theory, although I remember getting one caught in my shorts one time and nothing bad happened so either they don't sting, or I have very tough gonads.

The Snitch ran over and dropped his newest shell into Houdini's briefcase. Houdini found a perfect snail shell, and that went in, too. I know it's weird that we weren't using buckets, but my mother was into Amway at the time, and they'd always send stuff in these small plastic briefcases with a handle on them. I don't know why, but Houdini went nuts for these things.

"Just fill that one container and that's it," my mother warned, knowing that if she didn't give us a limit, we'd have half of the Jersey shore in our car on the way home.

With nothing better to do, The Snitch and I searched for shells too, helping Houdini to build up his collection. My father even woke up at dawn to walk us over to the beach before it was officially open to see if we could find some good ones. Most of the time we ended up watching for bubbles in the sand and digging up sand crabs instead, but it was still fun to be on the beach when it was virtually empty. Just us, some surfers in wet suits and a bunch of old guys waving metal detectors around above the sand.

We went to Seaside Heights every year for most of my childhood. We always stayed at this semi-run-down hotel across from the beach – the only one on the strip that would let my father pay day-to-day. That way, if the weather was still good the day before we were supposed to come home, he could wake up in the morning, look at the sky and pay for another day – or not.

The first thing my mother did when we got to the shore was to hit a souvenir store and buy three of the brightest hats she could find, and then make us wear them as long as we were on the beach. This was her way of being able to pick us out of the beach-going crowd with a single glance, and make sure we were all present and accounted for.

This really sucked for me, because I was almost 13 and at an age where I wanted to look cool – I didn't want to wear a stupid beanie hat with fluorescent green and white alternating panels on it that said, "Ahoy Matey" or some shit like that. I had my own *aviator sunglasses* for God's sake.* How was I supposed to be taken seriously by cute girls if I had to wear some stupid hat?

Of course, I was pasty white, weighed about 70 pounds, had zero muscle and wore a black and white nylon speedo that showed off my tiny mushroom cap. I'm sure it was the *hat* that was the problem.

My mother finally relented, and let me off the hat hook, and I felt free but kind of lost, like I had just gotten out of prison. I could finally let my Keith Partridge hair blow in the ocean breeze. I could meet girls. I could be just another anonymous tourist on the beaches of New Jersey. I could finally release all the pent up coolness that had been repressed by the hat. So what I'm saying here is that absolutely nothing changed.

Vacations with my family were fun, but they eventually wore you down and beat you into submission. Every day it was the same routine. We'd wake up, get dressed, pile into my father's nine-passenger station wagon, and go to the Whistle Stop for breakfast so we could listen to everyone complain that their french toast was cold. After that, we'd drive back to the hotel so everyone could take turns using the bathroom, then we'd change into our bathing suits and walk across the street to the beach. It sounds easy, but when you're dealing with four kids, two parents and *their* parents, it was a logistical nightmare to get everyone pointed in the same direction in less than two hours.

After the second day, The Snitch and I had pretty much lost interest in the seashell collection. Houdini, however, kept up the search, and when he found a particularly great specimen that was better than something he already had, he would do a swap and replace. He was building the ultimate collection. We didn't mind, because it kept him busy and also out of our hair.

Instead, The Snitch and I rented inflated rafts and rode the waves, which was always a good way to meet girls. When you're just drifting around out beyond the breakers, waiting for the next big swell, you could accidentally-on-purpose float over towards a cute girl and strike up a conversation. It was a pre-teen meat market out there.

---

*I was one cigarette holder away from being a 13-year-old version of Hunter S. Thompson

Sometimes, you'd meet some other guys around your age who where there for the same week as you, but it always seemed like the girls I tried to talk to were, coincidentally, all going home either that same day or the next. Funny, that.

On the fourth day, wonder of wonders, I met a girl. Her name was Sue, and she was blonde and pretty, and a year older than me. And she had boobs, one of which I got to see.

Our first extremely romantic conversation consisted of me screaming "AHHHHHHHHHHH! LOOKOUT!" right before my head rammed into her legs at about 20 miles per hour and she went down under my raft. When we both surfaced, sputtering and half-drowned, I began to apologize, but stopped dead when I realized her left boob had escaped its confinement. She realized it about the same time I did, and snapped her top up, completely mortified. Due to our mutual embarrassment, we bonded and ended up hanging out for a few days. I had a brand new camera, and she liked to get her picture taken, so I actually went home with an honest to god picture of a *girl*, smiling at *me*. It was a monumental moment.

We were in love, and when she left, we promised to write to each other. I think the culmination of our long distance romance was me writing her one letter and her writing me one less than that. It had been good while it lasted.

Our family's last day at the beach was always the same if the weather co-operated. We'd wake up, go to breakfast, come back and pack, check out of the hotel, put everything in the car and then head for the beach one last time. We'd spend all day riding the waves and sitting in the sun, then we'd head home, driving at night to avoid the rush-hour traffic on the Garden State Parkway. We were sticky with suntan lotion and itchy with sand, but it was worth it to squeeze an extra day in there.

On this trip however, Houdini had a little surprise for us. Our last day had turned out to be a beautiful, sunny, picture-perfect August day – blue skies and about 95 degrees. When we got back to the car, my father opened the driver's side door and the stench hit him in the face like a physical punch. Something was clearly rotten in the state of Denmark, and heaven was most certainly not directing it.

My father had no idea where the stench was coming from; he unrolled all the windows and turned on the air conditioner and it abated somewhat, but was still far from gone. He thought about driving home that way, but then re-membered Houdini's seashell collection, and resigned himself to unpacking the car right there in the parking lot. When he had unloaded all of our lug-gage, and worked his way down to the small storage area under the rear-most seat, he pulled out Houdini's briefcase. First in, last out, unfortunately.

133

When my father opened the case, the already unbearable stench jumped out at him like a jack-in-the-box covered in rotten meat. Turns out that nobody had been paying much attention to what sort of shells Houdini had been adding to his collection. Apparently, for the last three days of our trip, he had been collecting "really cool, double-sided black seashells," that were, in fact, live mussels. Needless to say, the unfortunate specimens in his collection were no longer even *remotely* alive. My father quickly closed the case.

Holding it at arms length, he walked to a nearby garbage can and dropped the entire case in, hard-won shells and all. He walked back and repacked the car without a word. He was tired, sunburned, and sand-covered. He was done dealing with kids, vacations and in-laws, and he just wanted to get on the road. When he was done repacking, he slammed the rear door down, looked at the three of us, pointed at the car, and finally spoke.

"Get in," he said. That was it. We had the air conditioner on and all the windows open most of the way home, but that disgusting smell stayed with the car for a week afterward.

To this day, I can't eat mussels. Even a plate of them passing by my table in a restaurant makes me think of August death. I blame Houdini for that. We had a lot of fun down there in Seaside, and I'd like to go back someday just for fun. I hear it's a little seedier in that area than it used to be, but even so, it'd be fun to walk up the rickety stairs at the Holiday Motel one more time.

Pets: Store Bought & Wild Caught

The Pet Problem

Let me tell you about the pets I had growing up, in order, by their relative level of deadness. I know what you're thinking – dead is dead. That is true, however some of my pets have been dead longer than others, and I submit to you that *older* dead stuff is deader on a relative scale than the *newer* dead stuff.

Also, the term "pets" is subjective. I had quite a few pets that were really not pets in the traditional sense. Rather, they were animals and/or insects which I had caught myself in the wilds of Colonie, New York.

In no particular order, my childhood opportunistic pets consisted of approximately 37 pet frogs, 28 toads, 1200-2400 tadpoles, five turtles, two crayfish, four bullheads, approximately seven snakes, three red efts, two salamanders, one duckling, one field mouse, and one praying mantis.

The officially sanctioned and parentally purchased pets included a buttload of tropical fish, a pet-store turtle that "ran away" the day after my mother read an article about salmonella, a random assortment of anoles, an even half-dozen gerbils, a dog, a cat, and a $6.00 blue-nosed parakeet that bit like a mad bastard.

I won't bore you with stories about all of these things, although there are stories to be told. Instead, I will pick from this hodgepodge of miscellaneous creatures to bring you a few of my favorites, and tell you how they met their untimely demise.

Let's start with my first "real" pets.

Funeral Flush

My mother bought me a fish tank for my room right around the time she got sick of me catching various creatures outside and calling them "pets." It seems that I wasn't very discerning, and as a result, my pet selection was limited only by my ability to capture something and carry it home. According to my mother, every single one of these creatures was disgusting and disease-ridden, so generally my ownership period for any given "pet" was from the time I caught it to the time my mother discovered that I had caught it. Normally, the discovery process would go something like this:

"Mom, do we have any toothpicks?"

"Yes, they're in the cabinet next to the plates."

"Do we have any raw hamburger?"

"Oh Christ, what the hell did you bring home now?"

I am not sure if fish can actually be considered pets, because you really can't do much with them except watch them swim around. Let me rephrase that. You *shouldn't* do much with them except watch them swim around. That did not, however, mean that we didn't do things to make fish ownership more exciting. If not for the fish, then at least for me and my brothers.

What I learned about fish in the very early stages of fish ownership:

1. *Fish will eat poop from other fish, and like it.* Sometimes they will realize it's not food and spit it out. Other times, they will not. Ergo, fish are disgusting and most likely disease-ridden. (Also, it's fun to try to get your little brother to drink the water.)

2. *Guppies will eat their own babies.* Additionally, other fish that are *not* guppies will also eat the babies, gulping them down as fast as they come out. Guppies, if you don't know, are "live birth" fish – no eggs involved. I distinctly remember the excitement and wonder I felt as the live babies poured from the mother guppy.

   "MOM! MOM! Come here! HURRY! THE MOTHER GUPPY IS HAVING BABIES! THERE'S HUNDREDS OF THEM! MOM! HURRY! OH CRIPES! OH, CRIPES THE FATHER GUPPY IS EATING THEM! THE FATHER GUPPY IS EATING THEM! NOW THE OTHER FISH ARE EATING THEM TOO! GET THE NET! OH JEEZ, NOW THE MOTHER IS EATING SOME! MAKE THEM STOP! MAKE THEM STOP!"

   Think about that. When I was nine years old, I witnessed what had to be the shortest and most ignoble life possible on the face of the earth.

a) You are born.

b) You are immediately eaten by your family members.

c) You get pooped out and immediately eaten again.

3. *While the fish are in the water, you cannot pet the fish*, no matter how hard you try. They will run from you.

4. *While the fish are out of the water, you can pet them all you want* – but they don't like it.

5. *Fish are slimy.*

6. *If a fish is missing, he was either eaten, or he jumped out.*

Check for other, newly fat fish. Then check for dried out fish on the floor around the tank.

7. *A fish funeral consists of flushing them down the toilet.*

The toilet was my mother's solution to not just fish, but *all* pet funerals. I swear she would have tried to flush cats and dogs if she thought it wouldn't involve hacksaws and plungers. If it would fit, it got flushed – No muss, no fuss. She liked it this way, because the alternative was a long, drawn out burial ceremony in the back yard, which was not ideal, especially in the cold weather. It got to the point where every time we heard a toilet flush in the house, we'd run to the bathroom.

Snitch: "What died? Did something die?"

Me: "Can I flush it? What is it? Snitch got to flush it last time."

Snitch: "I did not. YOU did, remember? It was Houdini's hamster."

Houdini: "You flushed him? You told me it ran away."

My Mom: "It did run away."

Snitch: "Yeah, it ran in little circles right down into the sewer."

My Mom: "Snitch, shut up."

Many variations of this conversation happened over the years.

At the time of the first fish tank, none of us knew anything about fish. We didn't realize that fish are as bad as humans, in that it seems like fish get along with everything else in the water except for other types of fish. In a lake or an ocean, chance encounters between enemy fish usually end in an unnoticed and completely undocumented death to one fish or the other. In a tank, it's pretty easy to document the winner of any confrontation. In general, you can spot the winner because he is the one that is not missing completely. He is also not the one drifting around upside down with his fins chewed level with his body. (Unless, of course the fish he was fighting against is missing completely.)

In fact, there are *whole books* written on the subject of which types of fish you can have in the same tank without facing some sort of impending carnage. We obviously had no idea, and figured that as long as the fish were the same species, there would be no issues. While this rule of thumb works well in most cases, there are a few exceptions we learned about early on. One such exception is the Betta. This fish taught us that some fish have levels of self-loathing that run so deep, they can't even be put in a tank with other fish that are *exactly like them*. These types of fish are generally kept in little tiny bowls, isolated from all other fish, where they barely have room to turn around. These fish actually hate themselves so much that they will attack their own reflections. For some odd and completely unfathomable reason, these fish are sometimes called "fighting fish."

So, long story short – unless you are running some sort of illegal fish-based betting ring, do not put these fish in your regular tank with others of their kind. Or with anything else, for that matter.

After I realized that the baby guppies might not die instantly if they had a place to hide, I put some fake plants in strategic locations, and got a small auxiliary tank that hung on the inside of the main tank. When the babies emerged, I'd grab the net and scoop up as many as I could. I'd drop them in the little tank, where the other fish would stare at them hungrily, like zombies looking through a car window at fresh brains. Because the large, hungry fish lacked crowbars and opposable thumbs, I managed to amass quite the quant-ity of adolescent fish in this fashion. I was even successful in breeding a small collection of "fancy tails" that ultimately turned out to be little more than ick magnets. (If you don't know what "ick" is, it is an aptly named fish disease that rots holes in fish fins. Eventually, it can get so bad their fins rot completely away. It starts out as a small white dot on a fin and before you know it, you have a tank full of small, tumbling filets drifting around aim-lessly, eating food as it floats by and bumping into each other by mistake.)

So anyway – lots of fish.

Houdini used to like to watch my fish. He also used to like to *feed* my fish, which was cool with me because I had grown bored with watching them eat their own poop.

One day I was watching him feed my fish, and he was doing the same thing he did a million times before. The tank had a top on it that housed a fluorescent light, and a trap door so you could drop food through without re-moving the top. Unfortunately, the door had broken and as a result was taped securely in place to keep the more depressed fish from jumping to their deaths. This meant that the entire top had to be removed to feed the fish. Houdini removed the top, as usual, and dropped fish food in the tank. This time, however, when he attempted to place the top back on the tank, it slipped from his hand and plunged into the water.

Every single one of my guppies instantly flipped over and floated to the top like cheerios in a bowl full of milk.

I distinctly remember Houdini beginning to reach into the water to retrieve the light. I don't know if the fuse had already blown at that point or not, but I remember yelling and practically tackling him before he could stick his hand in the water.

Mass casualties. All the fish were floating. Stunned, dead, we had no idea. Our money was on dead. *Very* dead. We unplugged the light, pulled it from the tank and looked at each other. There was no way to cover this one up – we had to tell our mother.

It was the largest single flush funeral in the history of our household. I think Houdini wanted to give them each an individual burial, because he felt he had some flushes to catch up on, but after about the third one my mother just dumped them all in because she was tired of standing there wasting time and gallons of water.

My fish-owning days were over.

The next time I saw that particular fish tank in my room, it was bone dry and had a layer of sand on the bottom of it. It also contained a water dish, a food dish and a large branch that was the hip place to be – if you were a lizard.

Karma Chameleons

After the fish vacated the premises, I decided I wanted a rat. The kid down the street had a rat, and it rode around on his shoulders and ate peanuts out of his mouth.

I had just seen the movie Willard, and even though it had scared the shit out of me, I figured that I didn't have as many personality problems as Willard did, so I was pretty sure I could avoid his fate without too much effort. Given my confidence that a pet rat wouldn't turn on me, I thought a rat would be the best pet ever. My mother, to put it mildly, disagreed.

She had watched my grandfather kill rats in their basement when she was a kid and she was having none of it. Even though the one I wanted was a black and white domesticated rat and not a brown sewer rat, it made no difference to her. A rat was a rat was a rat, and there was no way in hell I was ever going to get one, regardless of the color of its fur. Even at the pet store, she would get completely creeped out just watching them stand on their hind legs in their glass tanks, their little noses twitching as they sniffed the air. Basically, if the animal came equipped with a hairless tail, I wasn't bringing it home.

My grandfather was the same way. I had a couple of gerbils at one point, and whenever I'd take one out of the cage, he'd flip out. They were nothing more than small rats to him. Just because they lived in brightly colored plastic tubes and ran on stationary exercise wheels didn't mean they were pets. They deserved swift death, and nothing more.

Because I realized my rat-love would remain unrequited, I decided to test my luck with all things reptilian. Ted from across the street had an iguana, and it too rode around on his shoulders. I thought about asking for a parrot for the same reason. I have no idea what my fascination was with shoulder-riding pets. (I currently own a Siamese cat that, coincidentally or not, rides around on my shoulders.) I wasn't entirely sure I wanted an iguana on my shoulder, because frankly they were a little scary, but I still thought they were the coolest thing ever.

Whenever my mother dragged me to the mall, I'd convince her to leave me at the pet store while she ran around. I'd divide my time between looking longingly at the rats and examining the reptiles. They had everything from pythons to Iguanas, and even though reptiles as a general rule didn't seem to move much, I still wanted one.

I thought having an iguana would be like having a miniature dinosaur in a tank. They were way out of my price range though, and my mother was glad of it.

Finally, after a significant amount of begging and pleading, my mother took me to the pet store and grudgingly allowed me to buy a pair of anoles with my own money. While a far cry from an iguana, they were sort of cool in their own right. I went to get a lizard branch while the clerk boxed up the two lizards I had picked out. I also picked out a warming light, which was a little different than what had originally come with the fish tank. Apparently, lizards like to bask in the sun, and you have to provide them with an alternative to the real thing.

I carefully counted out the cost of the lizards from my hard-earned allowance money and paid the clerk, and my mother paid for everything else. As we were leaving the store, I remembered something important.

"Mom, I forgot the food! We need to get them some food," I said.

"Okay, what do they eat?" she asked.

I'm not exactly sure what she envisioned, but I think she was expecting me to run back down the aisle and grab a small box of Purina Lizard Chow off the shelf.

"They eat mealworms," I said. "But what they *really* like are live crickets."

"We're getting your money back," she said flatly. "I am *not* paying good money for bugs."

It didn't help when she finally saw the crickets. We went into the back room with the clerk and he uncovered a 20 gallon fish tank that was literally crawling with thousands of them. If you've never fed a lizard, then you probably don't know that the crickets you buy in the pet store don't look much like the black ones you chase out of your house in the summer. The pet store crickets are a tannish color, and they tend to be quite a bit more active than regular crickets.

"Jesus Christ, they look like *cockroaches*," she said with obvious horror. "You are *not* buying those."

I argued my case. "The crickets can't climb up the glass, so you don't have to worry," I said. "The mealworms just go in the bowl. They can't get out either."

Finally, after another five minutes of me pleading with her to not ask the clerk for my money back, she agreed.

"Just this once, and that's it," she said. "I am not going to be buying any filthy bugs for you after this, so you'd better figure something out. The mealworms are one thing, but that's my limit."

The clerk asked me how many crickets I wanted, and I didn't know. He told me to start with 50. That sounded good to me, since I knew nothing about the dietary habits of lizards. He packed the crickets in a separate box, along with a wet paper towel and a few pieces of cricket food that looked like rabbit pellets. Then both boxes went into a bag. My mother eyed it uneasily.

"They can't get out, right?" she asked.

"The bag is taped shut, mom," I said, exasperated.

That seemed to mollify her, and so we rode home, me holding the audibly skittering bag of lizards and bugs on my lap, and her paying very little attention to the road.

When I got home, I immediately started setting up the tank. I spread some sand on the bottom, and put my new stick in. I got the new light hooked up and found a small container for water and another for the mealworms. I opened the lizard box and gently placed them into their new home. They immediately started doing what they do best, which was absolutely nothing. When I put the bowl of mealworms in, one of the lizards climbed a little way up on the branch. The other one just sat there in the sand. Basking or some shit.

I wasn't quite sure what I had been expecting, but damn, these things were boring so far.

I decided to drop a cricket in the tank to see what would happen. I envisioned a feeding frenzy, with two starving lizards fighting to the death over the single available cricket. I picked up the cricket box and tapped the top to make sure they weren't sticking to it, then opened it up. I plucked one unlucky fellow from the teeming throng and dropped him in the tank. Instead of trying to avoid instant death, he ran across the tank and climbed directly onto the back of the lizard that was sitting in the sand. The lizard, however, was apparently basking so intently that he didn't even notice.

Then they both just sat there.

I decided that was enough excitement for one day, so I left them alone to get acclimated and figured I'd check on the fate of the daredevil cricket after we had dinner.

When I had finished eating and watching *I Dream of Jeannie*, I went back to my room and looked in on the tank. Sure enough, the cricket was gone, and I had missed it. Both lizards were on the branch now, and I wasn't sure which one had eaten the cricket. Neither one looked appreciably more self-satisfied than the other, so I decided to drop another one in just to make sure they both got their share.

Unfortunately, when I turned to open the cricket box, I realized something.

It was already open.

And empty.

I panicked. I had 49 crickets on the loose, running around in my room. I panicked a little more when I realized that I hadn't closed my bedroom door. My mother was going to have a fit. I ran across the hall and banged on The Snitch's bedroom door. I told him what happened, and after he got done laughing, he joined me in the hunt. We caught what we could, but an hour later, we only had a sum total of seventeen crickets. The rest had completely disappeared.

We could only assume that they were hiding under the bed, under the base-boards, or maybe behind the dresser. Or – and this was too horrible to contemplate – they had made their way out of my room through the open door.

My mother was in the kitchen standing by the sink, cleaning up our plates after dinner. I walked up behind her.

"Mom?" I said, desperately trying to think of a way to put a better spin on this. "Guess what?"

"If you're going to tell me something disgusting about your new lizards, then I'm not interested."

"No, it's not about the lizards."

"Good," she said brusquely.

"It's about the crickets," I mumbled, looking down at the kitchen floor.

"Stop mumbling," she said without turning around. "Speak up."

"It's about the crickets," I said, a little louder.

She turned around then. Oh, yes.

"Look at me," she said. I looked at her.

"What...*about*...the crickets?" she asked, almost daring me to continue.

"A few of them... got loose," I replied.

"How *many?*" she asked, her voice thin, like the edge of a razor blade.

"All but seventeen," I replied.

She did some quick mental math. "Are you telling me that THERE ARE THIRTY-THREE BUGS CRAWLING AROUND IN MY HOUSE RIGHT NOW?"

"Thirty two," I said. "One of the chameleons ate one. I think."

"You *think?*" she said. "Here's what *I* think. I think you are going to find every single one of those bugs before you go to bed tonight. I don't care if you have to stay up all night. Get busy, Mister. If you're lucky, maybe your brother will help you."

So The Snitch and I hunted for crickets. We expanded our search outward, finding one or two in the bathroom, another few in his room. Eventually, we had found another ten, but the rest evaded us.

My mother finally relented and let us go to bed with the rest of the crickets at liberty. The box went outside on the back stairs.

I didn't get much sleep that night. The Snitch and I had apparently missed a few in my room, because as soon as I turned the light out, they started chirping. It was maddening, because when I turned it back on to track them down, they'd stop.

The next morning, I must have looked tired.

"Didn't you sleep?" my mother asked.

"No. The stupid crickets kept me up all night. They wouldn't shut up."

"Good," she replied. "It serves you right. I hope you're not too tired. You still have a lot of crickets to track down."

For the next week or so, we'd randomly spot one here and there, hanging around the cat food dish in the kitchen, or zipping under the fridge, which really skeeved my mother out.

I never bought bulk crickets again, although the lizards seemed to be fine without them. The anoles didn't live very long though. A year, at most. I'm not sure, but they may have died of boredom. It was hard to tell when an anole had actually died. Sometimes they just up and died right where they were, sitting on the branch with their eyes closed. You didn't really even notice anything was different until they started to dry out. One day your lizard would be sunning himself, the next day he'd still be sunning himself only with less breathing. Not really the ideal pet.

I *did* learn something about mealworms that had never occurred to the nine-year-old me. For the longest time, I couldn't figure out where all the beetles in my tank were coming from. Eventually, I realized that the meal-worms actually *turned into* these beetles. Another thing I learned is that if they get loose, these beetles will seek out food sources like Raisin Bran, for instance, and they will lay eggs and then you will have a lot more meal-worms than you or your immediate family probably ever wanted.

Don't ask me how I know this.

Doc.

If you knew me, you'd probably consider me an outdoorsy kind of guy. I like backpacking and canoeing, hiking and snowboarding. When people see that, and then find out I don't care that much for dogs, I think that wrecks their stereotype of me. "How can you not like dogs?" they ask. "You are clearly a walking, talking Orvis ad, so what's up with that?"

Well, it's like this. I don't like dog slobber, I don't like dog smell and dog hair. We had a dog growing up. A big, stupidsmart* German shepherd/Collie mix named Doc.

Doc was the "family dog." My grandfather got him for us, and he was a great pup and fun to play with. When he grew up, he was mostly just my dad's dog. I really had no interest in dogs, and therefore thought it entirely unfair that two of my assigned chores revolved around taking care of him. I'm not sure whether it was my mother or father who thought it would be up-roariously funny to put me in charge of the dog's entire digestive process from start to finish, but that's what they did. It was my job to feed him every day, and it was also my job to clean up the resulting giant piles of crap every weekend. Sometimes I could get my brother to trade with me for the dishes and garbage duties, but that was rare, and usually involved a lost bet on his part.

Let me tell you, this clean up duty was a *lot* worse than it sounds because in retrospect he was clearly too much dog for our property at the time, and we never should have owned him. He needed a place he could run, and even though my father took him out for a run in the woods almost every night when he got home from work, it wasn't enough. We would take him out for walks but that never ended well. One random squirrel and we had two choices: Drop the leash, or be dragged down the street until we were almost skinless. Sometimes, we'd try to get him to pull us on our skateboards, which never really worked since he had two speeds – a dead stop and an all-out run, which he combined in unique and unpredictable ways.

During the day, he stayed in a penned area in the yard that he eventually wore down to a urine-soaked hard pack. And since the generally accepted in-terpretation of "clean up" was "bury," I quickly learned that you can only dig so many holes in a 16x16 foot area before you are just digging up the crap you buried the week before. It was horrible. It looked horrible, it smelled horrible, and I cursed my parents and that dog every day of my young, slave-driven, poop-shoveling life.

---

* a made up term to describe a dog that can somehow learn to do 10 different tricks, yet never learn how to not bark incessantly at every random squirrel that passed by.

I loved winter and hated spring. This was because in winter, the crap was frozen and didn't stink as much. Also, each new snowfall covered the crap piles so I didn't have to clean them up. That was all well and good through about the middle of March, but when the snow thawed and combined thirty-seven layers of frozen dog shit into one layer of dog crap soup, that clean up effort became one of SuperFund proportions.

The daily feeding was another issue. Was I allowed to simply shake a bag of dry food into a bowl, or plop a can of Alpo into a doggie dish? No, I was not. Instead, my father created "the mix," which I now firmly believe he did just to mess with me. The method for creating the mix was as follows:

1. Take a food storage bag from the cabinet and dump in a can of dog food that smells like roadkill and has a consistency of cold refried beans with pockets of nasty orange gel.

2. Take a cup of dried Gravy Train dog food and dump that into the bag.

3. Add a small amount of water.

4. Knead the bag until (a) the entire contents is completely mixed, or (b) the bag gets a hole in it and some of that nasty smelling orange gel squirts out on you, causing you to gag repeatedly.

After I made the mix, I had to turn on the backyard spotlight, walk out to the dog pen in the dark, and squeeze that pasty mixture out of the bag and into his bowl, all the while trying not to step in any fresh piles that may have been produced from the previous night's bag.

My mother, of course, thought it was hilarious to wait until I got about half way to the pen before turning off the spotlight. She would wait about 30 seconds and then turn it on again. This was apparently fun for her, and she would do it almost every night, no matter how much I begged her to stop. One night, as soon as she plunged me into darkness, I just dropped the food and ran like hell and hid behind the shed. When she flipped the light on, there was no sign of me – only the bag of dog slop sitting in the middle of the lawn. I stayed there until she came out to look for me, and then I jumped out from behind the shed and scared the crap out of her. After that, she laid off the light flipping for a little while.

Anyway, there's one more thing to add to the pile of things that annoyed me about this dog. He liked to run, as I mentioned, but he also liked to run in one direction – away. Since the only one he would listen to was my father, this meant when he escaped from the back yard during the day when my father was at work, my mom would pack us all into the car and we'd end up chasing him around the neighborhood. I still hear the cries of "HEEEEERE DOC! HEEEEEEERE DOC!" in my nightmares. He got picked up by animal control once, and once was enough for him to learn how to avoid that in the future, and he never got caught again. He was a smart dog. After a while, the guy in the truck would just call us to tell us he was out again. Doc would eventually come home, covered in mud or something worse, and we'd be forced to give him a bath, which tended to soak us as much as it did him.

My dislike of Doc only deepened as the years went by. When I was in college and still living home, he would wake me up either by howling in the middle of the night, or barking at six o'clock in the morning. I was hoarse from opening my window and screaming at him to shut up. It would work for approximately 30 seconds, and then he'd start up again. It was great for a hangover, let me tell you.

As luck would have it, I was the only one home besides my father on the day Doc died. Early that morning, my father came to get me out of bed and said, "We have to bring Doc to the vet. Something's wrong with him." I threw some jeans on and groggily followed him down to the garage, where the dog sometimes slept at night. He was lying on his side, whimpering and flailing around like he had no control over his legs. He was foaming at the mouth, and snarled every time you tried to touch him. "I think he had a stroke," my dad said, and I remember thinking that maybe I liked that stupid dog a little after all, because why else would I have a lump in my throat and feel like I wanted to cry? It was hard to see him in pain like that. We carefully picked him up and loaded him into the back seat as he whimpered. As my father drove, I sat there with my hand on Doc's head talking to him, telling him it was OK, and that he was a good dog. There was nothing the vet could do except put him down.

He was annoying and smelly and hard-headed and a giant pain in the ass 99% of the time, but even so, he was a part of the family and we were used to having him around. Come to think of it, he had a lot in common with my brother Houdini.

I'll never forget Doc, but I definitely wouldn't want another dog like him. I think I like the *idea* of a dog, but not the reality of a dog. In other words, I want Lassie but I know I'll end up with Marmaduke.

Little Johnny is Growing Up

Hormones, Music and Girls.

There comes a time in every boy's life when he wakes up one morning and decides that girls are no longer disgusting and vile, and are instead mysterious and intriguing. Generally, this realization is accompanied by a full cord of cut, split and delivered morning wood, but sometimes that's just coincidence. He will begin to question their motives, to study their habits, to try to understand what it is that make them tick. This will not work, and every attempt to understand them will ultimately fail*, but he will try nonetheless. They will alternately captivate and infuriate him, and there will be nothing he can do.

This new lusting for the fairer of the species may also be accompanied by a growing appreciation for music, particularly love songs and the bands that perform them, as well as the onset of strange and horrible bodily changes. It is at this point in his young life where he may listen to the radio incessantly, become moody and withdrawn, and spend an inordinate amount of time in the shower.

Eventually, all this will even out, and he will be old enough to go on dates. First, to school dances and movies, and then – when he's a bit older and driving – to rock clubs and make-out destinations, where he will do all the things that his parents explicitly told him *not* to do.

With that said – Mom, Dad, I apologize for everything I've done, and everything I've yet to do. Everyone else, welcome to my burgeoning adolescence.

---

* Not only now, but for the rest of his life.

It Only Takes a Minute, Girl

I was a radio junkie when I was a kid. I would rush home to listen to Casey Kasem on Saturdays, and late at night, I'd try to pick up the skip signals, pulling in stations from Chicago, Maryland, NYC and other exotic locations.

Check it out. She's gone. It only takes a minute. Remember what I told you to forget. Heaven must be missing an angel. Don't take away the music. Fool of the year.

Not exactly the typical soundtrack of adolescence for a middle class white kid growing up in the 70's, but for me, it was the first music I ever lived for. The songs were all by the same group – Tavares. Five brothers who sang exquisite harmony, Tavares were the lesser-known contemporaries of Earth, Wind & Fire, The Commodores and The Spinners. I heard "It only takes a minute" on the radio, I won their LP by being caller number five, and the rest was history.

I was nine years old, and Tavares sparked my budding musical interests, and then lit them up like a flare. This was the first music that got inside my spine and made me want to do the white-boy shuffle. I knew all their hit songs and had most of their records. I have no idea why they struck me like they did, but I think it was something about their ballads. I didn't realize they were the precursor to disco, or I may have dropped them right there. Disco didn't really exist yet. This was a smooth, polished type of R&B.

It had the best of both worlds – upbeat songs that made me want to jump around, and slow ballads that made me pine for the girl I was afraid to even make eye-contact with. At nine, I could get behind both of these things wholeheartedly.

In addition to being the first music I ever listened to, they also have the distinction of being the first live music I ever saw, and the first concert I ever attended. When I heard on the radio that they were coming to town, I badgered my mother into letting me attend. She listened to some of the music to make sure it was appropriate, then agreed, with reservations. I had to find someone to go with, I had to be dropped off and picked up at a precise time, and she would be the one doing the driving. I jumped on the chance, and called my best friend Mike to see if he wanted to go.

Mike had never heard of them, and in fact, I don't even know if he listened to the radio at all. But he agreed to go, we got the blessing from Mike's mother, and then we waited not-so-patiently for the night of the concert to arrive. Our tickets showed up in the mail a few days later, and it was a thrill to simply hold them in my hand. I examined them for hours. They were bigger than movie tickets, and had the name of the band written right on them. I was hoping to get an autograph.

The night of the concert, my mother pulled up in front of the venue and we got out. As she pulled away, something struck us as odd. There was something out of place, something weird, something that we didn't put our finger on right away. We stood there and looked around, trying to figure it out.

Almost simultaneously, we realized what the problem was. I glanced at my blond-haired, blue-eyed friend, and he was looking back at me, wide-eyed.

Leaning close to me so he wouldn't be overheard, he whispered, "Everybody is *black*."

"Yeah," I replied, in total awe.

We were the only white people within a quarter mile radius. The entire crowd consisted almost exclusively of black couples. There were no kids. And definitely no little *white* kids.

We attended a tiny elementary school, and I think there was probably one black kid in the entire school. This was the most black people we had ever seen in one place. We quickly walked inside, careful to avoid looking anywhere but straight ahead, and tried to find our seats.

As we were moving through the crowd, people noticed us. They were laughing, shaking their heads and pointing, and doing a fair amount of whispering of their own. *"I think they're lost." "Yo, The Captain and Tennille aren't playin' tonight." "Hey, look at the little white dudes. That's some funny shit."*

We found our seats and sat down. They were pretty good. Something like tenth row, but they were kind of in the middle. It was ok at first, since we had gotten there early, but eventually the seats around us filled up. We sat there, our necks on swivels, just staring at the people around us. People dressed in tuxedos and glittery dresses, leisure suits of all types, short skirts, long skirts, tube-tops, fancy hats and everything in between. There was so much to look at, I think our senses went into overload. There was a ton of smoke in the air too, and not all of it smelled like the cigarettes both of our mothers smoked.

The house lights went down, and the band started playing. The stage lights exploded into colors, and the brothers came out, dressed in identical white suits and sky blue shirts, instantly dancing. They moved as one, a syncopated machine on a Teflon stage, sliding and clapping with precision, spinning on cue. They broke into *Whodunit*, and I was gone.

I was singing the words to every song, and even though I couldn't see very well because everyone was standing, I could make out enough of the stage to know it was the greatest experience of my young life. After about the 5th song, I started noticing the people around me – mostly because *they* were noticing *me*.

Finally, a big, bald, black dude with a full beard leaned over and yelled, "Can you see?"

"Not really," I yelled back. "We're too short."

He said, "We gonna get you to the aisle."

Before I realized what was happening, he had us walking on the backs and arms of the chairs, helped along by the folks in our row. When we reached the aisle, we jumped down. It was amazing. We could see the entire stage, and there was nobody in front of us. I couldn't believe I was actually watching the people who were responsible for *The Love I Never Had*, a song I played incessantly during my first crush on a girl. We stood for a while, and then a security guy the size of a car dealership noticed us. He walked over, and we thought for sure he would make us go back to our seats. Instead, he motioned for us to follow him, and he proceeded to escort us to the front and told us we could sit on the floor right there in the aisle, dead-even with the front row.

So we did. For the entire show.

They played their concert, and ran off stage, and the crowd went crazy. A few minutes before the band came out for the encore, the big bouncer came over to us and said the band had invited us to sit on the edge of the stage for the last song. It was a dream come true, for me at least.

I've been to more concerts than I can count, but a first concert is like a first kiss, or losing your virginity. You never forget the first time, no matter how good or how bad it is. Those three moments are always with you. If you're lucky, and they're all good, you get the hat trick.

So even though I helped usher in what was to be the Disco Age, I'm not sorry. Whenever I hear a Tavares song, I'm instantly transported back to the innocent age of nine, and that one concert, that one magic moment in time, when I sat on the stage with my idols and they didn't let me down.

And She Knows How to Use It

Everyone loved Laurie. Teachers, parents, girls, boys – *especially* the boys. She was short and cute with dark hair and dark eyes, and had a great smile. She had flawless, porcelain skin and she was nice to everyone, even the geeks. And she smelled good too. Like Agree shampoo and bubble gum.

We were both prisoners in the sixth grade, and we shared a colored table. I know that sounds romantic, but unfortunately, it wasn't just the two of us. There were other kids sharing the same table, but at least I got to sit across from her every day. She made learning fun.

The powers that be were always doing things to us in grade school. Social experiments that were supposed to get kids to "accept change" and "embrace diversity" and "cooperate as a self-directed, coherent team." I think the table experiment was one of those. It was supposed to break down barriers. Help the introverts and the extroverts interact. Force the cool kids to talk with the losers. The fat and the skinny, the beautiful and the ugly, side by side. Cats and dogs living together in sin. I'm not sure what the goal was, really, but sitting in groups like that was uncomfortable when you were used to stacking up in alphabetical order in rows of wooden desks and minding your own business.

I think it was kind of like the "new math." Nobody really knew whether it was working or not, the teachers didn't understand it any better than the kids in their class, and at the most basic level, the whole thing was geared toward trying to change the way kids learned. Unfortunately, kids didn't like learning the *new* way any more than they liked learning the *old* way, and so after a ten-year period where it never really got off the ground, everyone said fuck it and went back to the old way. At least then the teachers could present the same mind-numbing curriculum year after year, the kids could rely on their short-term memory to pass tests, and everyone understood what it was that they hated. (Don't even get me started on the big metric system push. Is it pronounced *kilommitters* or *killo-meeters*? I still don't know. I use it when I build furniture because it's easier, but I don't have to like it.)

Anyway, for this particular social experiment, rather than give us individual desks, they took six or so of our wooden, flat-top desks and put them in a rectangle and then fastened painted plywood to the top of them. Each table had a different color, and you were assigned to a color, but not to a particular seat. This meant that the first week of class was basically a free-for-all, and what played out resembled a wolf pack establishing their hierarchy, except much more vicious.

While no one seat was actually more desirable than any other, we invented reasons for our preferences. I, of course, liked the one I chose because it was directly across from Laurie. I had originally considered trying to sit to the left or right of her, but I wasn't high enough up on the food chain for that sort of placement, and I figured at least this way I could have someone nice to pretend to not stare at. Looking back at it now, I think the initial free-for-all may have been part of the experiment. Since the seats weren't assigned, you couldn't complain if someone took "your" seat, and they couldn't complain if you took theirs. The funny thing was, once we had decided upon a de-facto seating arrangement on our own, we sat in the same seat every day regardless of whether it was required, just like good little lab rats. I think the only time the teacher moved people around was if someone got too chatty with their neighbor. She'd make you switch seats with someone at a different table. Even then it was only a temporary move, like visiting a vaguely unpleasant foreign country for a few days. Soon you'd be back in your home town, showing your pictures to your friends, none the worse for wear.

Even though our elementary school was relatively small, the sixth grade class was too large for a single classroom. As a result, it was broken up into two. I would say that probably 95% of the boys in the sixth grade were in love with Laurie from afar. The other 5% were either gay and didn't know it yet, still thought girls carried cooties, or were Johnny Blane.

Johnny was the coolest kid in the school. Even his *name* was cool. Just say it out loud. *Johnny Blane*. It sounds like the name of a stunt driver, or a super hero. He had the best hair and the best clothes. He was tall, good-looking, and a veritable chick magnet. He was also the class bad-ass, and nobody messed with him. Every kid I knew simultaneously feared him, and wanted to *be* him.

Because every guy in the class had a crush on Laurie, and every girl in the class had a crush on Johnny, the universal law of attraction stipulated that as the alpha male and alpha female, Johnny and Laurie were required to be a couple. They were "going out," which is what we called it then. (Out *where*, we had no idea. We just knew that we would be going to that mythical place with each other.) And this wasn't just *any* romance. They actually did stuff, like looking at each other instead of the floor when they talked, holding hands and even *kissing*. And that was the other reason most guys wanted to be Johnny Blane. While we didn't know for sure what kissing Laurie would be like, we figured it had to be a lot better than making a loose fist and practicing on the area between your thumb and index finger.

(As an aside, I remember the first time I "went out" with a girl. It was a year later, in seventh grade. Her friend asked my friend if I liked her, and my friend asked me, and I said, like her, or *like* her-like her?, and he said *like* her-like her and I said I think so, and my friend went back and told her friend that I *liked* her-liked her and then it was settled because it turned out that she *liked* me-liked me too, and as a result of this common like-like, we were officially "going out" – but a week later, her friend notified my friend that she no longer *liked* me-liked me and my friend passed the word to me and so we officially broke up, even though we had never actually spoken to each other face-to-face. I never really *liked*-liked that bitch anyway.)

Normally, Johnny and Laurie were pretty much inseparable, but in the sixth grade, either by chance or teacher wisdom, they got separated, one to each classroom. This was a bummer for them, and tended to put a slight damper on their relationship, but it allowed the rest of us guys to openly gawk and flirt without the risk of getting our asses immediately pounded into a smoking hole.

Twelve is a weird age for guys. Some, like Johnny Blane, were mature for their age. They were bigger, acted older and seemed cooler than the rest of us. Others were still more or less little kids, playing with hot wheels and climbing on the jungle gym at recess.

Take my friend Danny, for instance. His main claim to fame was that he had a fully functioning toy steam roller.

It actually burned fuel and had a small boiler. The steam it generated ran an engine that powered the wheels. I wanted one of those things so bad. (Hell, I *still* want one.) That tells you much about his level of cool at the time (and about mine now).

Danny sat next to me at the big red table, and while Johnny Blane would hit on a girl by telling her that he liked her hair, Danny would hit on a girl by walking up behind her and *pulling* her hair. There was a subtle difference as far as seduction techniques go, and much to Danny's surprise, his results were uniformly bad. What worked in third grade didn't work in sixth, and he was confounded by this turn of events.

I was sort of in between those two extremes. I knew on an intuitive level that something was wrong with his approach, yet I was hesitant to offer advice, since I, too, had no idea what the hell I was doing. I knew enough to know that if a girl punched you in the arm, it meant she was interested, but it in no way meant that she wanted you to punch her back. This made complete sense, and at the same time it made *no* sense. I was still puzzling that one out, but I had the gist of it. I just didn't know at the time that it was only the first in a long list of things that I would never completely understand about women.

I was nothing if not average, and while I knew I liked girls, I was still pretty small for my age, and most girls were taller than me* which could be a little intimidating. To guys like me, a girl was a foreign, dangerously unpredictable creature, best observed from a safe distance, like watching a lioness hunting antelope on an African veldt – fun to watch, but you didn't want to get too close. Laurie was one of the exceptions, and I think that's one reason why I and everyone else had a major crush on her. She was approachable.

I was much too shy to actually talk to her on a regular basis, however I did have one thing going for me – her house was on my paper route. This meant that I got to see her once in a while outside of school on the days I was "collecting." If you've never been a paper boy, you don't know the joys of this thing called Collecting. Once a week, generally on Sunday, you'd ride around to all the houses on your route and try to get people to pony up the cash for the paper you'd been delivering to them for the past X weeks. You'd give them a little ticket for each week they were paid up, and that was basically your bookkeeping system. To this day I have no idea how the hell the paper company ever kept track of how much money they were making from year to year. It was the worst system ever, and barely one step up from trading beads and gold nuggets for furs and food.

---

*Unfortunately for me, that never changed. Thanks for being five feet tall, mom.

Getting this money out of people was tougher than it sounds, and some of them would go to great lengths to avoid paying you. You'd hear every excuse in the book, and be told to "come back later" more times than you could count. As a kid with no power, it was infuriating to be at the mercy of these deadbeat newspaper consumers. The best thing of all was when you actually got permission from the publisher to cut them off if they didn't pay you, and then what generally happened was they either dropped the paper delivery completely, or they started paying their weekly fees directly to the paper company. At least then you were out of the middle of it, but forget about getting a tip from them ever again.

When I collected at Laurie's house, I never had that problem. They were always up to date on their payments, and I'd generally hit them for their money once every week or so. I always hoped Laurie would be the one to answer the door, just so I could talk to her. We had many deep, meaningful conversations that I'm sure she would remember to this day. In fact, there's one in particular that still warms my heart.

Laurie, answering the door: "Hi."

Me: "Collecting."

Laurie: "How much?"

Me: "Dollar seventy-five."

Laurie: "Be right back."

Laurie: "Here you go. Keep the change."

Me: "Thanks. Here's your ticket."

We shared so much.

She always tipped me well, and even though I knew the money was coming from her parents, I preferred to imagine it was Laurie herself giving me a large tip because she didn't find me completely repulsive and totally unworthy of acknowledgement. A fertile imagination is a 12-year-old kid's best friend.

After she gave me the money, I'd saunter coolly toward my bike, and in a single, fluid motion I'd boot the kick-stand up with my right sneaker, step on the pedal with my left foot and start to roll. When I reached the end of the driveway, I'd shift my newspaper bag a bit, toss my right leg over the seat and glide smoothly away. It was my one impressive move. The bag-shifting technique was very important, and I had to be very careful to avoid getting it caught on the seat as I threw my leg over. Failing to do this had once caused both me and my bike to spectacularly crash to Laurie's driveway in a spinning, bleeding pile of spokes and papers. It was not one of my more graceful moments.

Sometimes Danny and I would ride our bikes to school together, and along the way we'd wonder if she was ever going to break up with Johnny, and wonder if anyone else would ever have a shot. We decided that the answer was probably not, and probably not. Our considered opinion was that she and Johnny were going to get married and that would be it.

Sixth grade minds are funny things – I *knew* I didn't have a prayer, and I was OK with that. I was happy just to have her acknowledge my presence in the classroom. Danny though, was a different story. While Danny also understood that she was way out of his league, that simple fact didn't mean he was going to give up. He could win her over, he reasoned. He could persuade her that he was special, that he was about more than just steam rollers and hair pulling. He was formulating a plan, he said. He didn't share it with me right away, but I knew he was just biding his time.

One morning, a month or so into the school year, we met up at the front of the school where we usually did, and he was holding a large brown shopping bag with the top rolled down tight.

"I gotta show you something," he said. "It's really cool!" He was holding the bag in both hands, and kept wringing it down close to the bottom and then unrolling it again. Nervous. Excited.

"What is it?" I asked. "Is it alive?"

"Not anymore," he said, a goofy grin spreading across his face.

That statement piqued my interest. "Let's see it." I said.

He slowly opened the top of the bag and reached in. I leaned over to see what he had wrapped his hand around, and saw brown fur. Then I saw blood. Gristle. Bone.

"Ewwwww!!" I said. "What is it?"

He pulled it from the bag triumphantly. "A DEER LEG!" he said.

He dropped it back in quickly, and rolled the top down again.

I fired questions at him in rapid succession. "Where'd you get it? Who gave it to you? What are you going to do with it? Can you get me one?" I didn't know why he even had it with him, since we didn't do show and tell anymore.

"My father shot this deer and it was hanging in the garage. When he cut the legs off, I stoled one," Danny said. "I think the other ones are already in the trash."

This alternately fascinated and disgusted me. As a kid I was never really exposed to guns or hunting because nobody in our neighborhood had parents that were into either of those things. So while I knew about deer hunting abstractly, I hadn't come face to face with it in real life, other than maybe seeing the occasional dead deer strapped to the hood of a passing car. I certainly never touched a severed deer leg before, and this was my chance.

"Does he know you brought it to school?" I asked him.

"No way! I stoled it last night and put it outside," he said. "I was hopin' no dogs would get to it or nothin."

"Can I touch it?" I asked.

He unrolled the bag, and stuck just the bloody end out. It was a pretty clean cut, like it had been chopped off with a cleaver or a saw, which it probably had. I touched the sticky, semi-dried blood on the end, and the fur. He put it back in the bag.

I went back through my list, and re-asked the most obvious question.

"So...what are you gonna do with it?"

He grinned and said, "I'm gonna put it on Laurie's chair when she's not looking."

I thought this was the best thing I'd ever heard. It would be hilarious.

As far as seduction techniques went, it wasn't great, but it would certainly make an impression.

And that's exactly what he did. He took it out of the bag when nobody was watching, placed it carefully on Laurie's chair, and pushed the chair in to the table. Her chair was between the table and the wall, facing out toward the center of the room. You couldn't see the deer leg at all until you pulled the chair out.

While the class was assembling and all the kids were seating themselves, Danny and I were already in our seats, waiting for Laurie.

We watched her walk toward her seat. We watched her as she pulled her chair out.

She started to sit, then she looked down at her chair.

She screamed.

Then she pointed at her chair, and screamed the teacher's name. The teacher ran from the front of the room to look where Laurie was pointing. The teacher blanched a bit and took a step back. "Is that...a leg?" she asked tentatively, looking around at us.

"Is that an ANIMAL LEG?" she said, her voice rising, half angry and half hysterical. "WHO PUT AN ANIMAL LEG ON LAURIE'S CHAIR?"

Nobody said a word. The overhead fluorescent lights buzzed quietly. In the silence, you could hear the murmur of other classes, other teachers talking, the sound of chalk tapping on distant chalk boards. In other words, the comforting school noises made by people who did not have severed deer legs perched on their chairs.

I realized with absolute certainty that there was no way Danny was making it out of this unscathed if he was found out. Between his father, the school officials, Johnny or Laurie herself – someone was going to cause him a world of hurt if they ever figured out he was the kid who brought the deer leg to school and used it to traumatize a classmate.

"I did it," Danny said.

All eyes turned toward him. Had we heard him right? Had he just *admitted* to this act? He had. He wanted Laurie to know. The teacher pointed at him and said, "Stand Up, Danny."

He did, and she gave him further instructions.

"Take that...leg, and...*dispose*...of it," she said, tightly. "I don't care where." She reconsidered. "No, actually, I *do* care where. Take it outside to the dumpster. Then go directly to the Principal's office."

"I didn't mean anything by it," he said. "I just thought it would be funny. I thought that -"

"I don't want to know *what* you thought," the teacher said. "Just get that disgusting leg off of Laurie's chair and go to the Principal's office. NOW."

So Danny picked up the leg, tucked it under his arm and headed for the door. He wasn't embarrassed, or scared or even sorry. He had pranked Laurie, and that was way better than pulling her hair.

I don't remember what punishment was meted out. When we were in the sixth grade, the teachers and principal were still allowed to beat your bare ass with that big, two-handed paddle with the holes drilled into it to cut down on wind resistance. I don't know if he got an ass beating or not, but I do remember that his parents were not pleased, and my guess is that Johnny Blane wasn't either.

I went to school with Johnny, Laurie and Danny for the next six years. Johnny stayed cool, Laurie stayed cute and nice to everyone, and Danny stayed just a little this side of weird. Kind of like me, I guess.

As romantic gestures go, a severed deer leg was certainly unique. In Danny's case, it was well-intentioned, if perhaps not well thought-out. Think about it this way: Danny's best gift for his favorite girl was a prank. When you're 11 or 12, who's to say whether or not a prank can be a great gift? You might not find it funny at the time, but eventually you might. Laughing is fun. Why wouldn't it make a great gift? I think there's something to be said for that.

Sometimes it's not all about the chocolate and the flowers and the jewelry and compliments. When you're dealing with real people and real feelings, sometimes it's about awkwardly presented offers of friendship. My advice is to recognize these for what they are, and make of them what you can, even if someone is giving you a metaphorical severed deer leg** to get you to notice them. As I've recently learned, you never can tell where your best friends will come from in this life.

Even though Danny's gamble didn't work and he and Laurie never became any closer, I'd bet a month's pay that Laurie never forgot it. There's something to be said for that, too.

**If someone gives you a *real* severed deer leg, and you're not 12, call the cops.

My First Suit

When I was about 15 and needed a suit for my first semi-formal school dance, my mother towed me and Houdini to the Boy's department at Sears. We looked around for something suitable, but the pickings were slim. Everything was either too small or too big. I was always pretty average, so most stuff in my size sold out quickly. I was wandering around aimlessly, while my mother perused the racks. Suddenly, I heard her say, "Here's one! It looks PERFECT."

She had found the only suit in the store that was my size.

Unfortunately, it was currently being worn by a store mannequin, who clearly wasn't going to be needing it for a dance the next day.

My mother hunted around for a sales person for a few minutes, but patience was not her strong suit. We were standing by the vacant register, waiting for help, but none was forthcoming in the 30 seconds she actually had patience for.

She looked at me and said, "Go take that suit off that dummy."

"No way!" I said. "I'm not undressing a dummy in the middle of the store."

Obviously, neither was she. She turned to my brother, who was five years younger than me, and embarrassed by absolutely nothing. "Go grab the jacket," she instructed. He dutifully sauntered over to the mannequin and pretended to look at the inside of the coat. Within seconds, he had the coat almost off, but the left hand was giving him trouble. He yanked the jacket, turning the sleeve inside out. The mannequin teetered on its base, then the coat broke free. Unfortunately, so did the mannequin's hand. He brought them both back.

My mother turned the jacket right-side in, and fished out the dummy hand, discarding it inside a round clothes rack. "Try this on" she instructed me. I did as I was told. Against all my most fervent hopes, it was a perfect fit.

This was not good.

"It's a perfect fit!" my mother exclaimed happily. "We HAVE to get those pants."

She turned to look for my brother, but he was already over at the dummy, fiddling with the fly on the pants. It appeared to be stuck. People walking by were looking at him, and my mother and I were pretending that he wasn't ours. The pants were not coming off easily, but he was not deterred. He knew his mission. My mother would have these pants, at any cost. He untucked the shirt, and unbuttoned the bottom of it so he could get a better look at the zipper. Still no go. It was stuck good.

He looked over to my mother for instruction, but before my mother could even formulate the next stage of her plan, he came up with his own. He tipped over the mannequin, and dragged it forward until it came crashing down off its base. Holding it under its arms, he dragged it backwards toward the rear of the store. My mom nonchalantly followed my brother and the dummy, as if following an eleven-year-old who was dragging a disheveled, handless mannequin across the store was something she did every day. I followed too, wearing my spiffy new suit jacket and looking around for a hole to crawl into where I could conveniently die of embarrassment.

Safely hidden behind a rack of bargain shirts, my mother started working on the pants. The zipper was indeed stuck, but the reason wasn't apparent. We were all huddled over the mannequin's crotch, trying to figure out why the pants weren't cooperating.

"Jiggle it," my brother said helpfully.

"I AM jiggling it," my mother replied.

"Do the feet come off?" she asked him, as if Houdini had suddenly become an Expert Mannequin Technician of the highest order.

"I think so," he said, moving down to feet level. He gave the left one a tug. "I'm not sure," he said. "You try it."

My mother ducked around to his end, and my brother and I went back to work on the zipper. It was mostly him, because I was too embarrassed to really put my heart into it. My mother started yanking on the foot, while my brother was simultaneously tugging on the zipper. The mannequin was banging around on the floor like it was in the throes of a full-blown epileptic seizure.

Suddenly, we were interrupted by a loud "Can I HELP you?"

Startled, we all looked up at the same time, our attention momentarily drawn away from the dummy violation in progress.

The sales lady was not amused.

"No, we're just looking," my mother replied, twisting off a dummy foot.

"You can't DO that," the sales lady said.

"We can't look for a suit for my son? This was the only blue suit left in his size," she said, twisting off the other foot.

"No, you can't do THAT," the sales lady replied, pointing at the foot in my mother's hand. "What you're doing to the dummy. You're not supposed to remove the clothes from the mannequin. You should have asked for assistance, because there is a special way to remove the clothing without damaging it." She was clearly pissed.

"Well, there were no sales people around when I needed help, so I decided to help myself," my mother replied reasonably, sliding the pants down the legs and off, not missing a beat.

She stood up, holding the suit pants. She messed with the inside for a second, and the zipper slid down. "Go try these on," she said to me, handing me the purloined pants and pointing me in the direction of the changing rooms. I practically ran to the changing room, desperate for any excuse to remove myself from the middle of this conversation.

I took my time. I sat in the dressing room, wondering if there were a way I could tunnel through the wall and escape. I sat there until I heard the muffled conversation go from slightly heated to warm to cool. My mother was good that way. She could take someone who was flamingly pissed and have them laughing all in the space of five minutes.

When I figured it was safe to return, I came back wearing the pants. The sales lady was just propping the footless, handless dummy against the wall. My mother helpfully rooted around inside the clothes rack and came up with the hand. She offered this to the sales lady, who clicked it back on to the wrist. My mother then turned her full attention toward me, critically eyeing the hard-won pants.

"They'll do," she said. "We'll just take them up a bit – they're a little long, but other than that, they fit nice. Now we just have to find you a shirt and tie." She was already turning back toward the mangled mannequin.

The sales lady was one step ahead of us, and had already removed the shirt and tie. She handed them to my mom, who handed the shirt to me.

"I'll put the tie on you when you come back out," she said.

I trudged back to the changing room without a word.

I ended up wearing my full dummy ensemble to the dance, and even though my mother's methods were unorthodox, I can't fault her taste. I rocked that powder-blue polyester suit for all it was worth.

Mr. Smooth.

I had my first date with a real girl in eighth grade. Before that magical moment, I pretty much exclusively dated my best friend's older sister without her knowledge. I also dated a poster of Linda Ronstadt that I hung on the wall near my bed.

I was 14, and in the school band. I was something they called a "percussionist" which meant that if an instrument existed that required hitting it with something to get it to make a noise, I was the one who played it.

We all wanted to play drums, but not all of us were so lucky. They would always arrange us in order of ability, and you would either get the coveted snare drum position, or you'd be relegated to the bass drum or the crash cymbals. If you were really talentless, they'd hand you a triangle and tell you to smack the shit out of it when and only when the conductor pointed directly at you. I didn't play the triangle, but I crashed a lot of cymbals in my day.

There was one other instrument that was even higher on the totem pole than the snare drum. It was only used in one song per concert. It was the full drum set. This particular drum set was a five-piece Gretsch with two crash cymbals, a 20" ride and an actual honest-to-God high-hat. The holy grail for all seven of us, from the snare drummers down to Timmy triangle. This set was played by an angel with flowing brown hair and a perfect smile. She also wore eye makeup, which was pretty revolutionary for eighth grade – at least back then.

I was in love. Or lust. I'm not sure which it is when you're 14. Maybe both. Maybe neither. All I knew was she was the best drummer out of all of us, and she looked like a rock star goddess in her silk blouse and Jordache jeans.

At any rate, I decided I would gather up every one of my quaking nerves and ask her out. On a real date. A movie. Something grown up. It had to be something impressive, because she was clearly out of my league.

We didn't have cell phones back then, so privacy on the phone was essentially non-existent. My mother was into real-estate, and also into talking on the phone, so she was either constantly on it, picking it up when *I* was on it, or waiting for a call so I couldn't use it. That's some serious pressure when you're trying to get up the nerve to dial a number you just looked up in the phone book. Not to mention the fact that I had five numbers with the same last name and had no idea which one belonged to her, so it was all trial and error. I had to gather up my nerve for each and every one, and be ready to turn on the charm at a moment's notice.

I remember sitting on the floor downstairs in the dark, next to the phone in my father's office, trying to get my hands to stop shaking. It was the only phone in the house where my conversations couldn't be heard by everyone in the family.

I only had five numbers to work my way through. It should have been easy, but very time I touched the phone, my heart would start trying to pound its way out of my skinny chest. I rehearsed what I was going to say over and over. I literally had a script – complete with possible responses. I was a little geek even then. Without realizing it, I had invented the flowchart. It looked something like this:

Hi, is Karen there?

(if wrong number, hang up, cross number off list)

(YN)

> If no: leave name and number.

> If yes: This is Johnny, is Karen there?

If she comes to phone:

> Hi Karen. It's Johnny from band. I was wondering if you might want to go see a movie on Saturday.

If what movie?: (list of movies)

If busy: Oh, ok. Maybe we can do it on Sunday or next week.

> If no: OK, thanks anyway. See you in school.

> If yes: OK, what movie do you want to see?

Things to talk about if she doesn't hang up right away:

band, drums and music, TV shows

I had *pages* of this. As you can probably imagine, things didn't go quite as planned.

1st number:

> "Hello?"

> click.

Crap! Why did I hang up?

> 1st number again:

> "Hello?"

> (hyperventilation)

> "Hello? Is anyone there?"

> "Hi. This is Karen. Is Johnny there? Wait, I mean.."

"I think you have the wrong number, sweetie."

click.

One down. So she thought I was a girl. So what. Shake it off.

2nd number:

"Yeah?"

click.

2nd number again:

"Who is this? Stop calling me, you little shit."

click.

*Two down. Even if she **does** live there.*

3rd number:

"Hello?"

"Hi this is K – Johnny. Is Karen there?"

"Yes, she is. Hold on, please."

"Hi, this is Karen."

"Hi Karen. It's Johnny from band and I was wondering if you might want to go see a movie on Saturday."

"Johnny who? Did you say Fruhmband? I don't know any Johnny Fruhmband. How old are you? I think you have the wrong Karen."

click.

Jeez! Come on! How is that even possible?

Finally, I got the right number and the right Karen.

"Hello?"

"Hi, is Karen there?"

"This is her."

Those three words caused terror to leap into my chest. I used all my will-power to not slam the phone down on the receiver. This contingency was not planned for – it was not on my cheat sheet and I was flying blind.

How could I not have foreseen that she might actually answer? Idiot!

"Hi, it's Johnny from band do you want to go to a movie Saturday or if not Saturday then maybe Sunday or maybe next week if you're busy...(long ragged breath) but if you don't want to ever, that's ok."

click.

Crap! Why did I do that?

168

Ten minutes later, right around when I got my heart to start beating normally again, the phone started ringing.

Just when I had steeled myself to pick it up, the ringing stopped. My mother yelled down the stairs, "Johnny! Are you down there? There's a Karen on the phone and she says you got disconnected."

"H-Hello?"

"Hi Johnny. It's Karen. We got cut off. Did you say something about a movie? Because I can go."

"Mom, I've got it. Hang up."

"Yeah, I was.....um, wondering if (hyperventilation)...if you might want to....(frantically digging through notes) see a movie."

"What's that noise?"

"Mommmmmm, HANG IT UP!"

"Sorry, I think something is wrong with the phone."

"Oh. It sounded like papers rustling or something."

"No. Phone. It's the phone. So. (rustle rustle) W-What movie?"

"I don't care. It has to be PG and have to be home by eight, though."

"OK. I'll look and call you back."

"Is your mom driv – "

click.

As you can see from those sample exchanges, I had nowhere to go but up. During the next few scheduling calls, I got progressively smoother. I worked out the bugs. I gained confidence. I threw away my pages of notes.

I was a stud.

By the time the weekend rolled around, I was feeling pretty good about things. So good, in fact, that I entertained going for the fabled "good night kiss" that I had heard so much about. How hard could that be? After all, I had one other kiss under my belt. It was from seventh grade, but still it counted, even if it had been an awkward, open-eyed, two-second lip press while sitting on a couch in broad daylight, right before I ran out the door and rode my bike home as fast as I could.

Getting that kiss was all I could think about. Plus, there would be ample opportunity to hold hands and stuff in the movie theatre right? I mean, isn't that what people did? They didn't watch the movie, they sat in the back and just kissed a lot and maybe felt each other up. Maybe I would even feel a boob. The possibilities were endless.

It had taken all my courage to actually call Karen and ask her to the movies. Once I was past that hurdle, I immediately started thinking about the next one. While my imagination thought of all sorts of ways the actual date could unfold, my anxiety about it threatened to sabotage the entire thing. I couldn't believe she actually agreed to go with me.

My biggest problem was that I was the oldest of three brothers, and as the oldest, I didn't have anyone to go to for dating advice. Every one of my friends was as clueless as I was. We didn't know about the yawn/stretch move, or how to let the arm around her shoulders eventually slip down to more interesting territory. All this was as yet undiscovered, at least for me. It was complete trial and error, which is never a good thing on a date.

I think that's what makes first dates awkward for everyone, regardless of age. Even when you're older, you unconsciously have your repertoire of moves, and you have no way of knowing whether any of them will seem good or bad to the person you are trying to impress on that first date. When you're 14, not having that baseline to work from can be debilitating.

After subsequent phone calls (sans hang-ups) to nail down the movie and show times, I asked my mother if she could drive us. Being driven around by your mom was embarrassing and I wasn't looking forward to suffering the indignity, but short of taking a taxi or forcing Karen to ride on the handlebars of my bike, that was the only way we'd be getting there since neither of us were old enough to drive. My mother said no problem, she could drive us there and pick us up after the movie.

I did have one stipulation, however. I told her she couldn't look in the rear view mirror. "Exactly what is it you think you're going to be doing back there?" she asked. I had no idea, but I wanted to be prepared. I had all sorts of possibilities rattling around in my head, and absolutely none of them was "sit with your hands in your lap, staring straight ahead, completely paralyzed in fear" although that was probably what my mother was envisioning. She eventually agreed. OK, no staring in the rear view mirror.

With that little detail taken care of, the next bit of business was more pressing, and quite a bit more awkward.

The day of the date, I broached the subject boldly. I walked into the kitchen and sat down at the table where my mother was sitting, drinking her morning coffee.

"So tonight, when we bring Karen home, can you, um, not watch me walk her to the door?" I asked.

170

"What do you mean, not watch you?" she replied.

"I want to walk her to the door. You're going to be watching me. I'll be nervous if you're watching me. So I don't want you to watch."

She laughed. "OK, I won't watch."

'I don't believe you," I said. "I know you'll watch, even if you say you won't. Even if you're not watching, I'll still think you're watching and I'll still be nervous."

"So what do you want me to do?" she asked. "Drive away and come back for you?"

I, of course, did not see this for the sarcastic comment that it was, and latched onto the idea wholeheartedly.

"Yeah! Do that!" I said. "Just drive around the block or something and then come back and pick me up."

I didn't tell her that I would be going in for the kiss, but I think she just assumed.

"OK," she said, looking at me doubtfully. "If that's what you want. I'll drop you off and then wait until you're almost to the front door, then I'll drive around the block and wait a few minutes. Then I'll come back. After she goes inside, just walk to the end of the driveway and I'll pick you up."

So that was the plan, and it was good.

That night, the movie we had decided upon started at 6:30. Karen had gotten permission from her father to come home a little later that night, and he had spoken to my mother to make sure she was driving us, so everything was set. The movie was something called "The Goodbye Girl." I had no idea what it was about, but Karen picked it so it was ok by me.

We pulled up outside Karen's house at around 5:45, and I jumped out and ran to the front door. I reached out a trembling hand and rang the doorbell. Then I waited. After what seemed like an eternity, I heard footsteps coming from inside. An older woman answered the door, and said, "Yes? Can I help you?"

"Hi, I'm here to pick up Karen for the movie," I said.

She looked puzzled. "Who?" she asked.

"Karen. I'm Johnny. I'm here to pick her up for the movie."

She had an odd look on her face, and suddenly that small, tight ball of fear in the pit of my stomach started unraveling at high velocity.

"There isn't anyone here by that name," she said.

I stared at her, not fully comprehending.

"I think you must have the wrong house, hon," she added helpfully.

I think you must have the wrong house.

Oh my god, I thought. *No. No. No. How? How could this be?*

I had managed to get her address wrong. We were at the wrong house. This was not good. My mother was sitting in the car, engine running, watching the exchange. The woman must have noticed the look of dread on my face because she spoke again.

"Who are you looking for? What's Karen's last name?" she asked.

I managed to spit out the last name. Her face lit up, and for a second I thought that against all odds, the woman recognized it. Then she said, "Let me get my phone book." The big ball of fear slowed its sickening spin, then reversed direction. I thanked her and ran back to the car to tell my mother what was going on.

I stuck my head in the passenger side window of the car. "Wrong house!" I said. "We're looking her up in the phone book." I ran back to the front door. The woman had returned with a phone book, and had already looked up Karen's last name. I looked at the list and picked the one I remembered as hers.

She went back inside and dialed her number. After a brief conversation with Karen's mom, she came back. "You switched the last two numbers, honey. Her house number is 423 not 432," she said. "Tell your mom she needs to go to almost the end of this street."

I ran back to the car, jumped into the back seat, and we were off. We had wasted quite a bit of time, and the movie was starting in about 30 minutes. When we got to the right house, Karen was sitting on the front steps waiting. Before I could even get out of the car to go get her, she had jumped in the back seat with me.

"Sorry we're late," I said, completely ready to just leave it at that.

Unfortunately, my mother was *not* completely ready to just leave it at that. She felt compelled to add, "Yes, Johnny had your address wrong and we ended up at the wrong house and then had to look your last name up in the phone book."

"Yeah, I know," Karen said. "My mom told me."

For those of you keeping score at home, Johnny just stepped up to the plate.

Multiple moms making me look like a complete idiot: Strike one.

We made the trip to the cinema in record time, my mother yammering away the whole way asking Karen questions about school, her family, and everything in between. She didn't look in the rear view mirror, but she also didn't shut up. On one hand, I was miffed that I wasn't able to get a word in edgewise, but on the other hand I was glad my mother was talking, because then I didn't have to. Even at that young age I knew that I had a much higher chance of looking like an idiot if I opened my mouth than if I just kept it shut.

My mother dropped us off and drove away. I walked up to the ticket window and paid for both tickets, and handed one to Karen. As we walked into the theatre, I remember thinking about how weird it was being in there with a girl and not a bunch of my friends.

I took her hand as we walked, and she didn't recoil in horror, so of course I instantly started feeling pretty good about the evening so far, even though everything up to this point had been incredibly screwed up. We stood in line for some popcorn and a couple of sodas and then stood in line again to hand over our tickets. The ticket taker said "Number two on the left" and we were off.

When we walked into the darkened theater, the previews were already playing. It was musty, and romantic, and all I could smell was a combination of popcorn, her shampoo and the scent of her leather jacket.

I leaned over and whispered "Where do you want to sit?" hoping to steer her toward a couple of seats in the back.

"Let's sit down near the front," she said, and started walking towards the screen.

Something here was not going according to plan. We were not supposed to sit where everyone in the place could see us, and be completely lit up by the reflected light of the silver screen. We were supposed to sit in the back where it was dark, and nobody was paying attention. My dream was hemorrhaging before my eyes, and I didn't know how to stop the bleeding. I followed her to the front and sat down.

Front row: Strike two.

I asked her if her popcorn was ok, and she said yes. Apparently her drink was fine too. Finally, after I asked her a dozen different questions in that vein, and she responded to every one with a single word answer, our movie started. I was glad because I was running out of stupid questions.

Then she started fumbling around in her purse. After a few seconds she pulled something out.

Her glasses.

She put on her *glasses*. I was only 14 and a complete idiot, but even I knew what that meant. She was here to watch the movie. That's it. There will be no making out, feeling up, feeling down, necking, or whatever you wanted to call it. With a little luck, there might be some hand holding. With a LOT of luck, maybe I could figure out a way to put my arm around her.

The fact that I was apparently dating a blind girl: Strike three.

We sat there for a while, and eventually her hand crept out and put itself in mine. I was frozen in terror. A few minutes after that, she took my hand, raised it over her head and draped my arm around her shoulder. It was a little awkward, since she was taller than me, and it put my arm at a very strange angle. I felt like I had her in a headlock, but still, it was something. I know that normally after strike three you're out, but this was at least a foul ball.

My heart was about to break out of my ribcage, but this was good. My left hand was inches from an actual boob. I could feel the boob calling to me in the recesses of my mind. Calling to me, telling me to just nonchalantly drop my hand from where it was resting on her shoulder and let my fingers do the walking; On the outside at first, to get some shirt boob, then on the inside if she didn't seem to mind.

I couldn't do it. I sat there through the whole movie and I don't think I actually saw any of it. Instead, I had a front row seat to the prize fight between my force of will and my chickenshit hand. My hand would start to inch its way toward Boobville, and then suddenly it would chicken out and snap back to her shoulder like I was a marionette with rubber bands instead of strings. This epic battle raged, non-stop, for two hours. By the end of the movie, my arm was numb, my back was sore and I had a stiff neck from sitting in that totally awkward position due to the height discrepancy.

Before I knew it, the movie was over. We stood up and walked outside. I had failed to even touch shirt boob. I had put my arm around her, true, but that wasn't quite the same thing. Actually, I didn't even do that; she did.

"Pretty good movie," she said.

"Yeah," I agreed. "Pretty good."

Then we sat in total silence for ten minutes, waiting for my mother to pick us up.

It was dark by the time my mother got there. "There she is," I said, and the relief was palpable.

True to her word, my mother still didn't look in the rear view mirror. Not that it would have mattered at that point, because somewhere between the end of the movie and the drive home, Karen and I had erected some sort of wall between us that appeared to be manufactured completely out of solid awkwardness. For some reason, the girl I talked to every day at school had suddenly become unapproachable when she was sitting next to me in the dark. I sat there with my hands in my lap, staring straight ahead, completely paralyzed in fear. My mother looked straight ahead according to plan.

Before I realized it, we were pulling up in front of Karen's house. There were cars in the driveway, so my mother couldn't pull in, which worked out well for our plan. Karen got out of the car and apparently didn't realize that I was planning on walking her to the house. I base this theory on the fact that as she left the car, she slammed the door.

This didn't work out so well for me since I was only half way out of the car at the time. The door closed on my shin, and the window frame hit me in the side of the head. After my mother successfully stifled her laughter, and I assured them both that I was not bleeding or concussed, I asked Karen if I could walk her to the house. She agreed.

About halfway to the door, my mother initiated the first step in the plan, and drove away to give us our privacy. Although I pretended to ignore the fact that my mother just took off down the street, Karen seemed to notice it right away. She kept looking over her shoulder as my mother's car reached the end of her street, turned left, and then disappeared from sight.

We were standing on her front steps, awkwardly face to face. I had my hands on her hips, and my hands felt like two blocks of solid wood. She had her arms hanging straight down at her sides like she was standing at atten-tion. I was looking at Karen's sweet, full lips, and Karen was looking wildly down the street.

"Does your mother know you're not in the car?" she asked me, clearly concerned. "Do you need to use the phone?"

"Yes, she knows," I replied, my concentration broken. "And no, I don't need a phone. She'll be back soon. She's going to drive around the block to give us some time," I lamely explained.

Karen remained unconvinced. "Time for what? Why did she just... drive away?" she asked.

"Um, well...because... I sort of asked her to," I said.

"Oh," she said, obviously confused. She still wasn't getting it. "OK, then. Thanks for the movie. I'll see you tomorrow." She turned toward the door, and one of my hands fell from her leather jacket.

I could see my chances for the good night kiss slipping quickly away, so I decided to go for it. As I moved forward, two things happened simultaneously. Startled by my sudden lunge, she backed away from my questing fish lips. At that same instant, the porch light went on, the front door opened, and her mom said, "Oh! I thought I heard someone out here! How was the movie?"

Then, using her keen powers of deduction, her mother realized that based on my current in-progress pucker status, she had interrupted the goodnight kiss.

"Do you want me to give you two a minute of privacy?" she asked.

"Yes," I said.

"No," Karen said.

Karen's mother laughed. "OK, then. Karen, thank Johnny for the movie and come inside." Then she realized that my mother's car was nowhere to be seen. "Johnny, where's your mother?"

"She drove around the block." I mumbled, as if that made perfect sense. "She'll be right back." Karen's mother looked at me quizzically, but withheld comment.

"Thanks, Johnny," Karen said. "I'll see you Monday in school."

"OK, Karen," I said. "Thanks for going with me. I hope you had fun."

She didn't answer, but she did smile a little as she closed the door. Or maybe it was more of a smirk.

The door clicked shut, the porch light went out, and I turned and walked to the end of the driveway to wait for my mother.

I stood there for a few minutes waiting.

Nothing. The wind picked up.

I stood for a few minutes more, and I was starting to get pretty cold. Still nothing. Cars came, cars went. None of them contained my mother.

Come on, mom! I thought. *How long can it take you to drive around the block?*

Finally, the porch light came back on and the front door opened. Karen's mom yelled out. "Johnny! You can't stand out there in the cold. Come in here and wait."

Completely embarrassed, I did the perp walk all the way back to the house as Karen and her mother looked on. "Thanks," I mumbled, as I stepped inside.

Just as I was about to close the door, my mother pulled up. I spun around and literally ran down the driveway to the waiting car. Before I had even closed the car door behind me, I was yelling at her.

"Where were you?" I practically screamed. "You said you were going to just drive around the block! You were gone for ten minutes! Jeez! I felt like an idiot!"

"This neighborhood looks different in the dark, and I ended up one street over," she said laughing at my obvious distress. "All the houses look the same. So how did it go?"

"Can we just go home?" I asked.

"That good, huh?" she said, sounding sympathetic. She flipped on the radio as we pulled away, and Frankie Valli's *My Eyes Adored You* was playing. The song ended, and I reached out and snapped the radio back off, sulking.

A few minutes later, she spoke up again. "Trust me, chief," she said. "It'll get better."

And you know what? It did.

Not right away – but eventually, it did.

I was a Teenage Spiderman

When I was freshman in high school, our parents told us we were moving out of the old neighborhood to a bigger house that was 15 minutes away. The Snitch, Houdini and I were not happy. When you're a kid who can't drive yet, that ten miles may as well be 300. All your old friends that you used to hang with are, for all intents and purposes, gone. We didn't move far enough away to have to go to a different school, so it wasn't as bad as it could have been – we still got to see our friends every day – we just didn't get to hang with them after.

As all things contracting go, our new house wasn't done on time, and the people who bought our old house had to move out of the one they just sold, and they wanted to get busy living in the one they had just purchased. We were in a curious situation – we had a new house being built, and yet at the same time we were homeless. We needed to find a place to live. For *two whole months.*

Obviously we couldn't afford a hotel for that long, so we did the next best thing – we imposed upon our friends, and went to live with Markie's parents. There were six of us – me, my parents, my two brothers and my sister. Markie had a sister and brother too, so the two girls got one room, my parents got Markie's room, Markie's little brother slept in his parent's room, and the rest of us got:

The Basement.

At first it was an adventure. The four of us, sleeping downstairs in a poor man's bachelor pad. It was fun. For about the first week. After that, we quickly realized how much it sucked to live out of a musty box. At least Markie had the luxury of going upstairs to his bedroom to get his clothes out of an actual closet. The rest of us smelled like old library books after the first couple of weeks. After about the fifth or sixth time of waking up in the middle of the night with a numb arm from the shitty army cot I was sleeping on, I was ready to get the hell out of there.

There was a coating of light grey fuzz over just about everything down there. The sheets on the cot always felt cold, and while we had a television, there wasn't much else down there except boxes full of crap, a workshop, and spiders the size of pie plates. Big, black, hairy fuckers that you just knew were waiting for you to go to sleep so they could slide on down to the all-you-could-eat buffet. After the first couple of weeks of getting bit to shit every night, we got Markie's pellet gun and we'd take turns shooting those fat, hairy bastards off the wall. Pellets were good for that. Since they're made of lead, they didn't ricochet around like bb's. They just flattened out and fell straight down.

We did other things to amuse ourselves too. The Snitch had grown up to be a little bit of a stickler for the rules, and he was always paranoid about missing the bus, or being late to school. I think he would have died on the spot if he ever missed the bus. So one night after he went to sleep, Markie and I set all the alarm clocks in the basement two hours ahead, including The Snitch's watch. Then the next morning we woke him up when it looked like he had about ten minutes to make the bus. He went *apeshit*. It was a good prank.

Another time, he fell asleep at around six at night. An hour later, we woke him up, and pretended like it was the next morning and we were getting ready for school. I think we even got him to go upstairs and take a shower. He was pretty pissed at us, but he got over it, eventually.

As I mentioned, Markie's step-dad had his workshop down in the basement too, and he had a brand new radial arm saw that he was really proud of. I think he got a chubby just looking at it. One day, I had this idea, and we took about five or six nails and cut them in half, all at different angles. Then we took a tiny spot of superglue and put one half on top of the table, and glued the bottom half of the nail underneath, directly under the top half, so it looked like a big nail was pounded right through the table. The illusion was flawless.

Then we just waited.

We were upstairs when the bellowing started. Doug was downstairs screaming for all of us to get our asses down there pronto. We knew instantly that he had found the nails. We walked down all nonchalant, and asked him what he wanted. He was practically foaming at the mouth. He had a vein the size of a fire hose throbbing in the middle of his forehead, and his face was the color of blood. He was royally pissed. He kept yelling, "Who DID THIS? WHO DID THIS?" over and over. He was so shocked at the sight of his brand new saw with these nails sticking out of the table that he never even thought to try to pull them out.

After he yelled for a few minutes longer, I just reached out my hand and with one quick back-and-forth motion, wiped the nails off both top and bottom. I think I did it just in time too, because he looked like he was about ready to start kicking serious ass. The look on his face was priceless. His jaw just dropped and he stopped dead in mid-rant. He just shook his head, turned, and walked back up the stairs without another word. I'm guessing he didn't think it was as funny as we did.

Markie's sister was a year older than me, and apparently she was scared of spiders, since she wouldn't even come within ten feet of the basement door.

Of course, Markie was always fighting with her, and after this one fight, he wanted to get even. I had an idea.

The next time we saw one of those big black spiders, instead of blowing its guts all over the wall with the pellet gun, we were going to put it to better use. He was instantly on board with this. The "next time" turned out to be about an hour later, since those hairy bastards were pretty much everywhere you looked.

We didn't want it alive, since it would end up running under something and she probably would never see it. We needed it to be dead, but *look* like it was alive. This particular specimen was an extra chunky one, so we didn't want to waste him. We got a can of Raid and gave him a shot. He came down off the wall with a plop, and we scooped him up. He was dead but still flexible. We quickly placed him on a piece of cardboard, and used a toothpick to spread his legs out to what looked to be a natural stance. We left him to dry overnight. The next day, we went to school. Revenge is a dish best served cold, and all that.

The next night, after his sister went to sleep, Markie snuck in her room and put the spider on the spare pillow next to her. He figured she'd wake up in the morning, scream bloody murder, and we'd all have a good laugh. It didn't quite work out like that.

Somewhere around two a.m., we were all jolted out of a sound sleep by a blood-curdling scream. Apparently his sister had gotten up to go to the bathroom, and when she came back, she grabbed the pillow the spider was resting on. She felt something brush against her face, and fall down into her hair, so she flipped the light on to see what it was.

When this gigantic hairy spider fell out of her hair onto the bed, she completely lost her mind. She flipped out and started screaming at the top of her lungs. We heard Doug running down the hallway, probably thinking that his teenage daughter was being attacked by an intruder. When he burst into the room, Markie's sister was sitting jammed in the corner, knees to her chest, screaming her head off and sobbing uncontrollably. Once she stopped hyperventilating, Doug was able to get the story out of her.

I knew at that point that Markie had withheld information, and he was going to pay. He had told us that she was afraid of spiders, but not the extent of her fear. We had no idea that she would come within a half psi of blowing a tube in her head, all because of a harmless little spider. This was very close to a full-blown phobia, and she wasn't going to be able to sleep in her own bed for weeks. So much for the "ha-ha-have-a-good-laugh" original plan. Someone was going to hang for this one. In retrospect, I should have known this would happen, because a few years earlier, while we were up at her grandmother's camp, she jumped out of a moving boat when she happened to see a spider in it.

I have to hand it to Doug – he knew instantly that the spider had been planted, and he knew instantly it was Markie who had done it. I think he suspected that I may have had something to do with it, but he couldn't prove it. Markie took the rap on that one, even though it was my idea.

We moved out a few weeks later, and it was pure heaven to have my own bedroom again. It was by no means pleasant when we were going through it, but looking back, we had some fun during our mandatory two months in the hole.

The Snitch Had Balls of Steel.

I know that sentence is hard to believe, given all you've learned about The Snitch in the last 180 pages or so, but it's true. When the chips were down, The Snitch sacked up and pulled it off.

The drinking age in New York changed twice – the first time it went from 18 to 19, the second time from 19 to 21. Luckily for me I was born in the spring which was apparently a good time to weasel your way past shitty legislation. There may have been a period of a few months between 20 and 21 where things went a little dry for me, but for the most part I rode the wave.

On the one hand, I think it's a crappy law. I think that if you can enlist in the armed services and die for your country at 18, then you should be able to go out and get shit-faced if that's your thing. On the other hand, I remember what it was like to be 18, invincible, and driving a 4,000 pound slab of late 60's Detroit rolling stock. Not a good combination.

As a result of the drinking age being the exact age I was, I drank. Mostly because I could, but also as a by-product of seeing a lot of shitty bands in a lot of shitty clubs. At the time, most of my friends were either away at college or working full-time jobs, and they weren't really into the rock club scene anyway. As a result, I was always looking for someone to go with me.

I decided that The Snitch would be my wing man. At that point we were both old enough to have outgrown most of the contention between us. He no longer ran to our parents when Houdini and I committed misdemeanors, and he was tired of watching the drinking age out-run him. He was a prime candidate for a fake ID. Plus, I figured I would never get Houdini into a bar at the age of 15, no matter what his fake ID looked like.

I've seen a lot of fake IDs in my time. I've seen some that were great and some so bad they wouldn't fool a blind bouncer. I've even made a couple for friends that were pretty damned convincing. I made one for my then girlfriend (now wife) by switching her picture into an out-of-state license that we found somewhere. Other than her having to repeatedly say "Yeah, I lost a lot of weight since then" – because the rightful owner was something like 142 pounds – it was perfect.

No such luck for The Snitch though. We thought about taking one of my old licenses and doctoring it up, but a lot of places were only taking picture IDs by then, and New York was one of the last states to switch over. I had been using my college ID for the last year or so, and it seemed more reliable than a driver's license with no photo.

After thinking about it for a bit, I had an idea. It was risky, and a lot of it would ride on The Snitch and his ability to keep his cool, but I thought it might work.

At the beginning of my freshman year in college, everyone was issued a student ID. Somehow, I managed to lose mine and I had to go to the registrar's office to get another one. At the time, none of this was computerized so if you lost your ID it was a major pain in the ass for all parties involved, because they had to re-shoot your picture. All the other stuff they had on file, kept in something that looked like a series of recipe boxes.

The way the replacement card procedure worked was like this: You would get your picture taken a few times, they'd show you the strip and you'd pick which one you wanted. Then they would take the info on the index card, type it into a machine holding an official ID card blank, and then have you sign it. They'd match the sig against the one on file, and then stick your fresh picture on it and laminate it. The whole exercise took about 10 minutes if there wasn't a line.

You can see the flaw in this procedure, right?

For about two weeks, The Snitch practiced signing my name until he had it down perfect.

Armed with his freshly-honed forgery skills and my birth certificate, we jumped into my 1969 Impala and drove down to the registrar's office. I gave him a pep talk along the way. "You can do this," I said. "It's a piece of cake. You have the signature down pat. You have my birth certificate. It's a slam dunk."

I could tell he was starting to lose his nerve. Ironically, all he probably needed was a stiff drink.

We sat in the car for a bit while he collected himself. Finally, he said, "OK, let's do it," and jumped out of the car. I watched him walk to the front door and disappear inside. I started the count down. I figured I had about a ten minute wait, since there didn't appear to be many other cars in the lot.

At about the 15-minute mark, I started to get a little worried. *He should have been out by now. He's been in there 15 minutes. We're busted. He got caught and we're busted and any minute now I'll be surrounded by campus security.* I nervously started the car, rolled down the windows and turned off the stereo.

At the 30 minute mark, the door swung open and The Snitch ran to the car. He jumped in and yelled, "GO! GO! GO!" I didn't waste any time taking that advice to heart, even though my heart was in my throat instead of where it usually hung out. I gunned the Impala and left the parking lot in a squeal of rubber and a cloud of dust.

"What happened? Did you get it? Tell me what happened!" I said over the roar of the side pipes. He didn't say anything. Instead he just reached into his pocket and held up The Perfect Un-fake Fake ID. Original lamination. My birth date. My details. His picture. It was fantastic.

I finally got the story out of him, and it was a very close call. He was nervous, and he almost bailed out and came back to the car empty-handed, but when he told the woman at the registrar's office that he lost his ID, she just asked him for his birth certificate and sat him down in front of the cam-era. He knew he was committed at that point. He had two choices – either go through with it, or take off and leave my birth certificate behind.

Our plan had worked perfectly thus far. However, my brother soon realized that it had one fatal flaw.

Remember I said that they took three pictures and handed you the strip and you picked the best one? Well, the other two didn't go into the garbage. The other two went into the card file with the rest of your information.

We were brothers, but he did not look like me. At all.

So he did the only thing he could do. He sat down in the chair in front of the registrar lady's desk, and stalled by pretending that he couldn't decide which picture he thought was best. While she was waiting for him to make up his mind, she pulled the info card out, and started punching in the data for the new ID. When he glanced over at the recipe box, he could see my face peeking out of the index card file, staring right at him. He had no idea what to do. His luck was running out.

But it didn't. Right when he was going to confess and beg for the birth cer-tificate back, she dropped something on the floor. When she bent down to pick it up, my brother reached out and grabbed the pictures of me from the file.

Balls. Of. Steel.

Then, as calmly as he could, he said, "I like this picture the best" and poin-ted to the last one on his strip of three.

The registrar lady took the pictures from him and cut out the one he liked, and then put the others in the file. She rooted around in there for a second, a look of concern on her face.

"What's the matter?" The Snitch asked.

"There are supposed to be other photos in here," she replied. "But I don't see them. They must have been misplaced. That's odd."

She shrugged, flipped a few of the index cards back and forth for a second, then rolled the card out of the machine and had him sign the back. She compared it to the one on record, then laminated the ID, handed it back to him and told him to have a nice day. He thanked her and left.

After he told me the story, I only had one question for him. "Why did you come running out of the building screaming for me to get the hell out of Dodge?" I asked. "Everything went great."

"I don't know," he said, shrugging his shoulders. "I just thought it would be cooler if we peeled out."

Luckily or not, I transferred to a different school the following year and never needed to get another ID from that office.

I still find it funny to think that somewhere, on a dusty shelf in a record hall basement, there might be a moldy box holding an index card containing all my information – with a picture of my brother's smiling face fastened to it with a rusty paperclip.

We used the hell out of that thing for almost two years. The only catch was that we could never walk in together. We'd usually wait about 15 minutes before the second JV would make his appearance.

Obviously, whoever got to go in first bought the first round. It was only fair.

My Mother Was a Walking Sit-Com

It's MOM!

To Mom, Love, Johnny.

It doesn't seem like my mother has been gone for almost ten years. Of course, I've been saying something similar every year since she died, and I suspect I'll be saying it for a long time to come. I don't think it's something you ever stop saying when talking about loved ones that are gone from your life – especially ones that have played such a large role in determining who you are, as my mother did with me.

I've written before about how much alike we were – in our temperament, our outlook on life and our sense of humor – and I think that's why she still feels so close to me even after being gone for so long. I constantly see things that amuse me, and I know they would have made her laugh too. We had a lot of fun while I was growing up.

She was pretty spunky for being just over five feet tall, and would voice her opinion regardless of whom it pissed off. That's one trait we don't really share. I think that's because I'm only 5' 6" and I like my teeth right where they are.

My Mother, The Civil Engineer

I grew up in a residential neighborhood – one of those developments built back in the 70's where all the houses looked the same except for the color of the siding and shutters. Our house was about half-way down a fairly straight street, and as a result people tended to drive a little faster than they probably should have. There wasn't exactly a lot of traffic, but going on toward four or five o'clock, there were enough cars going by to make a game of kickball problematic, since yelling "CAR!" every two minutes and standing on the side of the street didn't really lend itself to riveting game play. Although I have to admit, yelling "WHAT DO YOU THINK THIS IS, A ROAD?" at the passing cars was very clever comedy indeed to a bunch of ten-year-olds.

Even as we mouthed off to the passing motorists, it was still embarrassing to us when my mother would do the same thing. Sitting on the front steps with her coffee, or raking leaves or planting flowers, she would always pause in whatever she was doing and yell "SLOW DOWN!" at the top of her lungs whenever someone would invariably go tooling by at what she deemed to be excessive speed. I was never sure exactly how she judged these speeds. I'm guessing it was dependent upon the color of the car and/or her mood at the time.

Eventually, my mother tired of the passing cars ignoring her. She took it as a personal affront that they did not immediately slow down upon hearing her bellowed commands. I think she expected them to back up and apologize to her for not driving 10 mph under the posted speed limit signs and then promise it would never happen again.

When that didn't happen, she complained to the cops. When the cops told her that the speed limit was 30 mph and that none of the cars they clocked had been over the limit, she decided that the speed limit should be lowered to 20 mph and any motorists exceeding this limit should be arrested immediately and have their cars impounded, because BY GOD she wasn't going to see her children or her neighbors' children run down like dogs. Unfortunately, the police didn't see it that way, and my mother and the local law enforcement officers reluctantly agreed to disagree on that matter.

She wasn't happy with that, however. So what did she do about it, you ask? Well, she did the normal and sane thing, obviously.

She collected signatures and got a spot on the agenda of the next town meeting and then proposed that the town petition the Dept. of Transportation on her behalf to consider lowering the speed limit on our street to 20 mph, and then – No, I'm kidding of course. That is not the way my mother operated.

What she did instead was this: *She drove to the local building supply store and bought about six bags of cold patch blacktop, waited until the middle of the night, and proceeded to make her own personal speed bump directly in front of our house.*

Under cover of darkness, my mother actually dumped bags of asphalt onto a public street, formed it into a long mound and tamped it down with the back of a shovel.

Needless to say, this project turned out about as well as you would expect. Lacking any formal training in speed bump construction techniques, the result wasn't so much a speed bump as it was multiple six-inch-high axle-busting speed mounds.

Surprisingly, someone complained, and it didn't take long for the new addition to our street to be addressed. The next afternoon, the police officers were back, and they weren't amused. Neither were the town's highway crew when they had to come out and scrape up the mess. Luckily, they got to it before it had hardened completely, otherwise it wouldn't have been that easy.

I don't remember much more about it, although the speed limit may have gone down a notch or two shortly thereafter. I don't think she did any hard time for it.

I don't remember missing any dinners, at any rate.

Stench, Flies and Animal Crackers.

One of the benefits to being the oldest kid in the family is that I got to do everything first. I was the first one to be allowed to cross the street by myself, I was the first one allowed to ride my bike to the drugstore, the first one allowed to stay out past dark, and the first one to take the car to the prom. One of the drawbacks, of course, is that all my "firsts" were tempered by the completely unfair notion that if *I* could do something, so could The Snitch, as long as he was accompanied by me. ("Watch your brother" and "Take your brother with you" become phrases I learned to hate.)

Obviously this loophole pissed me off, since he was more than two years younger than I was, and if there were any justice in the universe, he would have to wait exactly two years and 21 days to do those same things regardless of whether I were alive or dead. Also, the phrase "I thought I told you to watch your brother!" was probably used more often than it should have been, and was a testament to my short attention span and relative ambivalence about whether my brothers continued to exist on this plane.

One of the other dubious benefits, however, was being able to "watch my brothers" as they still had fun doing things that no longer interested me all that much. I realized that I was growing up, and that made me feel a little bit superior. [Warning: Santa Claus Spoiler Alert]

Do you remember when you found out that Santa wasn't real, and after you got over your enormous sense of parental betrayal, you realized that you were now on the inside? That was me. I was the spy who came in from the cold, the double-agent, feeding information to both sides, playing the cool confidant, the intrepid informant, the master of misdirection.

It was sometimes fun, sometimes a drag, but always interesting to watch as my younger brothers marveled over the reindeer hoof prints, the plate of cookie crumbs and the empty glass of milk, or the gnawed carrots and clumps of fur left behind by the Easter Bunny who, somewhere along the line, apparently contracted a really bad case of mange.

Since my mother was a stay-at-home mom, (or a "housewife" as they called them way back when) sometimes in the summer she would plan field trips just to keep us occupied. Mostly to maintain her own sanity, I think. When she'd had enough of our whining and fighting and complaining that there was nothing to do, she'd simply pack us all into the car and head out. One of the places she took us to was called The Catskill Game Farm.

If you grew up anywhere in New York, you probably have some great memories of this place. It was founded in 1933 by Roland Lindemann and closed for good in 2006. Back in the early seventies, it was still 50% regular zoo, 50% petting zoo, and 100% tourist trap, and as far as I know, that format never changed.

We went there quite a few times over the years, but only one of our trips really sticks out in my mind, mostly because it was an unmitigated disaster. We weren't bad kids, exactly, but let me just say that if leashes wouldn't have garnered my mother some dirty looks, they wouldn't have been an especially bad idea.

At the time of this particular trip, I was probably about seven years old, The Snitch was five and Houdini was three. As a seven-year-old, I was mildly interested in seeing the lions and elephants, but it was the thought of seeing giant snakes and lizards that really floated my boat at the time.

The Catskill Game Farm had a "Reptile House" which was sort of dark and cool inside, and had all sorts of creepy crawly things that my mother wanted no part of. She would go in with us, but was constantly looking over her shoulder as if she expected to be strangled by a boa constrictor that had escaped from its cage. I remember her seeing an empty cage that was being cleaned, and the next thing I know I was blinking in the bright sunlight, rubbing my arm and wondering how the hell I got outside. She really enjoyed watching us interact with the animals, and while I was initially a little apprehensive about it, it actually turned out to be kind of fun.

I've always had a sensitive nose, and a giant park full of animals in the heat and humidity of a mid-summer day in New York is not an olfactory experience you will soon forget. I know most of you are probably picturing a barn smell in your minds right now, but keep in mind that this place didn't just house mammals – you had reptiles and birds to deal with too, and each of them had their own unique and potent reek. In other words, if you've never smelled a pile of fresh rhinoceros shit baking in the sun, you'd be hard-pressed to imagine the stank of this place.

The first thing you do when you walk though the gates is buy the crackers to hand-feed the animals. My mother walked us over to the window and bought each of us a stack of crackers that I assume were made of processed grains and grass and things, because they were a greenish-brown color and smelled a little like rabbit food. She handed me my stack, handed The Snitch his, and tucked Houdini's into her purse. Thus armed, we ventured into the park, the three of us in tow behind my mother.

In addition to having animals in pens (the "zoo" part), they also had animals that just sort of wandered around (the "petting" part). What they failed to mention in the commercials was the "pooping" part. The animals that were just roaming around – the deer, goats and antelope-looking things – basically just let loose wherever they were standing, so it was almost inevitable that the first thing I did was step in a big pile of animal crap. I am not sure exactly what brand it was, I only know that it stunk. It was embedded deeply into the soles of my high-tops, and the smell of it made me want to puke. We sat down on a bench while my mother looked around for a stick to clean my shoe.

Behind a fence about 50 feet away, we could see a group of half-grown, domesticated deer surrounding some other little kid hapless enough to have flashed his crackers, and they were busy tearing him apart. His arms were in the air, crackers in each fist, and he must have had some extras in his pockets because they were basically undressing him where he stood. He wasn't tall enough to prevent the deer from taking his crackers, since they had already become adept at standing on their hind legs to get food, and he had a pan-icked look on his face like he thought he was going to die. His mother was just laughing and taking pictures. I don't think my mother noticed that this was happening, but The Snitch and Houdini sure noticed, and they didn't look too sure about it.

After my shoe was mostly clean, my mother stood us in a row and gave us the ground rules – one quarter of a cracker at a time, always place the cracker flat on your palm and let the animal take it so you don't get your fingers bit-ten, and crackers were expensive so we would only get one more batch each and that would be it. Houdini was pretty small yet, so my mother kept his crackers, planning to dole out small pieces as he requested them. She pointed her finger at me and said, "Johnny, you keep an eye on your brother."

Then she added the words I hated to hear more than anything in my young life.

"And hold his hand so you don't get separated."

"But Mom!" I whined, "I hate – "

"Don't you 'But Mom' me," she said. "You hold his hand this instant or we're going to turn around and go home."

As you can see by the expression on my face, the hand-holding requirement didn't go over so well. Also, nice ears.

I sighed, and grabbed one of his hands. Maybe a little harder than I needed to, but that wasn't my fault.

We walked past all the souvenir stores, the food court and the lockers and bathrooms, and finally, after what seemed like an hour, we reached some actual live animals.

"Get your crackers ready," my mother said, turning toward us. Suddenly, she noticed something. "Snitch, where are your crackers? How could you possibly lose them already? Did you drop them somewhere?"

"No," he replied.

"Did you give them to an animal?" she asked.

"No," he replied again.

"Well then, what happened to them?" she asked, exasperated.

"I ate them," he said, looking down at his feet.

My mother acted like he had just swallowed a cup of Drano.

"You ATE them? YOU ATE THEM?" she screamed, getting more agitated by the second. She grabbed him and told him to open his mouth. He did so, and it was quite empty. "You ate ALL of them? What in God's name were you thinking? They were for the animals!"

"I didn't know they were for the animals," he said. "I thought they were a snack."

She immediately tracked down someone on the staff, and frantically explained that her kid had just eaten a big stack of the animal crackers. He laughed and said it happens all the time, and told her not to worry about it. That seemed to calm her down. She walked us back to the cracker place, fished some more money out of her purse, and another stack appeared.

"Don't eat them this time," she warned, as she handed them to Snitch.

"I won't," he replied. "They weren't very good, anyway."

Here's something you have to know about my brother The Snitch. He was a vacuum cleaner for food since the moment he was born. To this day, I think the reason I eat so fast is because growing up, we all had to try to get our share before The Snitch got to it, otherwise there would be nothing left. That went for snacks, too. If you wanted peanut butter and jelly, or potato chips, or even a chocolate chip cookie, you would have to hide them, otherwise there'd be none left when you went to get one. My mother was constantly finding food stashed all over the place.

One trick Houdini and I used for a while, at least until he got wise to it, was to wrap whatever it was we wanted to hide in tin foil, and then tape a little piece of paper on it that said "Dog." My mother always used to save scraps for the dog, and they would end up in the fridge or freezer with a little tag on them so my father would know he wasn't supposed to eat it. The hardest part was learning how to write "Dog" in my mother's handwriting, but luckily it was a short word so it didn't take long to master.

With that, we walked toward our first batch of animals, a group of about five or six spotted fawns. They were small enough so we didn't get knocked over, but still – we were instantly mobbed, and it was pretty fun and a little scary getting poked and prodded and licked and nibbled by a whole group of fawns at the same time. (I know that sounds dirty, but it isn't.) Nobody was bitten, although the baby deer were even trying to poke their heads into my mother's purse in the hopes of stealing more crackers.

The Snitch wanted to go see the elephants, so we headed over to the elephant pen. The elephants were in the process of getting hosed down because it was hotter than hell, and there was a river of smelly water running out from under the chain link fence. It looked like they used something akin to a fire hose to douse them, because it seemed to be much more water than what you would get out of a normal faucet. The elephants were pretty impressive and while my mother, The Snitch and I were watching them move around in their slow, yet graceful way, Houdini managed to find one of the water spigots attached to a fence post and turn it on. A blast of water hit him full-force in the chest. He was so surprised he fell right on his butt and started crying, even as the water continued to shoot out of the faucet at roughly 1600 psi. My mother quickly turned the faucet off, but by that time he was soaked from head to toe, sitting in filthy elephant runoff, and had flies buzzing around him. As you can imagine, my mother was very pleased.

That was one thing they left out of the brochures. The incredible number of flies all over everything. When you have 1,000 acres of animals, that are, literally, full of shit, that's a lot of manure to deal with. When you figure the surface area of an average-sized pile of deer crap can accommodate about 300 flies (yes, I've done studies) you can imagine what the fly situation at this place was like. I don't doubt that they were hosing that place down with DDT at night, but it was still almost unbearable.

She stood him up, got him to stop crying, brushed the mud and worse-than-mud off him as best she could, and soldiered on. I remember seeing the crocodiles, and I remember seeing the exotic birds and the ant-eaters, and of course the snakes and lizards, but I couldn't tell you what else was there. I remember eating lunch and constantly trying to keep the flies off my food, but as far as other non-reptilian animals go, it was all typical zoo-type stuff and boring to me.

I do, however, remember the llamas. Or rather, one *particular* llama.

We went to the llama pen and my mother still had the last of Houdini's crackers in her purse. For some reason, she always thought llamas were fascinating, and she wanted to feed one. She walked up to the llama pen and held out a cracker to the first llama that seemed interested. The llama took one look at my mother and something very bad happened.

The llama put its ears back, made a weird noise deep in its throat, and proceeded to blast the entire contents of its stomach directly into my mother's face.

If you know about llamas, you know they spit. But saying "llamas spit" is like saying "Katrina caused a little flooding." Llamas don't really spit. Llamas projectile vomit.

She was so shocked she just stood there for a second, holding out her cracker, covered from head to waist in dripping, green, half-digested slime that used to be hay and crackers. She dry-heaved a few times, and I thought she was going to lose it, but she managed to hold herself together. And dear God, the *stench*.

196

She took a tissue from her purse and wiped the warm slime away from her eyes and mouth, and then cleaned herself up as best she could. It was right about then that The Snitch had just about all he could take, and he added to the party by upchucking his breakfast crackers and his undigested lunch all over the place.

She was done. Defeated. Beat down. We had been there for maybe a total of four or five hours, and we wanted to go home. We were shit-covered, slime-covered, puke covered, muddy, sick and tired. We hoofed it back to the car in the steamy heat and piled in. It was a very quiet and not particularly pleasant smelling ride home.

I think the llama incident is the only reason I even remember that particular visit. We went back a few more times over the years, although those trips were less eventful, and I only have the vaguest memories of them.

We stayed pretty far away from the llama pen, though, so that could be why.

The Butterfly Effect

In the late spring and early summer, my mother's interest in landscaping became all-encompassing. Spreading mulch, planting flowers, poisoning weeds and killing grubs became her passion. She loved flowers, and every year she would buy so many flats of flowers the garage floor would be covered with them the week before the planting and my father would have to park outside. In addition to the normal sort of planting that went on, there was always one wild goose chase. It was different every year. I called it The Quest.

The Quest was a name I made up for her incessant search for something unique for her landscaping. It had to be something nobody else had, and it was even better if it were something free.

As an example, for years we had something called a mimosa tree in our back yard. For those of you a few hours south or southeast of where I grew up, you probably see these things all over the place. They are a beautiful flowering tree my mother fell in love with and decided that she wanted.

The only problem is that nature did not intend for mimosa trees to grow in upstate New York. It's too cold, and they die. That's just the way things are. That little fact didn't stop her from trying, though. On our annual trip to the Jersey shore, she dug one up, brought it home and planted it in the back yard next to the pool. She did everything short of building a heated greenhouse around this thing to keep it alive. Believe it or not, she was remarkably successful. Every fall she would wrap the tree, put a chicken wire cage around it and fill it with leaves for insulation. This was apparently enough to keep the roots from dying, and even though the dead branches had to be cut back every year, we had it for probably a decade. It never did well enough to flower, and while disappointed, she was proud of it anyway. At some point it got too big for chicken wire and a particularly harsh winter ended the grand experiment. I guess you can't fight Mother Nature, although my own mother would have argued that point.

The Quest could get you in trouble with the law on occasion.

How? Well, "free" means different things to different people, and there's a fine line between "free" and "free, as long as nobody cares or you don't get caught."

When I was probably 15 or so, my mother and I were driving back from the store one day. Suddenly, my mother shouted what sounded to me like, "Lou Pins! There's Lou Pins!" I didn't know who this Lou guy was, but before I knew it we were pulled over on the shoulder of the highway, 15 minutes from our house. My mother got out of the car and ran a short way up a hill and examined some small, blue flowers growing in the sandy soil near a scrub pine. The next thing I know, my mother is back in the car. "We have to go get some pots and a shovel," she said excitedly. "Those are lupines growing right there on the side of the road."

That was my introduction to Lupinus perennis. Wild blue lupines. The way my mother was acting, I figured these flowers had to be so valuable they could probably be used as currency in a post-apocalyptic world. I went along for the ride. The Quest was not to be denied.

Thirty minutes later, we were back at the hill, and my mother was furiously filling pots and buckets with the bright blue flowering plants. She had about ten pots full, and was in the process of placing them in the trunk when the police car rolled up behind us, flashed its siren and lights briefly, then stopped.

The DEC officer got out of the car and walked up to us. "Ma'am, can I ask what you're doing?" he said.

"We're just collecting some wild flowers, officer. We saw them growing here on the side of the road," my mother replied.

"Are you aware that this is state land, and it's illegal to remove plants from state land without a permit?" he asked.

"Um, no, I wasn't aware of that," my mother said.

"And those plants you're digging up? Do you have any idea what they are?"

"Yes, officer, they're lupines." my mother said.

"Those are wild blue lupines, and they're an endangered plant species in New York," he said.

"Ah, I didn't know that."

This was getting better and better. Damn this cop and his bottomless botanical knowledge. I wondered if my mom would forgive me if I just bolted for the woods.

He continued. "Those flowers are the sole food source for the Karner Blue butterfly caterpillar, which is *also* endangered."

Entomology, too?

At that point I was thinking about our single phone call, because I was sure my dad would be bailing us out.

So far, we had removed plants from state land – strike one. The plants we had dug up were *endangered* plants – strike two. The endangered plants were the *sole food source* for an endangered butterfly.

Steeeeee-rike three, and that's the game. I felt like we were being busted for running meth across state lines.

My mother explained to the cop that she had no idea what she did was illegal; the cop said ignorance of the law is no excuse. He then explained about the various fines for just about all of our activities that day, and then after he had scared us, he took pity on us. Instead of tossing us in the back of his cruiser and impounding our car, he simply instructed us to immediately replant what we had removed, and promise to never do it again. We complied with both requests and made our way home without further incident.

Wasted time and effort aside, we had a good story for the supper table that night. My father just shook his head, knowing that only my mother could get herself in so much trouble so quickly with nothing but a shovel and her love of brightly colored flowers.

From that day on, my father let my mother buy pretty much whatever she wanted for the yearly landscaping. I think he figured it was probably cheaper than hiring a lawyer.

Thank You for Being a Friend

You Might Not Want to Hang Out With Me.

My childhood friend The Slug had his first brain tumor operation over a decade ago. I remember sitting there with him after they told him they were going to open up his head. "The doctor told me I might have some memory loss," he told me. "They also said I might have some personality changes."

"Don't worry," I replied. "If you still remember who I am when you wake up, I'll let you know if you're more of an asshole."

That's the sort of friendship we had. Constantly busting each other's chops. Unfortunately, three years ago the tumor grew back, and this time it was cancerous. He died on Oct 11th, 2007. We hadn't kept in touch as much as we probably could have, and a lot of that was my fault. He'd call, and I'll admit that sometimes I screened – and then put off calling him back. Other times I'd pick up and we'd chat, catch up a little, talk about getting together and then never end up doing it.

We had known each other since the seventh grade, but over the years our lives took drastically different paths. I found that we didn't have much in common any more, once you got past the shared memories of our childhood. It was a sad realization, but sometimes that's just the way life happens.

He was sometimes difficult to be around, and that was another part of it. His situation wasn't all that happy, and somewhere along the line I think he became bitter because life had short-changed him. Some of it was his own fault, to be sure, but a lot of it wasn't. I can't say I blame him. God knows he dealt with his health issues better than I would have, had it been me.

I probably wasn't as good a friend to him as I could have been, and I do regret that. Sometimes that realization comes too late and there's not much you can do about it except look around at the other people in your life and try not to let the same thing happen with them.

Those of you who have read my blog know that I also lost my best friend, Paul, in April of last year to a heart attack. That was a life-changing event for me (and for him.) We had been friends since the age of 13, and we still got together at least once a week. In October of 2010, I dumped his ashes at one of our favorite camping spots in the Adirondacks. He'd laugh if he knew he made his last backpacking trip in an old Sarah Lee Honey Roasted Ham container.

After his funeral, I found myself wondering whether it's better to just drop dead in your tracks like he did, or linger a few weeks in the hospital like The Slug, knowing there's nothing anyone can do. If you just drop dead, it's easy for *you*, but hard for everyone else. If you linger, then it's just hard on everyone. I guess in the latter instance, at least you get to say goodbye, but still – it's like a final reminder of all that you're being forced to give up. I don't know. I'm guessing nobody knows, really.

The Slug got to see his two boys one last time, so there's that. I hope that whichever option he thought was best is the one he got. He deserved that much, at least.

All that said, I think the best way I can honor their lives and our friendship is to tell you some of our stories. They both loved to laugh and loved to reminisce, so I'm going to tell you a few tales that will hopefully let you do the first and me do the second.

Knockin' on Heaven's Door

When I was 13, The Slug lived on a farm. He wasn't a farmer, nor were any of his family farmers – they just happened to live in an old farmhouse that had been converted to apartments. There was a lot to do on the farm, and I liked to go over there. Mostly this was because at my house, my mother always made it her business to know what we were up to. When I went to his house, we were pretty much unsupervised the entire time. The farm was the kind of place where you could get killed pretty easily if you weren't careful.

Case in point: There was a dilapidated barn that had a couple of old basketball hoops nailed to the opposite walls on the upper level, and you were fine as long as you remembered to avoid the *gaping three-foot-wide hole* in the middle of the floor during the full-court press.

Most of the other things we did to amuse ourselves revolved around dares of one sort or another. These dares always started out with a simple idea that rapidly went south. Here's an example:

Me: "Hey, did you ever touch the electric fence?"

Slug: "Yeah, you can't hold onto it for very long. It's pretty strong."

Me: "What's your longest time?"

Slug: "I dunno. 20 seconds, maybe."

Me: "I dare you to touch it now."

Slug: "No way. It rained this morning. The ground is soaked."

Me: "I'll bet I can hold onto it longer than you."

Slug: "What'll you bet?"

Me: "Whoever loses has to kiss elephant girl."

Slug: "OK, on the count of three. one…two…three…GRAB!"

Then after about ten seconds of us jerking around like epileptic marionettes – and a best-two-out-of-three – we would decide that nobody could really be expected to kiss elephant girl.

Me: "Man, that hurts."

Slug: "Yeah, my arm is killing me."

A pause.

Me: "You ever pee on it?"

You get the idea. But just in case you don't, I offer these other examples of farm-related dare-contests:

The "touch the bull on the ass" dare. This dare was dangerous. No two ways about it. This involved:

- Jumping the fence into the bull's field.

- Sneaking up on him from behind.

- Getting about halfway there before the bull noticed you.

- Running madly in the opposite direction as fast as you could, zig-zagging to avoid the giant cow pies that were pretty much every-where, while your friend shouted out play-by-play "how-close-are-the-bull's-horns-to-your-ass" commentary at the top of his lungs.

The "visit the cow graveyard" dare. There was a certain section way in the back of the field where the farmer just dragged the dead cows and left them to rot. The stench was a physical thing, like getting hit in the face with a wet towel, and it got on you and stuck in a very similar way. The object of the game here was simple: The first person who puked lost. If neither of you puked, then the object of the game was to see who could "bang the drum." And by this I mean throwing rocks at the thin, dry skin stretched over the skeletal rib cages of the oldest ones, in order to get that classic John Bonham bass drum sound to ring forth.

Anyway, that was a very long and drawn out way of saying we didn't have a lot of supervision.

While lack of supervision wasn't a problem for us, there *was* something else we didn't have a lot of, and that was a real shame, since this something else went hand-in-hand with being unsupervised. That something was quality porn.

As a couple of red-blooded, American 13-year-olds, our porn search was pretty much unending. No matter what we were doing, there was always some sub-conscious mental process working on how to get porn. Waking, sleeping, it didn't matter. It was a perpetual subroutine stuck in an infinite loop, and it pretty much governed our lives.

Why was it so hard to get porn, you ask? Well, we couldn't buy it, because we had no money, and besides, the store owners wouldn't sell it to us. We couldn't steal it, because we were basically good kids, and were afraid of get-ting caught. My father never had any that I knew of, and Slug's father had some, but he hid it pretty well and we could never reliably find it. Remember, as hard as it is to believe, this was before the internet put hardcore porn just a few clicks away. It was also a time when sex education classes didn't start until high school, as opposed to now, when they are practically taught in utero. This was the biggest mystery on the face of the earth to us. *Sex.* What it was. What girls looked like naked. How to *do it*, and what, exactly, *it* was. This was big stuff. Unless you had a generous older brother (and neither of us did), you were pretty much out of luck.

Every once in a while we would find the odd soggy, mildewed *Playboy* or *Penthouse* magazine in the woods. If the inside pages weren't too badly deteriorated, we'd rip out the pictures and put them in plastic baggies and hide them in the barn or bury them in the woods. We treated them like treasure.

We were, for all intents and purposes, Pirates of Porn.

This all changed when Slug happened to notice his next door neighbor opening his mail. There was a certain magazine-sized package in a black plastic wrapper that showed up every month, and Slug had caught a glimpse when his neighbor was opening it one day.

He was pretty sure that porn was actually being delivered to within 30 feet of his house.

He shared this news with me, but neither of us could figure out a way to get it. This was the closest we had ever been to fresh-off-the-press porn, and we were obsessed. We thought about stealing his mail, but we could never time the delivery right. Besides, it's not like he wouldn't miss it. And we were pretty sure that stealing mail was a federal crime, even if it was just a skin mag.

After coming up with nothing plausible, we forgot about it for a bit, and just let the subroutine loop.

One other game we used to play on the farm was called man hunt. Sometimes it involved a bb-gun, but sometimes it was just more of an elaborate game of hide and seek. There were plenty of places to hide and explore and we knew all of them. During one game, we were running around in the basement where the storage units were, and Slug's next-door neighbor happened to be down there putting some stuff away. The storage units were nothing more than a bunch of separated areas where everyone stored their off-season junk, but Slug's next-door neighbor had an actual room with a padlock on it.

We weren't really supposed to be down there, but for the most part, nobody cared. Slug's neighbor snapped his padlock on the clasp, nodded to us, and then was gone. I looked at Slug, and he was standing shock-still, staring at the door.

"What?" I asked.

"Did you see that?" he said, dazed.

"See what? I didn't see anything," I said.

"What he had under his arm. What he put in the room," Slug said, whispering like he was afraid he would be overheard.

"No, what was it?" I asked.

"A *stack* of Playboys," he said with awe. "Tons of 'em."

"No way," I said under my breath.

We stood there for a while, both of our porn-acquisition programs suddenly running full speed in the foreground, spiking our CPUs to 100%.

Finally, my brain processed something and spit it out.

"We could take the door off its hinges," I suggested.

"Duh. The door opens in," Slug said, quickly dismissing that idea.

Bing! Another idea popped out. "We could try to pick the lock," I said.

"It's a Master lock," he said, annoyed. "You can shoot a bullet through those and they won't open."

Then we both saw it at the same time. It was like a sunbeam from heaven had reached down and illuminated the padlock in a golden light.

The person who had installed the padlock clasp on the door hadn't done it correctly. You're supposed to install the clasp so the hinge folds back on itself, covering the screws. This installer however, was apparently no carpenter, because the screws holding the clasp to the door were just sitting there in plain sight.

We waited until the next day, and when Slug's neighbor went to work, we did too. We headed directly to the storage basement with a screwdriver and a flashlight.

Four screws later, the latch fell to the side, the dangling padlock still connected to the door frame.

The Slug pushed open the door and we walked in. He stopped dead in his tracks, and I practically walked into him. We looked around, and I don't think either of us could breathe.

We were surrounded by shelves full of indexed and labeled boxes, and in these boxes sat the biggest collection of T&A we had ever seen. Ten full years of *Playboy* magazines. A five year run of *Penthouse*. Uncountable copies of *Club, Swank* and *Hustler*. It was all there, alphabetized and cataloged by issue and year.

It was porn heaven, and we felt like gods.

We immediately set to work. We took one back issue from each box, and got out of there as fast as humanly possible. We put the screws back in the padlock clasp, and then went to a different area of the basement where someone was storing some old furniture and appliances. We stuck the balance of the magazines in the bottom drawer of an old electric oven, and sat down to peruse our ill-gotten treasure. It was an unforgettable moment.

For the next three months, we overloaded on porn. We would sit down there for hours, reading the articles, looking at pictures and swapping the mags when we were done. Sometimes, we wouldn't say two words to each other from the minute my mother dropped me off to the time she picked me up. We would read porn for six hours straight, break in again, put the old mags back, get new ones, and read for four more hours. Basically, we were addicted to crack, except it was a different sort of crack, we had free access to our drug of choice and it didn't cost us a cent. *Penthouse Forum* ruled my young world, and my head was exploding with forbidden knowledge. The only drawback was walking around with a stainless steel rod in my pants 24 hours a day.

As all good things must, it finally came to an end.

One day we went down to the basement and our oven stash was missing. We went over to porn heaven and there was a new clasp on the door – installed correctly.

So that was it for us. I don't know if he ever figured out exactly who it was who had been breaking in, but we never got in trouble for it. I suppose it wouldn't be the easiest thing to walk over to your neighbor's house and accuse their kids of raiding your gigantic porn stash.

We went cold turkey, since we had no choice. From skin-feast to skin-famine, from boob-rich to boob-poor, From enjoying the finest close-up glossy renditions of beautiful women-parts of all shapes and sizes and colors, to damp, mildewed, faded pictures that had been rained on for a week before we found them.

It just wasn't the same. After a while, we didn't even bother to pick them up anymore. We had dined at the table of Kings, and were now left to eat whatever rats we could catch in the castle walls. We went back to taunting the bull, but our hearts weren't in it. We were haunted by the ghost of porno past, and it would take more than an angry bull to fill that void.

We learned a lot about the ways of the world that summer, and I'll never forget it. I'm sure much of it was inaccurate and sexist, but goddammit, it was fun while it lasted.

Cow Pasture Golf Should be a Real Sport

When The Slug and I were about 15, we became obsessed with golf. I'm not sure exactly why – neither of us had parents who golfed on a regular basis. My grandfather was a really good golfer, and he'd take me out to the sand pit and we'd hit a bucket of balls every once in a while, but that was it.

I think it started when we found the old golf clubs in the barn. There was a driver, a three iron, a nine iron and a putter. What more do you need, right? We pulled them out, dusted them off and started hitting the old golf balls that were tucked in the pocket of the cracked leather bag. We had no idea what the hell we were doing, and we probably looked like a couple of complete idiots out there in the field, but eventually we began making contact. We even started reading books on how to golf.

Geeks, I know. But since the porn dried up, this was what we were reduced to.

This golf obsession led to one of the worst ideas we ever had, at least in retrospect. We didn't have enough money to play real golf, so we set up our own 'golf course' in the cow pasture. We used wooden stakes and rags as flag pins. It was a little three-hole course – out over the stream to the first hole, left across the field to the second hole, and then back across the stream to the last hole. That one was tricky because you were hitting back towards the buildings. Normally not a problem because...well, because we sucked, but occasionally dangerous for that exact reason.

I'm sure all this sounds pretty boring, and really, *playing* golf is only one step up on the boredom scale from watching it on TV, but our game had more interesting hazards. The first thing we had to do, of course, was to create The Rules.

The Rules didn't necessarily have anything to do with regulation golf rules. The rules were ours, and were as follows:

(1) If you hit a cow, you can subtract a stroke, because that's just awesome. (Cows can run. Way faster than you. Just so you know.)

(2) The fox hole and surrounding area is off-limits (We fully believed the old wives' tale that a fox seen during the day was rabid. Mulligans were definitely allowed in this instance.)

(3) If the farmer comes out and starts yelling at you because you hit the barn by mistake or a cow on purpose, whoever is ahead at the time wins.

(4) Play it where it lies. If the other guy catches you moving your ball, you lose.

That last one actually *is* a golf rule of sorts. It might just be a penalty and not cost you the game, but there is no pushing, prodding, tapping or scooping of the ball allowed. In friendly play, you bend this rule all the time. Not us. You play it where it lies, no matter what. That was our single most important rule, and also the most potentially disgusting.

Why? Because, as all good cow pastures are, this pasture was full of cows. And because it was full of cows, it was also full of that particular by-product of cows – namely, cow shit.

Very, very *large amounts* of cow shit.

Normally, this is not necessarily a *bad* thing, unless you happen to be walking in the field playing golf. Or if you happen to be a cow. In the latter case, it can be a bummer because you spend most of your day scrounging around for the *good* grass, by which I mean the grass you and the rest of your friends haven't crapped on. And these were meat cows, not milk cows. I'm not sure if that makes any difference in the consistency of their crap, but these cows seemed to exclusively drop giant loads of splashy brown custard. Maybe there's some cow expert out there who can tell me.

The same situation that makes grazing difficult also makes golfing difficult, especially with rule number four in full-force. Remarkably, we managed to play many, many holes of golf with no issues other than the normal ones of losing balls in the mud, in the stream and in the pond – and of course, the relatively un-normal ones of losing balls near the fox hole, hitting the barn or house, or having to poke a cow in the ass with a golf club in order to take the next shot.

Then one day it happened. The Slug teed up, hit a great drive about 150 yards, and scored a direct hit into a fresh pile. I saw the splash and burst out laughing. He just shook his head and said, "Awww, man. That's gross." I hit next, and my ball landed probably ten feet short of where his was. As we walked out, I reminded him of the rule. "Play it where it lies," I said. He looked at me in disbelief.

"It landed in a fresh pile of *cow shit,*" he said, as if I hadn't understood the ramifications of the splash.

"Yeah I know," I replied, grinning evilly. "And if you don't follow the rules, you lose." We were friends, but we were also pretty competitive. We had five bucks riding on best two out of three, and I had won the first round.

We jumped the stream, dodging the random piles of cow crap until we came to his ball. The stench was fearsome. His ball had hit and stuck, spraying cow crap three feet in all directions, forming a perfect crater around his ball.

210

"No way," he said. "I'm not getting near that mess."

"Then you lose, and that's best two out of three, and you owe me five bucks. Play it where it lies, or don't play it and pay up."

"You suck," he said.

"Yeah, I know. I'm hitting first. Something here stinks." I said.

My ball was resting on a clump of grass, so I got a good piece of it, and it sailed over the second flag and into the woods on the edge of the field. "Dammit!," I muttered.

"Serves you right," he said, walking gingerly toward his ball. "This is disgusting."

I couldn't help laughing at him. It looked like he was tip-toeing through a minefield.

I stood a safe distance away and watched him get ready to take his shot. His stance was far too wide, as a result of trying to keep his sneakers out of the splash zone. I expected him to swing gingerly, just to pop the ball clear of the mess, and take the stroke.

But he didn't.

In spite of his wide stance, he swung like Tiger Woods and connected with the ball. He also connected with about a half-pound of wet cow shit that sprayed everywhere. His shoes, his shirt, his hair, his pants – everywhere. I was laughing so hard, I was crying. Neither of us saw where his ball went.

He stood there for a second, arms out, looking down at his shit-covered shirt. Then before I could comprehend what was happening, he chopped down hard with the club, only this time it was in my direction. Before I could move, a spray of cow shit hit me, pretty much covering me from my armpits to my feet. I spotted a nearby pie and swung into it, spraying him again. By that time, we were both laughing hysterically, swinging shit-laden golf clubs at each other, frantically searching for fresh piles to send flying in each other's general direction. Yes, it was disgusting. Yes, the stench made us gag, but goddammit we never laughed so hard in our lives.

Eventually, we called a truce and then slogged back to his house. We hosed ourselves off outside as best we could, then went in to get some lunch. Luckily his mother wasn't home. He gave me a dry T-shirt and pair of jeans, and we dropped all the disgusting clothes into the washing machine. Then we sat down in the kitchen and made a couple of triple-decker peanut butter and jelly sandwiches. Tri-D PBJ's, we called them.

I think that was the last time we played cow pasture golf. Both of us got jobs at Star Market the following summer, and when we golfed we did it on a real golf course. Eventually, we even got pretty good at it.

We never forgot our humble beginnings though. From that day on, every time either of us picked up a nine iron we couldn't help but laugh to ourselves.

I'm not sure what happens to you when you die, but if golf is involved, I hope it's the regular kind.

Rocket Boys

When The Slug and I were growing up, we had a fascination with models of all sorts. Cars, trucks, tanks, planes, monsters, dinosaurs, you name it. Sometimes we'd set up a table in my parent's basement and work on them together.

The Slug was a perfectionist, and his attention to detail was insane. At one point, he told me he wanted to work as a model maker professionally, creating realistic miniature sets for the movies. He probably could have – he was that good. You couldn't see the seams on any of his models – he would sand and fill and prime and spray the thing like it was a real car. His engines had spark plug wires and oil stains. His tires had white letters. His dashboards had readable gauges.

No matter what type of model he was currently into, eventually they all came down to the same point – he would get bored with them and start customizing. He'd swap engines, he'd cut holes in car hoods and add scoops, he'd tub wheel wells and shorten rear ends to add slicks. It was like an episode of "Pimp My Ride" but in 1:24 scale. When he was done, you couldn't tell that it wasn't supposed to be that way.

In the meantime, I would be across the table trying to not glue the left half of a Chevy big block to the side of my face.

Soon, however, the static models lost their appeal. Even though they were still cool to look at and work on, the Slug wanted something that moved. We would look wistfully through the catalog of radio controlled cars and airplanes that he found somewhere, knowing that we'd never have enough money to own one. We were especially enamored of the Corsairs, since we were both huge fans of a new TV show called *Baa Baa Black Sheep.*

One day he called and asked me if I could come over because he wanted to show me something. My mom dropped me off, and when I walked into his room he was in the final stages of applying fins to a sleek black rocket that stood about two feet high. When I found out that the rocket would actually launch and come down on a parachute, I went out and bought my own rocket kit the next day. I made him promise that he wouldn't launch his until I finished mine. He didn't have a problem with that, since he still needed to fit up the nose cone and clear-coat his rocket again.

While it wasn't the neatest job, I had my entire rocket built in about three hours. I painted it gloss white, because that was the paint I had. I didn't bother with the U.S.A. stickers or anything else. It looked like a vibrator with fins. I didn't care. It was done and ready to fly.

The following weekend, we took them out to the cow field and set up the launch pad. We evaluated the wind-speed and direction, and angled the launch pad so that it would head slightly into the wind, the theory being that when the parachute deployed the rocket would drift back to us. He launched his first. Neither of us knew what to expect, since we had never launched a rocket before. We stuck the igniter into the back of the rocket, played out the wire and had a countdown from ten. We got to one, then we yelled "IGNI-TION!" and he hit the button.

Nothing happened.

He hit the button again.

Still nothing.

"Let me check it," I said and took three steps toward the rocket. I was just about to reach down to pick it up when all hell broke loose. The engine ignited, the rocket took off screaming into the sky and I fell on my ass as a cloud of dense white smoke billowed around me. The Slug let out a whoop behind me.

I looked up and saw that the nose cone had ejected and the chute had popped. I couldn't believe how high it was. It drifted back to us like we planned, then over our heads and past us and into the cow pasture. The Slug was laughing at me.

"You gotta hold the button in," he said. "You can't just push it and let it go. Sorry about that."

I could tell by his continuing fits of laughter that he really wasn't.

I stood up and brushed myself off. "Dick," I said, and punched him in the shoulder.

We ran out and got his rocket, and then came back to the launch site. When we launched mine, we knew what to expect. We set it up the same way, only this time we started from three. When I got to the end of the countdown, I pushed the ignition button and held it in. There was a loud WHOOOOOOSH as the rocket disappeared into the sky. And I mean that literally. It disappeared. No chute, no nose-cone ejection, no nothing. Just a smoke trail and the ringing in our ears. It was gone forever and we knew it.

"If you start laughing again, you're dead meat," I said.

After that, I did build more rockets and have many successful launches and – more importantly – recoveries. But as always, The Slug grew bored with it. There was something about vertical flight that just didn't do it for him. He wanted horizontal flight. That meant planes.

214

And obviously, given our current stock of spare parts, that meant Rocket Planes.

In the mid 1970's, the military came out with a new fighter jet called the F-15 Eagle that the Slug liked, and someone had given him a model of it for his birthday.

He hadn't built it yet, because he was mostly out of the "static model" phase, but sometimes kids move from one thing to another faster than their grandparents can keep track, and the gifts they receive can tend to lag a hobby or two behind.

He got the idea in his head to modify this model to take a pair of rocket engines, and I watched as he cut and sanded and melted and managed to make this model plane look like it was meant to be powered by rockets. He measured the jet engines and figured out that with just a little bit of modification, each one would hold a D-12 Estes rocket engine. He lined the body of the jet with tinfoil before he put it together and modified the cockpit and nose cone to pop off, so the chute could be deployed. He put so much time into this rocket plane that I don't think either of us really wanted to test it. Just looking at it and imagining that it might actually fly was almost more fun than launching it and having it be a complete failure.

Eventually, we decided it had to be done. The main sticking point was how to get both engines to fire simultaneously. There was no way we could get two igniters to go at the exact second when they were wired together, so we decided our best bet was to set up two launch buttons, one for me and one for him. We'd count down, then push the buttons simultaneously. Using fresh batteries, we figured that would be as close to exact as we could get. We waited for a day with almost no wind, and then set everything up.

We wanted to launch almost horizontally, but knew there was no way it could actually take off on its own, so we opted for about a 15-degree launch angle. We pointed it out into the cow pasture, just in case anything went wrong.

We had a piece of sheet metal set up as a back stop, and we used a straightened coat hanger as a launch guide. Once we had everything set, we checked the nose cone one more time, made sure the igniters were placed correctly and we played out the wire in preparation.

When we were set, we started the countdown. When we got to zero, we yelled "Now!" and slammed down our buttons.

I'm not exactly sure what went wrong. I only know that the thrust and burn time of a D-12 engine is not something to take lightly. Only one of the engines ignited, and when the plane came off the launch guide it immediately started spinning like a pinwheel. It went about six feet in the air, then came directly at us. We both dove out of the way, and the plane crashed into the ground right where we had been standing. It was well-made however, because it didn't fall apart on impact.

No, that would have been too easy.

Instead, it began cartwheeling madly around the field, bouncing end over end, starting a grass fire every time it touched down.

We were screaming at each other and running around in a 50 foot radius stomping out fires that seemed to be sprouting miraculously one after another. The plane finally came to rest, and a few seconds later when the ejection charge fired, the nose cone didn't pop free. Instead, the entire plane started burning furiously. When we were finally done putting out all the surrounding fires, we walked toward the ruined plane. It was burning with a greasy yellow flame and copious amounts of smelly black smoke. It was a molten mess.

We were looking around for something to put it out with – since neither one of us wanted to step on it – when the second engine ignited with a roar. We had completely forgotten about that one, and we both almost shit our pants right there. The engine case had burned through and the flame hit the solid fuel. The engine didn't have much more than melted plastic holding it in place at this point, so it took off like a bullet, spraying melted plastic and spinning and bouncing around the field. Luckily the grass was shorter there, so other than a few scorched areas, a huge cloud of white smoke, and a pile of melted slag that used to be an F-15, there wasn't much damage.

We talked about that F-15 for years. Even though we both outgrew rockets and models shortly after that, it was a good couple of summers. The funny thing is, every time we'd get talking and that story would come up, he'd get this look in his eyes. A look that said even after all these years, he was still trying to figure out a way to make it work.

I'd bet anyone reading this a hundred bucks that right up until the day he died, if I had suggested to him that we try it again, he would have been building that F-15 model the next day.

Whoosh.

The Lords of Brookshire.

Back in the days when the year was split into two seemingly equal amounts of time – the school year and summer – The Slug and I were always looking for something to do. Riding our bikes was OK, but not exactly thrilling. We spent a lot of time at the farm, but sometimes I couldn't go over there and he had to come over to my house, which was decidedly more boring. We didn't really have any video games like kids today, unless you count PONG, which was fun for about five minutes. (Kelso was wrong – even smaller paddles wouldn't have helped.) We had a basement with a ping pong table, but that was *inside*. Unlike the kids of today, we wanted to be outside whenever possible, but generally at my house that meant bikes or nothing. Boring.

That all changed when we got new skateboards. These weren't just any skateboards, and the reason they weren't just any skateboards is because of one thing:

Urethane wheels.

Why does that matter? Well, if you were riding a skateboard in the early seventies, you know. If not, I'll explain it to you.

Up until that point, our skateboards were made of narrow planks of wood and had rock-hard clay wheels with loose ball bearings. I am pretty sure the vibrations from these wheels permanently damaged my young brain. The combination of hard wheels, hard pavement and a stiff deck (deck, I said *deck*) meant that the whole contraption just...*buzzed* under you. Does anyone remember those old vibrating football games? Yeah, like that. It was like being electrocuted from the waist down.

Even so, we used to take turns pulling each other behind our bikes. First your feet would go numb, then your ankles, then your calves. Pretty soon you'd feel like you had pins and needles from your knees down, and your feet felt like blocks of stone. This was not a good situation to find yourself in given what inevitably happened next. One second you were holding on to a rope and being towed as fast as your friend could pull you, the next second one of your front wheels would hit a pebble, the board would stop dead, and suddenly you were trying to run at 20 miles an hour with brick feet.

If you planned for this, you had a shot of maybe getting in one or two good giant-steps before you fell on your face, so it was a good idea to at least try to head for some grass. If you *didn't* plan for this, it meant that at best, you were going to be picking gravel out of your palms and knees for two days – at worst, it meant a trip to the emergency room. This was the story of clay wheels, and it was not a happy one.

Enter urethane and sealed bearings. Urethane was like magic. Like rubber, but tougher, it allowed you to do two things – (1) go fast, and (2) go fast with control. You could slalom these boards, jump curbs, pull wheelies, you name it. The flexible fiberglass board in combination with these new, sticky soft wheels meant you had quite a bit of shock absorbency built right into the board, and the ride was incredibly smooth.

Those were the good things. There was an evil dark side, however, although we didn't recognize that fact until much later. Urethane gave you a false sense of security. It made you feel like you were better than you actually were.

In short, it made you feel invincible.

Right around the time we became invincible, they started re-paving our neighborhood. We couldn't believe it. It was a gift from the gods. A surface so smooth and blemish free it was like you were flying instead of riding. Both of these things conspired to convince us that we could tackle Brookshire Drive, a long, horrendously steep road that would take you 10 minutes to walk up and about 60 seconds to ride down. You had to slalom down this hill because if you didn't you would probably die.

We were never about the pipe or the park; in fact, we didn't even know those things existed. We were about one thing, and that one thing was speed. Well, two things, actually – speed and competition. So this of course meant that eventually, we'd be back to *one* thing again and that one thing was racing.

One day, after a successful slalom run down Brookshire, we were walking back up for the last run of the day before heading back to my house to grab some food. The Slug looked up at the hill and said thoughtfully, "I'll betcha we could just come straight down. "

"I don't know," I said. "It looks awfully steep. I almost got speed wobbles the last time, and I wasn't even going that fast."

"We'll tighten up our boards first," he said, taking his board wrench out of his pocket.

I was still skeptical.

"I'll bet you five bucks I beat you," he said, just to sweeten the pot.

"You're on," I said, looking up at the hill. I wasn't sure this was such a good idea, but there was no way I was going to wuss out.

We got to the top and tightened up our boards. I cranked down on mine so hard I don't think I could have turned if I had wanted to.

We were standing at the top, waiting for the last car to turn off Brookshire before we dropped in. I looked at The Slug. "You sure we want to do this?" I asked him.

"Hell yeah," he said, tucking his wrench into his pocket. "It'll be fun. Plus I'll have five bucks."

There was no limit on kicking off to gain as much initial speed as you could, and The Slug was faster than me to begin with. Luckily, I had the better board. I figured my only shot at winning would be if I could get ahead of him and stay there, since he was heavier than I was and if he got in front of me I'd never catch up.

"GO!" he yelled, and we kicked off. We were neck and neck going into the first drop, and by that time we had both feet on our boards, crouching low to cut down on our wind resistance. I was in the lead and wanted to keep it that way. I didn't look behind me to see how close The Slug was, but I could hear him coming up on my left. About half way down, the angle of the road changed and it got really steep, then leveled out for about 50 feet before dropping again. When we hit the first drop, The Slug pulled ahead of me, but I was keeping up. Still, I knew there was no chance I was going to catch him, and had already resigned myself to paying him five bucks. Suddenly, his board began wobbling from side to side and he came out of his crouch.

That was the last thing I saw before he disappeared behind me. I heard two giant steps as his sneakers hit the pavement – THWOP! THWOP! and then nothing.

I couldn't stop, I couldn't turn around. My board was too cranked down to turn quickly, so I did the only thing I could do – I headed for the side of the road toward the grass. I hit the edge and tumbled, rolling over and over on someone's front lawn. I stood up and looked behind me, then started running back up the hill toward The Slug, who was lying face down in the road.

Before I could get to him, he rolled over and picked himself up. He stood slowly, and I could tell he was hurt. The question was how badly. He limped toward me.

"HOLY CRAP!" I said. "Are you OK? What happened?"

"I think so," he said. "I got speed wobbles." He held out his hands.

His palms looked like hamburger. He pressed them against his T-shirt, leaving two red stains. "Nothing broken, I don't think," he said, slowly moving his fingers.

"How bad is my back?" he asked, turning around.

When he turned around I couldn't believe what I saw. "You don't want to know," I said.

I had thought his hands were bad, but apparently he had not only hit and rolled, he had skidded on his back first. His jeans and T-shirt were shredded – two giant, oval holes on either side of his spine, a thin strip of bloody cotton running down the center. There was almost nothing left of it. One of his back pockets was hanging off his pants, and his belt had torn itself free of the belt loops. He had scraped off a good portion of his back skin, too. I have no idea how he didn't crack his head wide open.

"My mother is going to kill me," he said, which was pretty funny, considering he almost accomplished that on his own.

"We'll go back to my house and fix you up. You can take one of my T-shirts. Your mother won't even know. "

We walked very slowly for a bit, then he stopped.

"What's the matter?" I asked.

"I don't know," he replied. "Something hurts on my ass."

"I'm not looking at your ass," I said.

"It's more like the back of my hip," he said, and pulled his jeans down a little and tried to look behind him.

I glanced over against my better judgment. The skateboard wrench he had stuffed in his back pocket had taken a quarter-sized chunk out of the fatty part of his hip. And the chunk was just...missing. I was looking into a pasty-yellow, gravel-lined hole in his skin.

"Oh man, that's gross!" I said.

He poked at it and said, "Yeah, it sorta is." Then he laughed.

"Man, that was fun," he said.

I couldn't believe it, but that's what he said. I thought about the sweet, smooth ride, and the feeling of all that air rushing by me as I sailed down the hill. Then I laughed, too.

"Yeah it really was," I agreed. "Well, more for me than you, but still."

We finally made back to my house, and got him "fixed up" to the best of our limited ability. It involved lots of hydrogen peroxide, folded up toilet paper and masking tape is all I'm saying.

Our mothers never did find out, although I don't know how that was even possible. I also don't know how he didn't end up with tetanus or something worse, considering all the foreign matter he had packed into his scraped hands and back. He had a dimpled scar on his hip for the rest of his life, and I'm sure he had gravel permanently embedded in his back, too.

I never got my money, but that was OK. I told him it was worth five bucks just to see a T-shirt shredded like that.

Tall Boys and Big Mouths

After I wrote that title, I realized it sounds like the name of a gay porno, but I'm leaving it.

Not too long ago, I was having a conversation with a friend of mine who has two sons around the ages of 15 and 17. In the course of the conversation, I asked him if either of them had come home drunk yet. He informed me that his kids didn't do that sort of thing, and that they knew better. So I sat him down and gently explained to him that Pamela Anderson's boobs aren't real.

I then told him that for the next few years, he will begin to notice a strange phenomenon. For some unknown reason, his Ketel One and Bombay Sapphire might start to taste a little weaker than he remembered. His top-shelf booze would seem watered down, almost as if, somehow, *water had been added.*

Breaking this news to him reminded me of a story. It's the story of the first time The Slug and I got mildly intoxicated before we were technically allowed to by law. We were 16 years old, and we both had just gotten our driver's licenses, but because of some screwy New York law, we weren't allowed to drive after nine p.m., unless it was to and from work or school or school functions. Today they call that a "junior license."

Since I had *my* parents, however, it wasn't nine p.m. for me – it was whenever it got dark. This wasn't bad in the middle of the summer when it didn't get dark until after nine, but it sucked when the days started getting shorter and I had to be back by seven. Suffice it to say I was home before sundown every single night that I wasn't working, with no exceptions. My parents even checked my work schedule. It was like my mother believed that if I drove after dark, I would be run off the road by teenage vampires with great hair and cool cars and then drained of my blood. The Slug, on the other hand, who had his own set of – shall we say – "less involved" parents, basically did whateverthefuck he wanted.

One summer night around nine, the phone rang. I picked it up, and The Slug said, "I'm on my way over. I gotta show you something."

"What is it?" I asked him. "You didn't put a third set of fog lights on your mom's car, did you?"

"I can't talk now," he said. "See you in 20 minutes." Before I could say anything else, he hung up. There was nothing left to do but wait.

About twenty minutes later, the doorbell rang and my mother let The Slug in the door. "Hello Michael. You shouldn't be driving after nine," she said.

He shrugged. "My parents don't care," he said. "Besides, I'm an excellent driver."

"That's not the point. It's against the law," my mother said.

"I'm on my way home from work," The Slug said, clearly lying.

My mother gave up her crusade and went back into the kitchen. I knew I would get the "you do realize that just because he does it, doesn't mean you're going to do it, too" speech later, but that was OK. That was later.

We threw a frozen pizza in the oven, then went into the family room, turned on the television and opened a couple of Mountain Dews.

"So what was so important that you had to come over and show me?" I asked him.

"Come out to my car for a second," he said, grinning.

"It's more fog lights isn't it?" I said, as we were walking out to his car. "Jesus, your mother is going to kill you. Her car already looks like a city snow plow."

"No, jerk off, it's not fog lights," he replied. "Check this out."

He opened the passenger side door and there was something on the seat covered with his sweatshirt. He pulled up the corner of the sweatshirt and re-vealed a six pack of these:

Six hand grenades. Six barrels of beer on the seat. A six of Mickey's Big Mouth. Malt liquor, baby.

"Holy crap!" I said. "Where'd you get those?"

"My father bought a shitload of it on sale and I just took one out from the bottom case. If he no-tices he'll just blame my brother anyway."

"So...what? Are you planning on us drinking it here? How? In case you haven't noticed, my par-ents are home."

"That's easy. Tell'em I'm staying over night. I'll call my mother and tell her the same thing. She doesn't need the car until tomorrow afternoon anyway – she's working nights this week. After they go to bed we'll sneak it in and drink it."

We went back inside, and by that time the pizza was done. We brought it into the family room, closed the sliding glass door between the family room and kitchen, and turned up the volume on *Don Kirshner's Rock Concert*.

After we ate, we basically just sat there nursing our Mountain Dews and waiting for my parents to go to bed. (A bunch of years later, we'd sit in that same room pretty much every Friday night and drink way too much Genesee Cream Ale [we called them "Genny Screamers" for obvious reasons] and wait for the new Whitesnake video to come on. What? Can you blame us? Tawny Kitaen was hot. Too bad she's a shoe-throwing bag of crazy now.)

At any rate, I told my parents that The Slug was staying over, and eventually, they wandered off to bed. I was still paranoid about bringing the beers in, because my father had a tendency to roam the house at all hours of the night. It wasn't uncommon to be watching TV and suddenly see him standing at the kitchen counter in his tighty-whities at three a.m. making a peanut butter and margarine sandwich. Yeah, I know. Don't ask. That habit of his would cost me a girlfriend later in my life.

Since the paranoia won out, I came up with the bright idea of us going outside and drinking the Mickey's while sitting in The Slug's car. We slipped out the back, and took the dome light out of the car so we could leave the doors slightly ajar and make it easier to get out to pee without making noise. By that time, the beer was only slightly cooler than room temperature, but we didn't care. It was the first time either one of us had ingested more than a single bottle of beer, and we wanted to know what all the fuss was about. We chugged the first one.

Nothing.

So we chugged a second one. That's the good thing about the Bigmouth. It's like drinking beer out of a glass. Actually, it's probably closer to drinking piss out of a mason jar, but you get what I mean.

Still nothing. Not even a little tipsy. Granted, we didn't exactly know what to expect, but "absolutely nothing" wasn't it.

"We only got one left each," The Slug said.

"Let's do it," I said, letting out an enormous belch.

We toasted Mickey, and drained the last of the six. Then we sat there just listening to the radio and waiting to be drunk.

After a while, The Slug asked, "You feel anything?"

"Not really. I feel like I need to burp again, I know that."

"Your father got any beers inside?"

I looked at him in disbelief. "I'm not stealing my father's beer. He'd freakin' kill me."

"He won't even notice. He never drinks beer unless there's a barbecue or a party," The Slug said, being annoyingly right.

I thought about it, and that seemed to make sense. I'm not sure why.

"OK," I said. "Lemme go look. I'll be right back."

I sneaked back in the house, went down to the basement and opened the spare fridge. I struck the mother lode. A week earlier, my parents had a big get-together on July 4th, and the fridge was filled with the leftover booze. I grabbed the first six pack of cans that I saw, and ninja-walked my way back out to the car. I opened the door and jumped in, being careful not to slam the door.

"What did ya get?" The Slug asked.

I held up a six-pack of Schlitz Tall Boys. The beer that made Milwaukee famous. I didn't know a city could become famous for diarrhea but there you go. These things were huge – they dwarfed the Mickey's Big Mouth bottles. 24 ounces of carbonated drain cleaner in each can.

We each popped one and chugged it, then opened another to drink more slowly. I had to pee, so I got out of the car and pissed on the back tire like a dog. I noticed that my eyes felt a little weird. Kind of like my head was floating sideways, but my feet weren't. I got back in the car.

"Did you piss on... uh, piss on yer feet?" The Slug asked me slowly. "Cuz I think I smell it."

"No, I pished on your car," I said, wondering why I was having trouble talking. Probably because my cheeks were kind of numb. "I think there wass...I think maybe some splashing."

"That's gross," The Slug said. "I gotta piss too. Be right back."

He opened his door quietly and stood next to the car, pissing straight out into my father's driveway. I stage-whispered out the window, "Don't piss on my father's driveway!"

"You just pissed on my mother's *car*," he said over his shoulder. He had a valid point, so I sat back and took another pull on the can.

After we finished the rest of our respective tall boys, we were feeling decidedly more drunk. We laughed hysterically at mostly nothing, and I had the good sense to realize that we were making way too much noise and we needed to move away from the house and my parent's open bedroom window.

"We gotta walk thissoff," I said, getting out of the car. "Let's check out the new devel...devilpment...the new houses."

"Good idea," The Slug said, grabbing the rest of the six and slamming his car door out of habit. "Shit!" he said. "Sorry!" This was, of course, the funniest thing in the universe at that particular moment, so we stumble-ran a little way down the street, laughing until we couldn't breathe.

At the time, our house was in a brand new development and there were about a half-dozen other houses around the corner that were in various stages of construction. We figured we could find one that was recently framed up and maybe hang out on the porch roof and finish our beers.

We quickly realized we couldn't walk in a straight line. Somewhere along the way, The Slug decided it would be fun to spin around and then try to walk. He did this until he fell on the grass and couldn't get up.

"What time issit?" he asked me, lying on his back on someone's front lawn.

"No watch," I said, "but I see a clock in a car. I'll go look."

I know that doesn't sound like it makes much sense, but there was a Corvette parked in a nearby driveway and I could see it had a lit up digital clock in it. I went to look, but the clock was too small to read through the window. So obviously I did the non-drunk thing and opened the door to get a better look. The Slug yelled, "Shit! Don't get innit! Are you nuts?" But it was too late. I was already sitting behind the wheel, trying to make out the time glowing on the dash. I yelled back to him, "It's 12:30. Or 13:30. It's one of those."

Finally, The Slug got up and staggered over. "Get out! Get out of the car," he said desperately.

"Why?" I asked.

"Dome light!" he said. I looked up and it suddenly dawned on me that I was sitting in someone else's expensive car in the middle of the night, in plain view of anyone who happened to hear something and look out the window. I didn't want to go to jail, so using what was left of my good sense, I got out of the car. We continued zig-zagging our way down the street.

We headed toward the new construction. We had cracked open two more cans and even though it was a pretty dead subdivision as far as vehicle traffic goes, we were still a little freaked out carrying cans of beer, so every time a car came, we assumed it was a cop and we'd run and hide behind a bush or a parked car.

At one point we were running across a lawn trying to dodge a car, and at the last second I saw one of those short "stay off the grass" type border fences that are about shin-high. I jumped over it, but The Slug didn't see it and went down hard, his beer can flying. Before I even knew if he was OK, I started laughing. I'm a good friend. It seemed as if everything was the funniest thing I had ever seen. I sat down hard on the grass and waited for him to get up, trying not to spill my own beer.

The slug rolled slowly to a sitting position, and rubbed his shin. "Stop laughing, asshole," he said. "And give me a swig of your beer." I gave him the can and he tipped it back and chugged it, just out of spite. "HEY!" I yelled. He laughed and flipped me off, then tossed the empty can back at me. He stood up and juicily belched A through H of the alphabet song.

We had two beers left.

"We prob'ly shouldn't open these ones anyways because of the open container," The Slug said blurrily.

"What're you talkin' about?" I asked. "That doesn't make no sense. No sense at all."

"It's a law," he said. "One my brother told me about. You can't walk around with a open beer, or wine or nothin'. It has to be in a bag. If the cops see you they arrest you on the spot."

"Really?" I said. "No shit."

"No shit," he said knowingly. "But there's...here's whatcha do. You put yer thumb over the hole in the top of the bottle or can, see, and then the cops need a warrant to make you move your hand. Then it's like a Mexican stand-off. As long as the hole is covered up, they can't arrest you."

"That doesn't sound real," I said, doubtfully.

"Swear ta God," he said.

By this time we were both slurring our words, and while we didn't really think our reasoning was impaired since neither of us had been completely shit-faced before, we definitely noticed that it was getting harder to walk since the ground kept moving in odd directions under our feet. The Slug took the last two beers and stuffed them inside his shirt so we didn't have to dodge cars any more. It didn't really matter at that point because we had reached the row of new houses, and it was a pretty desolate stretch of street to begin with.

We walked toward the first house that didn't have a door or windows yet and went inside. We didn't have a flashlight, and there were no street lights, but the moon was full. It's amazing how well you can see once your eyes get acclimated to the moonlight. Still, at first we moved around with outstretched hands, since neither of us were very steady at that point. We stood in the foyer for a few minutes waiting for our eyes to adjust.

"Let's find the stairs to the second floor. We can climb out that front window and sit on the porch roof," The Slug said. "Then we'll drink the last two."

We started wandering around, looking for the stairs to the second floor, but then discovered that there weren't any yet. The second floor had been laid down, but there was just a hole above and a hole below. The hole below had a 2x4 ladder dropped into it.

"Let's grab that home-made ladder," I said. "Lean it. Climb it. Boom, on the porch." I was pretty incoherent at that point.

The Slug apparently understood what I was getting at and was down with it, so he took the beers out of his shirt, and we tried to pull the ladder out of the basement hole.

At first we thought it was just too heavy, but after a few minutes of drunken analysis and significant straining, we determined that it was, in fact, nailed in place. It seemed we weren't going to the porch roof after all. It's probably a good thing, because at that point, we didn't have much in the way of balance or good sense, and excessive heights probably wouldn't have been a great idea.

Instead, The Slug had a different idea. "Let's go down ta the...the basement and check...check'er out. It'll be dark. Spooky. He waggled his fingers in front of my face. "OooooOoooooooo," he added, helpfully.

"OK, but you first," I said, looking into the inky hole. I could see the first two rungs and that was it.

The Slug carefully turned around, got down on his hands and knees and started backing towards the hole, feeling for the opening with his feet. He looked like a dog trying to figure out if it had to crap or not. When his feet touched air, he fished around for the first rung and got his foot on it. "Got it!" he said triumphantly. He started down the ladder.

I was on my hands and knees looking down the basement hole from the other side, and I watched him until he disappeared. I stuck my head into the hole. "What's down there?" I asked, hearing my voice echo back with a flat, strange reverberation. The blood was rushing to my head and making it spin.

"I dunno. I dint get ta the bottom yet," he said, "Going slow so I don't – "

Right when he said those words, I heard a grunt, then he yelled "OH SHIT!" and then I heard a giant echoey splash, like someone doing a belly flop into a half full indoor pool. Which is basically what had just happened. It was the absolute last sound I expected.

"SHIT!," The Slug said. "It's FLOODED! There must be three feet of water down here!"

I heard more splashing and more swearing. I couldn't help myself. I started laughing. I laughed until I couldn't breathe. I laughed until my head spun. I laughed until I saw stars.

I laughed until I vomited into the basement hole, then kept laughing.

"WHAT THE?....DID YOU JUST BLOW CHUNKS?!" The Slug screamed. "YOU PUKED! YOU ALMOST PUKED RIGHT ON ME, YOU ASSHOLE! OH SHIT! OH SHIT, THERE'S PUKE IN THE WATER! I THINK I HAVE PUKE ON ME!"

He sounded like a wounded alligator thrashing around in a small pond. Then I heard him retching, and he puked too. I got sick again, avoiding the hole this time. The Slug catapulted out of the basement. He cleared the hole but stayed on his hands and knees and retched again, letting loose a stream of beer punctuated with an incredibly loud BRRRRAAAAAAAAPPPP! sound that triggered another bout of insane laughter for both of us. If you've never laughed your ass off and puked your guts up at the same time, it's an odd feeling to say the least. I've been drunk-sick a few times since then, and there's never anything funny about it, so I'm pretty sure that's not normal.

By the time we stopped laughing and puking, the entire house was spinning. "Oh man," The Slug said. "This sucks so much." I indicated my agreement with an incoherent groan. It was about the only sound I could manage. Puking takes a lot out of a man, I guess.

Without a word, The Slug reached out with his foot and pushed the last two beers down into the basement. They kerplunked in the water and that was it. That was the last time either one of us drank Schlitz or Mickeys.

We lay there for a while, too tired and sick to move.

"Whatever you do, don't close your eyes," he said.

So of course, I closed my eyes. Then I dry heaved, and opened them quickly. "We have to walk," I said, vowing to myself that I would not blink again for as long as I lived.

We got up and made our way out the front door. We were both holding our stomachs and I'm sure we looked pretty green. The Slug was soaked with basement water, vomit and who knows what else. Luckily, it was a very warm night so he wasn't cold. We finally walked far enough so there were street lights again, and we took inventory. There didn't seem to be any visible chunks, so that was good.

The Slug held his elbow up to the light and inspected a small gash.

"You OK?" I asked. "Prob'ly a good thing the water was there or you would have landed right on your back on the concrete."

"Yeah, nothin' much," he said. "Just the elbow. I'll wash it when we get back. My stomach's sore, though. I still feel sick, but I'm not as drunk, I don't think."

I felt better after heaving my guts up, too. I looked at him closer and concentrated, trying to focus. Something looked...weird. Then I realized what it was and started laughing again. "What?" he said, defensively. "What's so funny?"

I pointed at his shirt and pants. He looked down and realized that he was completely covered in sawdust from lying on the floor of the house while soaking wet. Even the back of his neck was covered in sawdust. He looked like a breaded chicken breast.

"CHICKEN BREAST!" I screamed. That struck him funny, even though I don't think he knew what I was talking about, and he started laughing too, and pretty soon we were rolling on the grass holding our stomachs and crying with silent laughter.

"SHAKE AND BAKE!" I yelled, and this brought new fits of hilarity. We finally just lay there, exhausted, looking up at the moon and watching it dance around the sky in small, sickening circles.

We stopped looking at the moon.

At that point we decided that we should probably head back to my house so he could get some dry clothes, and we could try to avoid getting sick again and just go to sleep. We didn't know about hangovers yet.

As we were walking up the street toward my house, I saw our cat sniffing around by the mail box.

"Here, Kitty!" I said, walking toward the cat.

(Yes, that was his name. Kitty. Original, I know, but that's what we named him. I don't know if it's just a stunning lack of originality, or just a type of practicality that kids eventually outgrow, but they always want to name their pets descriptively. I remember my friend Glen wanted to name his new pet rabbit "Sucky" because it seemed like all he did was drink on that water bottle thing, but his mother nixed that one pretty quick. When he got the second rabbit, he probably should have named him "Humpy," because all he did was hump the shit out of the first rabbit every twenty minutes, and then fall on his side and go to sleep until it was time for another humping session. Humpy "ran away" shortly thereafter.)

"Here Kitty!" I repeated, then turned toward The Slug. "Help me get the damned cat," I said. "My mother doesn't like to leave him out all night." We started creeping up on him so he wouldn't run away, hoping to corral him from both sides so he didn't have anywhere to run. We were about six feet away from the cat when The Slug froze.

"Don't move," he said, quietly. "Don't. Move."

"What? Why?" I asked, confused.

As still as a statue, he didn't even look at me when he spoke. *"Skunk."* he whispered.

I froze. I looked again. He was right. What I had thought was our black and white cat was, in fact, a black and white skunk.

We both stood there silently, hardly daring to breathe as the skunk snuffled and sniffed and dug at the soil in front of the mailbox not six feet in front of us.

"I'm gonna run for it," I whispered.

"NO!" The Slug hissed. "No. If you do, we're getting sprayed for sure."

I gave in and we waited it out, standing there like two frozen idiots. Eventually, right about the time when we both were about to cramp up and get doused for our trouble, the skunk wandered across the lawn and into the little patch of woods on my parent's front lawn.

"Holy crap, that was close," The Slug said.

"Yeah," I agreed. "Lets go inside before it comes back."

We walked around back to the sliding glass door, all the while scanning the yard for the skunk, and let ourselves into the house. All was quiet.

There was no sign of my father on one of his two a.m. PB&M runs, so we opened the slider to the kitchen, and sat down at the kitchen table. I went down in the basement and got The Slug some sweats and a fresh T-shirt and he tossed his wet, smelly clothes outside, next to the back stairs. I gave him a blanket and pillow from the closet and crawled upstairs to bed.

The next morning when I woke up, it was close to noon and The Slug was gone. I had a horrible headache, and my stomach muscles hurt, but otherwise I felt pretty good.

I went downstairs to get some breakfast, and my mother was in the kitchen drinking a cup of coffee and talking on the phone. I walked into the family room and looked out the sliding glass door, just to make sure The Slug's clothes were gone. They were, so I walked back into the kitchen, poured myself a cup of coffee, and sat down at the table. My mother glanced at me, then held up her finger and mouthed the words "One cup, that's it." and went back to her conversation.

She used to tell me that coffee would stunt my growth, and I used to tell her that it wasn't the coffee stunting my growth, it was the fact that she was only five feet tall that was doing all the stunting.

Kitty was sitting on the other kitchen chair, sleeping soundly. Oddly, he didn't look much like a skunk. I'm not sure why. OK, I *am* sure why, but that's neither here nor there.

I vowed to never drink again. You can guess how that worked out.

Gearheads in Training

As we got older, The Slug and I got heavily into muscle cars.

We studied them with a passion, and knew just about everything there was to know about them.

We attended local car shows, we drag-raced on deserted streets, and we even took a road trip to Super Chevy Sunday in Englishtown, New Jersey after getting my father to co-sign for a car rental because neither of our cars could be counted on to actually make it there.

This last story will explain why.

It's a story about me, The Slug, and his mother's 1972 Cutlass Supreme Convertible. Picture a perfect powder-blue paint job, a spotless white leather interior, matching top and white-letter tires on stock rally wheels.

Do you have that car perfectly pictured in your mind? OK, now picture it dented and rusted and covered in chalky blue paint with floorboards you could see the road through. Now add a convertible top made almost entirely of duct tape and sporting a rear window cut from a section of clear shower curtain.

That was the car we cruised around in.

As tired as his mom's car was when we were finally old enough to drive, it still had a Rocket 350 engine with a four-barrel carb that applied approximately 200 horsepower directly to the pavement via two almost completely bald Goodyear tires. While 200 horses doesn't sound like much today, in 1972 the government was starting to clamp down hard on the "horsepower wars," and they had just switched the method in which they measured horsepower the year before, and everything was up in the air.

The consumers didn't know how to compare horsepower numbers, and most of the car manufacturers were seriously under-rating the actual power of their engines just to sneak them past the regulators.

Even so, 200 "stated" horses was plenty enough to get us into trouble, even with an automatic tranny. To make the engine sound louder, we'd flip the air filter cover upside down. This made the car idle like shit when it was cold, and it probably didn't help with the fuel/air mix, but it sure did make the engine sound bad-ass when you hit the gas – at least from inside the car.

I mentioned that the tires were bald, however they didn't start out that way. We tended to... *accelerate* their wear just a little bit.

The Slug had discovered that if you put the car in reverse and coasted backwards, then dropped it into neutral while you were still rolling, you could then rev the engine up to the red-line and slam the transmission into drive while simultaneously stomping on the gas pedal.

While admittedly rough on the transmission, the end result was that the car would sit in one place for about 10 seconds with the tires spinning, billowing clouds of foul-smelling, white smoke that would eventually engulf the entire car. As the car gained traction and the tires started to squeal, we would scream "WHOOOOOO HOOOOOOOOO!" at the top of our lungs. I don't know why, but it seemed like the right thing to do at the time.

Usually, "the time" was approximately three in the morning outside our ex-girlfriend's house (yes, we dated the same girl. No, not at the same time. That I know of.)

Failing that, we'd perform this maneuver outside Pat C's house, because his father really, really hated when we did that.

Actually, I'm pretty sure his father just hated us on general principles. He would get pissed at Pat for having such asshole friends, and then Pat would get pissed at us (and probably himself) for the very same reason.

Eventually Pat's father just started calling the cops on us and that put a damper on our late-night wake-up calls, but the street outside his house was covered in thick, black, intertwining tread marks for years afterward.

Just to give you a little more background on our relationship with this car: We would drive it in the middle of February with the top down just for fun, the heat on full-blast, huddled in the bubble of hot air that formed behind the windshield. We'd do donuts on the ice patches in the mall parking lot, trying to slide sideways and hit the dry pavement fast enough to put the car up on two wheels. In the summer, The Slug would sit on the back of the front seat and steer with his feet while I worked the pedals with my hands based on his commands.

(Dad, if you're reading this, take off your coat and sit down. There's no need to drive to my house right this instant just to tell me what a disappointment I am and take away my car keys for the rest of my life. I know it was horribly irresponsible, and I'm sorry. Also, driving that way requires a lot more skill than you might think.)

At the end of the night, we'd scrape the melted rubber off the outside of the rear fenders, and The Slug would head home. When we went out, we always preferred to use his mother's car because my car was tiny and orange, and had a top speed of about 49 mph before it felt like it was going to just say fuck it and disintegrate. The Cutlass, on the other hand, was glass smooth right up to the point where the red needle slammed itself into the right hand side of the speedometer. With at least a half mile of straight blacktop, it had a top-speed of about 130 miles per hour. At that speed, it was a sick-scary, floating, mostly unstable ride that made the hair on your neck stand up and your asshole pucker. But it was smooth.

At any rate, it never really occurred to us that we might actually do some permanent damage to something that didn't belong to us.

Until, that is, we did permanent damage to something that didn't belong to us.

In retrospect, it wasn't the most brilliant decision to try to get the car air-borne. I know that now.

(As an aside, here's a picture of what my '69 Impala looked like shortly after my father finally gave it to me:

Or course, you'd have to picture it covered with fluorescent orange Rolling Stones tongues to get the full effect. As bad as that car looks, the 120-lb or-ange Subaru I was driving during the reign of the Slugmobile was much, much worse. When I finally got the Impala, The Slug had also moved on to his own car, which was a beat-to-shit gold 1971 Chevelle SS with floor-boards so rotten you could Flintstone-pedal that bitch if you had to. Of course, the first thing he did was completely rational: He sunk all the money he had in the world into a monster-rebuild of the engine, even though he had no place to live. But that's a different story.)

OK, so where were we? Oh yes. About to get airborne.

About 20 minutes from my house, there was a two-lane road called Route 155, and unlike Route 66, this road was arrow-straight for about three miles, whereupon it intersected another, busier four-lane local highway known as "Central Avenue" At this intersection was a traffic light, and Route 155 con-tinued straight for about a tenth of a mile past that.

Because Central Avenue was busy, it got beat down and always ended up covered in giant potholes every spring. That meant they had to repave it, which they did. When I was growing up, it seemed as if one lane of that road was always under construction. Route 155 didn't get as much traffic and they didn't have to repave it as often. That meant they had to smooth the intersection every year, and every year Central Ave got a little higher than 155. By the time we were loose on the streets, that discrepancy in pavement height had turned into quite the ramp. Long ago we had discovered that if you hit the traffic light at the right time, you could sail through it on green and maybe get a little air between you and your seat.

One night we were out cruising in the convertible and had just pulled onto 155. He squealed the tires pulling out, because that's just the way he drove. I barely noticed it any more – I just instinctively braced myself against door. The Slug looked over at me and said, "What's the fastest you've ever gone?"

I could tell he was bored. I was a little bored too, so I thought about it for a second, then replied with the truth, because I knew what was coming. "110. Last summer. On my way up to camp."

A few of us spent two or three weeks every summer up at his uncle's camp on Lake Champlain, and I'd always drive up there late Friday night after my shift at the gas station ended, usually around 11 or so. This "three hour" trip took me, at most, an hour and a half. All I'm saying here is that some speed limits were occasionally broken in order to get to where the beer was.

The Slug looked at me and said, "A hundred and ten, huh?" then he floored it, and in about seven seconds we passed the 60-mph mark. I know this because I was looking at the speedometer when he said, "Sixty." A few seconds later, I stopped paying attention to the speedometer and just started watching the road. The wind was incredibly loud, and under it I could hear the engine screaming. When I was just about to lose my nerve, I heard him yell "One-fifteen!" and let off the gas. The car backfired once, and started slowing down. I relaxed, and un-puckered things I hadn't known could actually pucker until that moment. We weren't slowing down fast enough however – because by that time we were impossibly close to the traffic signal, which had turned red, and the re-puckering began. He slammed on the brakes and we screeched to a halt, mostly sideways, and directly under the red light.

A few of the things I learned that night: Everything seems faster when (a) it's dark, (b) you're not the one actually doing the driving, and (c) you have the top down. He put the car in reverse, straightened it out and backed it up a few feet so we were on the correct side of the traffic light. Luckily, since it was almost four a.m., there were no witnesses to our text book car-chase stop. The light turned from red to green, but the car didn't move. We just sat there in the cool air, the car idling roughly, our faces illuminated a sickly green by the traffic light. The Slug was staring at his watch.

I glanced up at the light, which was turning red again. "What the hell are you doing?" I asked him.

"Shhh," he said. "I'm timing it."

We sat there through two more changes of the signal. Green. Yellow. Red. When he convinced himself that it was consistent, he turned the car around and headed back where we came from, watching the odometer on the way. At a certain point, he stopped, and did a k-turn so we were once again facing the traffic light. It seemed, rather suspiciously, to be exactly a quarter mile away.

I'll say this about the Slug: He knew to a tenth of a second how fast his mother's car was in the standing quarter mile. In fact, that was true of every car he drove after that as well – the quarter mile, the zero-60, the top end, you name it, he knew them all. By that time I had a pretty good idea of what was going to happen. As if to confirm my unspoken thought, he grinned and said, "How much air do you think we can get?" After he said this, he put his seatbelt on. *That* was a little unsettling.

He was going to time the light and hit the center of the intersection at top speed while it was green. We were going to see how far we could fly.

General Lee style.

I didn't answer him right away, which was OK, because I don't think he was looking for an answer. He was busy looking at his watch. Finally I swallowed and said, "I guess we'll see" and put my own seatbelt on. Tight.

"Tell me when it turns red," he said, staring at the second hand on his watch.

I shoved my feet as far under the dash as they would go, bracing myself, and watched the light. The instant the light changed, I yelled, "NOW!" at the top of my lungs and pushed myself deep into the well-worn bucket seat.

The Slug just looked at me and burst out laughing.

"I have to wait about 10 seconds after it turns red in order to hit the green light at top speed," he said, still laughing.

For some reason, I had been expecting the car to launch forward like a junkyard dog on a short chain the instant I told him the light had changed, but when that didn't happen I felt like a moron. We tried it again, only this time I knew what to expect and when the light turned red, I marked the occasion by saying, "now" in a relatively normal tone of voice.

Approximately 10 seconds later, all hell broke loose. He crushed the accel-erator and the car took off, straight down the middle of the two-lane road. About 15 seconds after that, we were barreling toward a red light at close to a hundred miles an hour. He had timed it right though, and just before we got to the light it turned green. Unfortunately, the street wasn't quite as deserted as it had been when we started the run. We hit the intersection at about 110 mph – with an audience.

Luckily, none of the cars idling at the light were of the law enforcement type, so at least we had that going for us.

I think we were airborne for about an hour. At least that's what it seemed like. We were going so fast we almost forgot to yell. I've never been in free-fall while strapped inside a car – before or since – and it was a pretty unset-tling feeling.

We came down hard. No, that's an understatement. We slammed into the pavement nose first and bounced the underside of the engine off the ground. The second we hit, the hood popped up a little and one of the headlights went out, and the engine was instantly THIS LOUD. The Slug struggled to main-tain control of the car and we slewed to the left, then to the right, then swung back to the left again. Finally, The Slug stood on the brakes and we plowed to a stop in some poor bastard's front yard.

We looked at each other. "We gotta get out of here before someone calls the cops," The Slug said. I agreed wholeheartedly. I didn't need my father bailing me out of the county lockup.

Miraculously, the car was still running, although it now sounded like a helicopter. We were sure we had blown the engine. We drove in silence for a while, mostly because we couldn't hear each other talk over the engine noise. We pulled into an empty mall parking lot to assess the damage. At that point it was starting to sink in that he was going to have to explain to his mother how this had happened to her car.

We parked under a floodlight and opened the hood, the engine still run-ning. It was loud, but we discovered the problem in short order, and luckily it wasn't as bad as we had originally thought. We could see fire shooting out between the block and the exhaust manifold. We had blown a manifold gas-ket, and broken off one of the mostly-rusted exhaust headers. The metal skirt under the front bumper was pretty smashed and we weren't sure about the ra-diator, but at least it wasn't leaking. The front wheels were still mostly poin-ted in the right direction, and the front suspension seemed OK. The shocks weren't great to begin with, but they didn't appear to be any worse for wear. We had gotten lucky, and decided to call it a night.

He dropped me off a half block from my house so he wouldn't wake up my parents with the rolling helicopter, and then drove home.

The next day, the phone rang, pretty early for a Sunday. I picked it up, and The Slug's mother said, "Hello John. I'd like to talk to you about what happened to my car last night."

You'd think with all that puckering and un-puckering the night before, my butt would have been tired, but I guess not, because right then I experienced the mother of all puckers.

We had forgotten to get our stories straight.

If she had asked me what happened, I would have been screwed. I had no idea what The Slug had told her. Worse, if he got busted, he would lose his car privileges, probably for the rest of his natural life. Luckily, she thought I was more trustworthy or something because she only asked me to confirm his story.

"Michael told me that you were just driving down Central Avenue when the car blew a manifold gasket." she said. "Is that true?"

"Yeah, it scared the heck out of us," I lied. 'We were just driving down the street and it went."

"OK, then. I was just making sure he wasn't lying to me about what happened," she said curtly, then hung up.

I felt a little bad, since she was going to have to pay for it, but also relieved that she believed me, and that was the important part. The Slug and I would live to cruise another day.

The convertible didn't last too long after that. It had frame problems, transmission problems, a bearing knock and major body cancer on top of all that. I don't remember exactly what happened to it, but I think his brother sold it for parts. The Slug's replacement car was a 1971 Chevy Nova that his mother found for him. It had a straight six under the hood.

We got into less trouble with that one since it was a bit of a dog, but in retrospect, that was probably his mother's plan.

Mr. C's Great and Wondrous Show

While Paul and I were still living in our respective parents' houses, he'd always invite me over for his family's holiday celebrations.

Every year, his parents would host their 4th of July cookout, and I would spend most of the day over there stuffing my face with hot dogs and hamburgers and pasta salads and chips. Before we turned 18, we'd steal beer when nobody was looking, chug them in the basement, and hide the empties behind the bar. Later on, when we were legal, we'd bring our own beer so we didn't have to drink his dad's Black Label.

All in all, it was a good party, and we looked forward to it. The food was always good, and the fireworks afterward were the highlight of the day. I don't think I missed a single fourth of July there throughout all of high school and college.

After dark, when the coffee was brewing and the desserts were on the table, Paul's dad would break out a metric ton of illegal fireworks and put on a show for everyone in attendance. Most of the neighbors came over to watch, too. Everyone would applaud and oooh and ahhh over them, and Mr. C loved every minute of it. Because it was a residential neighborhood, he always went easy on the rockets and tended to stick with the stuff that stayed earthbound. I'm not talking snakes and sparklers here, I'm talking things like giant spinners, jumping jacks, boards full of nailed up pinwheels, and ground blooms.

Paul liked rockets, though, so his dad always got him a few extra-large bottle rockets that he was allowed to launch over in the baseball field of the nearby school. Part of our yearly routine would be to head over to the field at dusk and launch one right before his dad's show started at the house. Then after the show, we'd go back over with the others and send them up, too.

One year, when Paul and I were probably around 14 years old, we got tired of the same old thing.

Light the single rocket, go back to the house and eat...it was all so boring.

In our minds, we had become too cool for that. As we were walking down the street toward the shortcut through the woods to the schoolyard, Paul said offhandedly, "I wonder what would happen if you lit one of these horizontally? Ya think it would go anywhere?"

"Probably not," I replied. "It would have to be on something pretty smooth or it would just spin around in circles."

"Smooth like the road," he said, looking up and down the street to see if there was anyone around.

There wasn't. Everyone was in their backyards with their grills going full bore. The fronts of the houses were deserted.

"Yeah, like the road," I agreed. "The road would probably do it."

The road that Paul lived on was about a quarter of a mile long, and straight as an arrow until the right angle turn slightly past his house. He laid the mammoth bottle rocket down flat in the middle of the street and took out his lighter.

"Think we should?" he asked.

I could already tell he'd made up his mind to do it, regardless of what I said.

"It's your rocket," I said, absolving myself of all responsibility. "I'm just here to watch."

For some reason, I think we both expected that the rocket would just shoot straight up the middle of the street and that would be that. A boom, a laugh, and it would be over. Looking back on it now, I have no idea why we would have believed that sort of trajectory was even a remote possibility. These rockets were powerful, and wanted to go up.

He checked again for cars and people, and when he didn't see any of either, he reached down with his lighter and lit the fuse. While we were clearly ignoring the majority of the safety instructions written on the rocket, among them being minor details like "CAUTION: VERTICAL LAUNCH ONLY," and "USE WITH ADULT SUPERVISION" we did follow the bit that said "LIGHT FUSE AND BACK AWAY." We very quickly put about 20 feet between us and the sputtering rocket.

If you've ever lit the fuse on a large rocket, you know there's always that second or two when the fuse disappears into the body of the rocket and nothing happens. You wonder if it's a dud, or if it's just taking its sweet time. You are torn between waiting for something to happen, or walking up to it to see what's going on.

The fuse disappeared into the rocket, and of course, nothing happened. We looked at the rocket, then at each other, and then back at the rocket. Paul said, "I think it's a d -" and then the street erupted.

The rocket took off down the road with a deafening roar amid a huge shower of silver sparks and a cloud of billowing smoke. This was made all the more impressive because the rocket only traveled about a hundred feet before it hooked left and jammed itself under the front tire of the neighbor's car with a loud, hollow, *PONK!*

It sat there spewing an ever-increasing shower of sparks as we looked on in horror. I barely had time to think, *"no, no, no, No, NO!"* before the rocket petered out.

We had taken a step or two toward the car before we remembered what came next – and decided that maybe moving toward this thing wasn't such a good idea.

What came next was not good.

As we watched, cringing, the rocket made a noise like a warm bottle of seltzer being stabbed with a knife, and then shot two dozen flaming red balls in all directions. The balls spun around madly, bouncing around under the car and jumping onto front lawns and driveways alike. Then, almost simultaneously, each of the 24 burning balls changed color to vivid green and exploded with a deafening bang.

At that point we figured the worst was over. We figured wrong.

We had been watching this unfold for what seemed like an hour, but had been, in reality, perhaps six to ten seconds. A split-second later, fresh activity began under the tire. We looked at each other in disbelief, thinking we should probably do *something*, but also knowing there was absolutely nothing we could do.

So we continued to stand there and watch as another huge cloud of smoke and a fresh burst of golden sparks shot out of the jammed rocket, right before it blew itself to tiny smoking pieces with an explosion that sounded like a stick of dynamite.

"HOLY SHIT!" Paul said.

I had no immediate reply to that that statement. It really said it all.

We waited another minute for the car to explode, and when it didn't, we walked cautiously toward it to assess the damage. Surprisingly, other than some gray powder burns on the tire, there wasn't any. There were some scorches on the road from the fire balls hopping around and exploding, but there didn't seem to be anything else burning. We figured we had gotten lucky and that maybe we weren't going to end up owing anyone a new paint job.

Unbelievably, we were still the only people on the street. We quickly gathered up all the bits of rocket we could find, un-jammed the wooden stick from under the tire and nonchalantly walked away, as if it had been someone else entirely who had almost blown up the neighbor's car and lit the entire subdivision on fire.

When we got back to Paul's house, we stole a couple more beers, and drank them in the basement while we rehashed what had just happened.

By the time we had finished the beers, we were done laughing and retelling the highlights of the story to each other. We had regained enough composure to rejoin the family, so we headed out back to watch his dad's show.

It was a great show, as usual, and the neighborhood crowd was out in full force. We clapped and hooted at every one he set off, even the ones we privately thought were kind of lame. Looking back on it now, it was great to be there surrounded by family and friends, with nothing but good times ahead of us.

The potential of those days was staggering.

That's It? WTF?

Then and Now

I thought for quite a while about how to wrap this whole thing up. Since it's more a collection of short anecdotes rather than something that has a clearly-defined beginning, middle and end, I'm finding it to be a difficult task – Mostly, I think, because the book is a collection of stories from my life, and my life isn't finished yet. At least as far as I know. I suppose it's entirely possible I'll accidentally choke to death on my toothbrush today, or fall into a wood chipper by mistake or something, but let's assume I'll be around for the foreseeable future.

Yes, let's assume that. That sounds like a plan.

I hope to have many more stories to tell, and those of you who have read my blog have had the privilege (or the misfortune, depending upon your point of view) to have read some of them. I realize there isn't much actual new content here, and I hope that all of you weren't too terribly disappointed.

On the other hand, you can't say I didn't warn you – I told you right up front not to expect too much.

Even so, I'd like to send a heart-felt thanks to all of you who shelled out your hard-earned cash for a copy of this book, especially in today's economy. If anyone feels cheated, just let me know and I'll invite you to our next cookout. I flip a mean burger.

It continues to be great fun writing my blog, and I appreciate the opportunity I've had to make you laugh, and make myself laugh in the process. If it weren't for all of you, I'd have written these stories in a vacuum, and nobody wants that. As far as I can tell, they're mostly full of cat hair and Dorito dust.

Be good to each other, and remember – stay away from Granny Grunt. She'll shoot you in the ass just as soon as look at you.

Peace,

I'd Like to Thank the Academy...
No Wait, That's Not Right.

I'd like to thank my brothers and my sister for helping to create these stories, and letting me tell my versions of them. I'd also like to thank Markie for being like a brother to us all. I'm sure each of you guys would have some contrary opinions about the specifics of these tales, so I'll apologize now if you think I've remembered things a little differently than they actually happened. I'm sure I got a bunch of it wrong, but in my defense, there were a lot of blanks to fill in. If I made myself seem cooler than you in these stories, well…that's because I *am* cooler than you. So I guess what I'm saying here is write your own damned books if you want. Seriously though, thanks for being the biggest part of my childhood, and the best siblings a guy could ask for.

Thanks to my parents for being the best parents in the universe, and (I never thought I'd say this) for not making me an only child. While I'm sure it would have been awesome, I probably wouldn't have had any of these stories to write down. Every minute of my childhood will be forever cherished. You did a great job raising us to be the best adults we could possibly be, and I appreciate every sacrifice you made for us along the way. Also, please consider every single one of the stories in this book fiction.

Thank you, readers of my blog; those who have been with my sorry ass since 2005, the ones who came on board after the JCP post, and the new people who stop by my blog every day. All you guys rock. It's your comments, observations and shared stories that keep me going.

Thanks to my blogging buddies at work, who encouraged me to start a blog that turned into something more fun than I ever could have imagined. Sarah at okayseriously.blogspot.com, Shamus at shamusissues.blogspot.com, Carly, Big Tool Scott and ErikwithaK, JP at Shop Dungarees, you guys made me laugh more than anyone else. Thanks for sharing the ridiculousness of your childhoods and daily lives with me.

Thanks to Dave at www.davehitt.com, Prisoner 7381, Gutu Notunobu, and all of my other proofreaders. (If you still find typos and grammatical errors, blame them, not me.)

Lastly, and most importantly, thank you Fuzz for supporting this crazy idea, and putting up with me on a daily basis. You've given me up to this keyboard more times than I can count, and I appreciate everything you do for me and for us, every single day. I love you.

15minutelunch.blogspot.com

Don't expect too much

Contact Johnny at:

johnnyvirgil@nycap.rr.com

Made in the USA
Lexington, KY
31 January 2012